lonely planet

Montenegro

Northern
Mountains
p111

Central
Montenegro
p91

Dubrovnik
(Croatia)
p127

Bay of
Kotor
p36

Adriatic
Coast
p64

Tamara Sheward, Peter Dragicevich

PLAN YOUR TRIP

ON THE ROAD

BOBOTOV KUK, DURMITOR
NATIONAL PARK P116

DAN TAUTAN/SHUTTERSTOCK ©

OSTROG MONASTERY
P107

MILA ATKOVSKA/SHUTTERSTOCK ©

DURMITOR NATIONAL PARK
P116

DELLA LINER/SHUTTERSTOCK ©

Contents

UNDERSTAND

SURVIVAL GUIDE

COVID-19

We have re-checked every business in this book before publication to ensure that it is still open after the COVID-19 outbreak. However, the economic and social impacts of COVID-19 will continue to be felt long after the outbreak has been contained, and many businesses, services and events referenced in this guide may experience ongoing restrictions. Some businesses may be temporarily closed, have changed their opening hours and services, or require bookings; some unfortunately could have closed permanently. We suggest you check with venues before visiting for the latest information.

SPECIAL FEATURES

Right: Bay of
Kotor, Kotor
(p46)

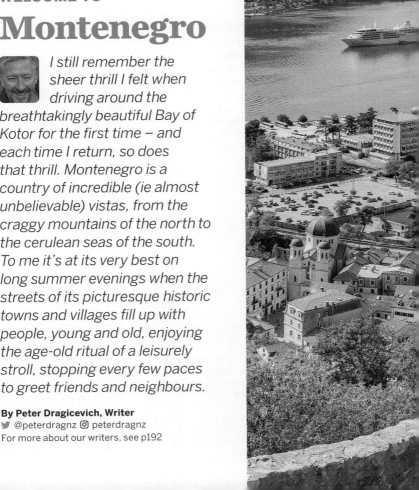

WELCOME TO

Montenegro

I still remember the sheer thrill I felt when driving around the breathtakingly beautiful Bay of Kotor for the first time – and each time I return, so does that thrill. Montenegro is a country of incredible (ie almost unbelievable) vistas, from the craggy mountains of the north to the cerulean seas of the south. To me it's at its very best on long summer evenings when the streets of its picturesque historic towns and villages fill up with people, young and old, enjoying the age-old ritual of a leisurely stroll, stopping every few paces to greet friends and neighbours.

By Peter Dragicevich, Writer
🐦 @peterdragnz 📷 peterdragnz
For more about our writers, see p192

Montenegro

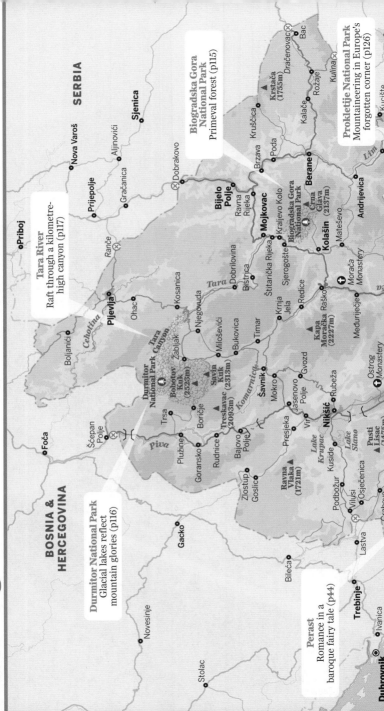

Tara River
Raft through a kilometre-high canyon (p117)

Biogradska Gora National Park
Primeval forest (p115)

Prokletije National Park
Mountaineering in Europe's forgotten corner (p126)

Durmitor National Park
Glacial lakes reflect mountain glories (p116)

Perast
Romance in a baroque fairy tale (p44)

SERBIA

BOSNIA & HERCEGOVINA

KOSOVO

CROATIA

0   25 miles
0   50 km

Locations (from map)

Priboj, Nova Varoš, Sjenica, Prijepolje, Gračanica, Alijnovići, Priboj, Dobrakovo, Dobrakovo, Bijelo Polje, Ravna Rijeka, Mojkovac, Kraljevo Kolo, Kruščica, Poda, Brzava, Berane, Krstača (1755m), Dračenovac, Bac, Rožaje, Kalače, Kulina, Peć, Plav, Kučište, Murino, Lim, Crna Glava (2137m), Biogradska Gora National Park, Kolašin, Mateševo, Andrijevica, Surdup (2182m)

Priboj, Ranče, Čehotina, Pljevlja, Ohac, Kosanica, Njegovuda, Miloševići, Bukovica, Dobrilovina, Bistrica, Tara, Štitarička Rijeka, Sjerogošte, Redice, Krnja, Jela, Raško, Medurječje, Morača Monastery, Kapa Moračka (2227m), Moračka Kanjon, Morača

Foča, Šćepan Polje, Plužine, Goransko, Rudnice, Boričje, Bajovo Polje, Trsa, Zabljak, Durmitor National Park, Bobotov Kuk (2523m), Savin Kuk (2313m), Treskavac (2093m), Komarnica, Šavnik, Mokro, Jasenovo, Gvozd, Polje, Rubeža, Nikšić, Vir, Presjeka

Gacko, Bileća, Zlostup, Goslic, Ravna Vlaka (1721m), Kuside, Podbožur, Vilusi, Osječenica, Lake Krupac, Lake Slano, Pusti Lisac (1475m), Izvori, Zagorak, Gorica, Danilovgrad, Ostrog Monastery

Novesinje, Stolac, Trebinje, Ivanica, Cavtat, Dubrovnik, Sitnica, Lastva, Grahovo, Han, Mt Lisac (1586m)

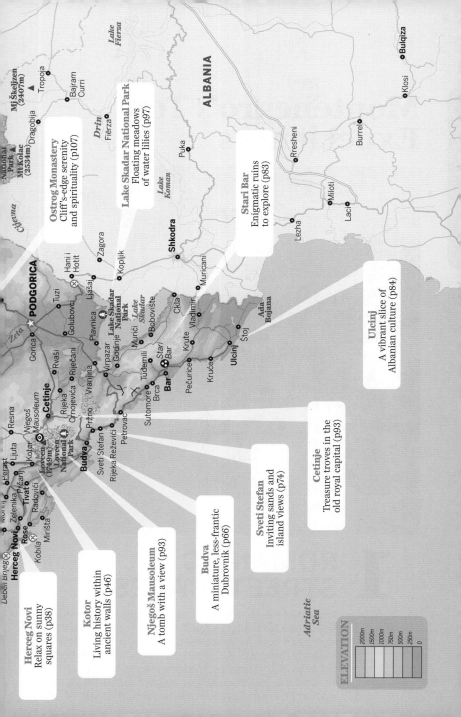

Herceg Novi
Relax on sunny squares (p38)

Kotor
Living history within ancient walls (p46)

Njegoš Mausoleum
A tomb with a view (p93)

Budva
A miniature, less-frantic Dubrovnik (p66)

Sveti Stefan
Inviting sands and island views (p74)

Cetinje
Treasure troves in the old royal capital (p93)

Ulcinj
A vibrant slice of Albanian culture (p84)

Stari Bar
Enigmatic ruins to explore (p83)

Lake Skadar National Park
Floating meadows of water lilies (p97)

Ostrog Monastery
Cliff's-edge serenity and spirituality (p107)

ALBANIA

Adriatic Sea

ELEVATION

2000m
1500m
1000m
750m
500m
250m
0

Montenegro's Top Experiences

1 ROMANTIC STREETSCAPES

Ancient stone towns set alongside azure waters abound along the Montenegrin coast. The walls and towers may have been built for practical purposes, but the effect is achingly romantic. Although the Venetians were booted out over 200 years ago, the influence of their tenure as overlords has bequeathed elegant architecture that wouldn't be out of place in the watery city itself.

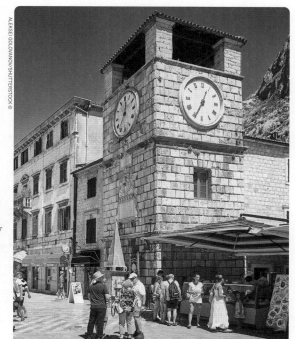

ALEKSEI GOLOVANOV/SHUTTERSTOCK ©

Kotor

Time-travel back to a Europe of moated walled towns with shadowy lanes and stone churches on every square. The way Kotor's Old Town seems to grow out of the sheer grey mountains surrounding it adds an extra thrill to the scene. p46

Right: Kotor's Old Town

BORIS STROUJKO/SHUTTERSTOCK ©

OLEKSANDR SAVCHUK/SHUTTERSTOCK ©

Perast

An oversized village comprised almost entirely of elegant baroque palaces and churches, pretty Perast forms a worthy centrepiece to the Bay of Kotor. The positioning is perfect, sitting at the apex of the inner bay looking straight down the narrow channel leading to the outer section. p44

Left: Bay of Kotor, Perast

Above: Marina, Perast

Budva's Stari Grad

Budva's walled Stari Grad (Old Town) rises from the Adriatic like a miniature Dubrovnik. There's an atmosphere of romance and a typically Mediterranean love of life palpable around every corner. When it's time to relax, there's a beach on either side. p66

Above: Stari Grad, Budva

2 ASTONISHING VIEWS

The country has a mountain in its name, so it should come as no surprise that there are plenty of lofty vantage points. The Dinaric Alps stretch through almost the entire country, at times dipping their feet in the Adriatic. A highlight of Montenegro is the simple joy of travelling along its many scenic routes, taking in the beauty and power of the landscape.

The Kotor–Lovćen Road

The serpentine road connecting Kotor with Lovćen National Park loops up and up, providing ever more jaw-dropping views over the Bay of Kotor. Vistas of mountains and blue water compensate for any white-knuckle moments caused by the narrow road and its sheer drops. p51

Above: Lovćen National Park (p93)

Njegoš Mausoleum

The second-highest peak of Mt Lovćen is the final resting place for 19th-century Montenegrin ruler Petar II Petrović Njegoš. The simple but affecting structure and monumental statuary do little to distract from the remarkable views over all of Old Montenegro. p93

Top right: Njegoš Mauseoleum

Sveti Stefan

The postcard-perfect fortified island village of Sveti Stefan is a wonder to behold as you drive along the coastal highway. Soak in those views, as the island itself is currently closed to nonguests of its resort. p74

Bottom right: Sveti Stefan

3 BEAUTIFUL BEACHES

Let's be honest, the opportunity to laze about beside crystal-clear waters is the main reason why tourists descend on Montenegro every summer. The entire coast is a scant 100km long as the crow flies, so the beaches can get a tad busy. If it's buzz you're after, you'll find that easily enough. Quieter nooks are harder to come by but beauty isn't in short supply.

Drobni Pijesak

Green hills and turquoise waters frame this secluded cove, hidden from view below the coastal road. p76

Top right: Drobni Pijesak

DUSAN RADEVIC/SHUTTERSTOCK ©

Lučice

Lined with cypress trees and oleanders, and with picturesque church-topped islets offshore, Lučice is a Mediterranean dream. It's reached by a short walk along forest paths from the resort town of Petrovac.
p77

Above: Lučice Beach

Ada Bojana

One of the few places where you might get a stretch of sand to yourself, this 3km-long island at the southern tip of the country is connected to the mainland by a bridge. The catch: the entire island is clothing optional. p88

Bottom right: Ada Bojana

4 TRANQUIL LAKES

NOMAD_SOUL/SHUTTERSTOCK ©

Montenegro's mighty mountains come with their own mirrors courtesy of some commensurately impressive lakes. Hiking tracks circle some of them, while others can be explored by boat or kayak. In contrast to the bustling Adriatic beaches, there's plenty of tranquillity to be found in the remote reaches of the national parks that surround them. They are also extremely important habitats for native wildlife.

Lake Skadar

Shared between Montenegro and Albania, the Balkans' largest lake is home to an extraordinary array of birdlife. On the Montenegrin side, a national park encompasses island monasteries, fortresses and old stone villages famous for their wine. p97

Durmitor's 'Mountain Eyes'

Reflecting the beauty of the Durmitor range's imposing grey peaks are 18 glacial lakes known as *gorske oči* (mountain eyes). The largest and most beautiful is the Black Lake near Žabljak. p117

Lake Biograd

Peaceful Lake Biograd is surrounded by one of Europe's most significant remaining tracts of virgin forest, nestled within the folds of the Bjelasica Mountains. p115

Above: Lake Biograd

5 WILD ADVENTURES

Montenegro has a wild side that lends itself to all manner of outdoor pursuits for the adventurous at heart. With such a diverse landscape crammed into such a small space, it's quite possible to go from river deep (rafting, canyoning) to mountain high (hiking, climbing, skiing, paragliding) and then plunge straight into the sea (diving, kitesurfing, parasailing). In any case, you won't get bored.

UTAMARIA/GETTY IMAGES ©

FOXYS FOREST MANUFACTURE/SHUTTERSTOCK ©

Rafting the Tara River

It's hard to get a decent view of the beautiful Tara Canyon, with its sheer tree-lined walls, up to 1300m high. It is most impressive from the water, which helps to explain the popularity of rafting. p118

Top left: Rafting, Tara River

Skiing in Kolašin

The swankiest of Montenegro's ski resorts lies just off the main highway heading north from the capital. p113

Bottom left: Kolašin 1450 Ski Resort (p114)

Hiking the Prokletije Mountains

They're called the 'Accursed Mountains' but for hikers and climbers this rugged range in Montenegro's far east leans more to the divine than the damned. p126

Above: Hiking, Prokletije Mountains

6 HEAVENLY ARCHITECTURE

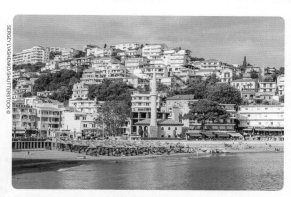

SERGEY VYASHENKO/SHUTTERSTOCK ©

Ulcinj's Many Mosques

There's a special buzz to Ulcinj, Montenegro's southernmost town – and one of the things that sets it apart from the other beach towns is the profusion of historic minarets punctuating its skyline. p85

Top left: Ulcinj (p84)

KIEVVICTOR/SHUTTERSTOCK ©

Ostrog Monastery

No photo can do justice to the wonder that is Ostrog. Set in a seemingly sheer mountain wall, it's impossible to frame a picture that reveals its great height without reducing the luminous white monastery to little more than a speck. p107

Bottom left: Ostrog Monastery

St Tryphon's Cathedral

Kotor's Catholic cathedral is a masterpiece of Romanesque architecture and is home to many lovingly crafted religious objects. p47

Montenegro's three main faiths (Eastern Orthodox, Roman Catholic and Islam) have left a legacy of architectural and artistic treasures all over the country. While Catholic churches are concentrated around the Bay of Kotor and Budva, and mosques in the north and east, there are Orthodox monasteries dotted all around – many of them in blissfully remote settings such as high up mountains, on tiny islands and alongside river canyons.

7 ENIGMATIC RUINS

Having been positioned at the crossroads of civilisations for millennia has left Montenegro with a plethora of ruined cities, towns and fortresses ripe for exploration. There are Illyrian towns dating back nearly 3000 years, Roman mosaics uncovered from farmers' fields, and broken battlements dating from the Byzantine, Bosnian, Venetian, Spanish, Ottoman, French and Austrian occupations.

Stari Bar

The ancient Illyrian-founded city of Stari Bar lies in enigmatic ruins atop a bluff surrounded by gnarled olive trees. Its current state of dilapidation dates from a bombardment in 1878. p83

Bottom right: Stari Bar ruins

Herceg Novi's Fortresses

Herceg Novi may be better known for its bustling waterfront promenade but huddled above it is a set of menacing fortresses with names such as Kanli Kula (the bloody tower). Down below are the collapsed remnants of the Citadela.
p38

Above: Kanli Kula (p38)

Haj-Nehaj Fortress

Chances are you'll have isolated Haj-Nehaj all to yourself, if you can find it. It's reached by a stony track up an isolated hill.
p78

Top right: Main gate, Haj-Nehaj

KATSIUBA VOLHA/SHUTTERSTOCK ©

8 OLD MONTENEGRIN HEARTLAND

SDURAKU/SHUTTERSTOCK ©

Montenegrin national identity formed on the slopes of Mt Lovćen, the 'black mountain' that gave the country its name. The massif's lofty wilderness areas are protected by a national park, while nestled within a series of high-altitude plateaus are the rugged villages and historic capital in which the Montenegrin tribes maintained a degree of independence from the Ottoman occupiers. You haven't really seen Montenegro until you've visited Lovćen.

Cetinje

Cetinje may have been stripped of its capital status but this erstwhile royal city still boasts the country's richest and most important museums, plus two superb galleries, a magnificent monastery and historic palaces. p94

Above: Cetinje Monastery (p96)

Njeguši

Producing the country's best *pršut* (smoke-dried ham) and cheese, this mountain village is synonymous with traditional Montenegrin cooking. p93

Rijeka Crnojevića

Set on the sinuous Crnojević River between Mt Lovćen and Lake Skadar, this picturesque hamlet was the winter escape of Montenegro's ruling family. p98

Need to Know

For more information, see Survival Guide (p163)

Currency
Euro (€)

Language
Montenegrin

Visas
Many nationalities are entitled to a stay of up to 90 days without a visa.

Money
ATMs widely available. Credit cards are accepted in larger hotels but aren't widely accepted elsewhere.

Mobile Phones
Local SIM cards are a good idea if you're planning a longer stay and can be used in most unlocked handsets. The main providers (T-Mobile, M:tel and Telenor) have shopfronts in most towns.

Time
Central European Time (GMT plus one hour)

When to Go

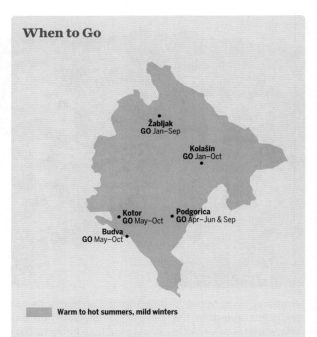

Žabljak
GO Jan–Sep

Kolašin
GO Jan–Oct

Kotor
GO May–Oct

Podgorica
GO Apr–Jun & Sep

Budva
GO May–Oct

■ Warm to hot summers, mild winters

High Season
(Jul–Aug)

➡ The warmest, driest, busiest and most expensive time to visit.

➡ Accommodation should be booked well in advance; some places enforce three-day minimum stays.

Shoulder
(May–Jun & Sep–Oct)

➡ The best time to come, with plenty of sunshine and average water temperatures over 20°C.

➡ Some beach bars and restaurants are closed and activities can be harder to arrange.

Low Season
(Nov–Apr)

➡ The ski season kicks in, with peak prices in Kolašin and Žabljak.

➡ Many hotels, restaurants and bars on the coast close their doors and prices plummet.

Useful Websites

Montenegrin National Tourist Organisation (www.monte negro.travel) Packed full of information, photos and some downloadable resources.

National Parks of Montenegro (www.nparkovi.me) All national parks are covered, with information about activities and fees.

Visit Montenegro (www.visit-montenegro.com) One of the most informative of the commercial sites.

Renome (www.renome.me) Montenegro's hugely interesting cultural tourism magazine.

Ethno-Gastronomic Route (www.ethnogastro-balkan.net) Has excellent off-the-beaten-track itinerary ideas based on cultural and foodie landmarks.

Lonely Planet (www.lonelyplanet.com/montenegro) Destination information, hotel reviews and more.

Important Numbers

International access code	✆00
Country code	✆382
Police	✆122
Ambulance	✆124
Roadside assistance	✆9807

Exchange Rates

Australia	A$1	€0.64
Canada	C$1	€0.66
Croatia	1KN	€0.13
Japan	¥100	€0.78
New Zealand	NZ$1	€0.60
Serbia	100DIN	€0.85
UK	£1	€1.12
US	US$1	€0.87

For current exchange rates, see www.xe.com.

Daily Costs

Budget: Less than €85

➡ Dorm or shared room in private accommodation: €12–21

➡ Pizza slice: €2.50

Midrange: €85–185

➡ Double room in midrange hotel: €45–100

➡ Sit-down meal in a traditional restaurant: €10–30

Top End: More than €185

➡ Double room or suite in an upmarket hotel: €100–600

➡ Fish meals that stare back at you while they're served: €25–50

Opening Hours

Montenegrins have a flexible approach to opening times. Even if hours are posted on the door of an establishment, don't be surprised if they're not heeded. Many tourist-orientated businesses close between November and March.

Banks 8am to 5pm Monday to Friday, 8am to noon Saturday.

Post offices 7am to 8pm Monday to Friday, sometimes Saturday. In smaller towns they may close midafternoon, or close at noon and reopen at 5pm.

Restaurants, cafes & bars 8am to midnight. If the joint is jumping, cafe-bars may stay open until 2am or 3am.

Shops 9am to 8pm. Sometimes they'll close for a few hours in the late afternoon.

Arriving in Montenegro

Podgorica Airport Taxis charge around €12 for the 9km to central Podgorica. There are no buses.

Tivat Airport Taxis charge €7 for the 3km to Tivat, €10 for Kotor and €20 for Budva. There are no buses.

Dubrovnik Airport (Croatia) There are no buses directly to Montenegro, but buses to Dubrovnik Bus Station (24km in the wrong direction) are timed around flights (40KN). From the bus station there are at least four services a day to Herceg Novi (€14) and Kotor (€18), two of which continue to Podgorica (€29). Herceg Novi travel agencies and accommodation providers can usually prearrange a transfer for €45. Herceg Novi–based taxis charge around €60 for the trip, but Dubrovnik taxis can be more expensive.

Getting Around

Bus Buses link all major towns and are affordable, reliable and reasonably comfortable.

Car While you can get to many places by bus, hiring a car will give you the freedom to explore some of Montenegro's scenic back roads. Some of these are extremely narrow and cling to the sides of canyons, so it may not suit the inexperienced or faint-hearted.

Train Trains are cheap but the network is limited and many carriages are old and can get hot. The main line links Bar, Virpazar, Podgorica, Kolašin, Mojkovac and Bijelo Polje, and there's a second line from Podgorica to Danilovgrad and Nikšić.

For much more on **getting around**, see 174

What's New

Recent years have been marked by social unrest, high Covid death rates and an absolute thumping for the local tourism industry. A change of government wouldn't ordinarily be such a noteworthy event but in Montenegro's case it's absolutely huge, given that it's the first time that it has ever happened.

Portonovi, Kumbor

A former Yugoslav military base along the bay from Herceg Novi has been transformed into a lavish resort complete with a five-star hotel (Europe's first One&Only), a marina, hundreds of private apartments, a beach club, swimming pools, tennis courts and a 'wellness' centre. Among the complex's many upmarket bars and restaurants is Sabia, helmed by internationally renowned chef Giorgio Locatelli (of London's Michelin-starred Locanda Locatelli fame).

Broadening palates

Despite the pandemic causing heartache for many restaurants, the last few years have seen a welcome increase in the diversity of cuisines on offer. Ten years ago there were only a couple of places offering anything other than Montenegrin or Italian cuisine in the entire country. Recent openings include Masala Art and Chi Le Ma in Podgorica, Dubai House in Podgorica and Ulcinj, Tapasake Club at Portonovi and China Rujin at Porto Montenegro (p57) in Tivat.

Ulcinj Salina Nature Park

These vast salt pans (p86) near Ulcinj have been awarded Nature Park status and declared a Ramsar Wetland of International Importance, ending a passionate battle to preserve them from a proposed development. Visitors can now borrow bikes to explore the 14.8 sq km site and to get close to the colourful flock of flamingos that call it home. They're just one of 250 bird species that have been spotted here.

LOCAL KNOWLEDGE

WHAT'S HAPPENING IN MONTENEGRO

Peter Dragicevich, Lonely Planet author

The last few years have been tumultuous ones for Montenegro, even by Balkan standards.

At the September 2020 parliamentary election the ruling Democratic Party of Socialists, who had been in control of Montenegro since the break-up of Yugoslavia, lost power for the first time in 30 years. The election followed on from an extended period of social unrest, with major protests against government corruption and against a law transferring control of some church property to the state – part of an ongoing tussle between the established Serbian Orthodox Church and the resurgent Montenegrin Orthodox Church.

Violent protests accompanied the enthronement of a new Serbian Orthodox Metropolitan for Montenegro at Cetinje Monastery in September 2021, suggesting that issues of ethnic and religious identity in Montenegro are far from resolved.

At the time of writing Montenegro had the unenviable distinction of being placed fourth in the world for Covid-related deaths as a percentage of its population, with over 3300 fatalities per million people.

Tivatska Solila Special Nature Reserve, Bay of Kotor

Similarly, new nature trails and information boards have improved the visitor experience at these former salt pans near Tivat Airport. After falling out of use in the 1960s, they became a dumping ground for construction and other waste but have since been cleaned up and are now an important wetland habitat for birds and native halophytes (salt-tolerant plants).

Dalmatian pelicans on the up, Lake Skadar

In more good news for our feathered friends, Lake Skadar's population of Dalmatian pelicans is bouncing back from near extinction a couple of decades ago, with a record number of fledglings born in 2021 bringing the population to more than 300. Birdwatchers taking a boat or kayak tour on Lake Skadar from spring through to June are almost certain to see them.

Lake Skadar accommodation

Accommodation in the vicinity of Virpazar continues to improve with Undiscovered Montenegro (p170) expanding the offering at their gorgeous Villa Miela Lake Retreat, and others such as Eco Villas Merak and Ethno Lodge AB popping up.

Kolašin ski fields

Skiing and snowboarding at Kolašin (p114) has gotten a whole lot better with the opening of a new ski resort further up the mountain (Kolašin 1600), linked to the older one (Kolašin 1450) by a new lift. The numbers in their names refer to their respective altitudes in metres. A fancy new branch of a famous international hotel chain is due to open high up on the slopes at Kolašin 1600 by the end of 2022.

A1 Motorway

By the time you're reading this, it's highly likely that at least some of the hugely expensive and highly controversial motorway linking the port of Bar to the Serbian border at Boljare will have opened. The most likely section starts immediately north of Podgorica and terminates just south of Kolašin, bypassing the beautiful but treacherous Morača Canyon. This should reduce the drive from the capital to the ski town by around 30 minutes.

Stara Čaršija Resort & Spa, Stari Bar

Atmospheric Stari Bar finally has quality hotel accommodation in the form of this rustic gem in the old market area. It's built in a traditional style and offers wonderful views to the ruins of the ancient city, plus an excellent restaurant.

LISTEN, WATCH & FOLLOW

For inspiration and up-to-date news, visit www.lonelyplanet.com/Montenegro/articles.

Covid-19 Response (www.covidodgovor.me) Government website outlining current public health measures in response to the Covid-19 pandemic including testing locations, mask requirements and restrictions.

Montenegro Institute of Public Health (www.ijzcg.me) Up-to-date information about current Covid outbreaks (in Montenegrin).

National Tourism Organisation of Montenegro (www.montenegro.travel) The official tourism site, with information about destinations, upcoming events and the Covid situation as it pertains to travellers.

Balkan Insight (www.balkaninsight.com/montenegro-home) Montenegrin news in English.

FAST FACTS

Food trend New Asian restaurants

Percentage who identify as Montenegrin 45%

Percentage who identify as Serb 29%

Population 621,000

population per sq km

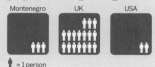

Montenegro   UK   USA

☗ ≈ 1 person

Month by Month

January

The ski season kicks off, heralding peak prices in Kolašin and Žabljak; it's low season everywhere else.

★★ Orthodox Christmas

Held on 7 January, the traditional Orthodox Christmas is marked by church services and unbridled feasting; the night before, oak branches (*badnjak*) are burned and prayers are offered for good luck and happiness in the coming year.

February

The ski season is in full swing in the north. Despite chilly temperatures in the Bay of Kotor (average highs of around 12°C), residents find reasons to celebrate.

★★ Mimosa Festival

Herceg Novi gets a jump on spring with this festival, which has been held, perhaps coincidentally, since the flower-power era of the late 1960s. Expect concerts, sports events, majorettes and lots of yellow blooms. (p40)

★★ Carnival

The traditional pre-Lent festivities continue to be held in the once predominantly Catholic towns of Kotor and Tivat. Expect Venetian-style masked balls (for adults and for children), concerts, theatre performances and parades.

March

The ski season continues up north but spring arrives elsewhere, with average highs jumping above 10°C in Podgorica and hitting around 15°C on the coast.

★★ Camellia Day

Not to be outdone by mimosa, the camellia gets its moment in the springtime sun with this festival held in both Kotor and Stoliv in mid-March. (p50)

April

You might get a few skiing days at the beginning of the month before the rising temperature melts the snow and speeds up the flow of the Tara River – leading to the start of the rafting season.

★★ Carnival of Budva

Bucking tradition in favour of warmer weather, Budva gets into the Venetian swing of things in late April, with parades, folk music, concerts and DJs. (p69)

May

Late spring is a great time to visit Montenegro, with average high temperatures in the 20s everywhere except the mountains. Rafting is at its most thrilling and accommodation prices move into the shoulder-season bracket.

✨ Spring Break Festival

The otherwise calm sands of little Kamenovo Beach get all stirred up during this two-day electronic music festival that attracts big-name DJs from across Europe. (p73)

June

Summer brings with it warm, dry days and rising accommodation prices on the coast, but not yet peak rates. Tourist-orientated businesses reopen, including beach bars and restaurants.

☆ Theatre City

Budva comes over all thespian for six weeks from mid-June, with performances held in such dramatic spots as the Citadela and in front of the Old Town's walls. (p69)

✨ Southern Soul Festival

The silly season kicks off in earnest at Velika Plaža's happening Copacabana Beach, with four full-on days (from late June to early July) of terpsichore and tunes. (p89)

July

The official start of 'The Season'. Peak rates kick in, temperatures soar, beach clubs crank into life and tourists flood the beaches. In the mountains, the weather is perfect for hiking.

✨ Sea Dance Festival

This fantastic, frenetic three-day electronic and alternative music festival on the sunny sands of Jaz Beach (near Budva) attracts tens of thousands of merrymakers. (p69)

☆ Kotor Art

Continuing through to August, Kotor's summer arts umbrella shelters several well-established festivals, such as Don Branko's Music Days (classical music) and Perast's International Klapa Festival (traditional Dalmatian unaccompanied singing). International companies head to the Children's Theatre Festival in early July. (p50)

✨ Fašinada

On 22 July Perast men row decorated boats laden with stones to Gospa od Škrpjela in a centuries-old tradition, adding to the artificial island created by their ancestors. The event is now accompanied by the Perast to Tivat yacht regatta. (p45)

August

August is the hottest and driest month, sometimes resulting in wildfires. The party continues on the coast and Lake Skadar is at its very best, but in Podgorica it gets unbearably hot.

✨ Boka Night

Kotor goes crazy on its night of nights – celebrated since the 19th century (and possibly before) – with a parade of lavishly decorated boats, Old Town parties and seemingly never-ending fireworks. (p50)

September

Temperatures drop back to the 20s and 'The Season' comes to an abrupt halt, with prices dropping and some beach businesses disappearing – despite the weather remaining lovely. It's a great time to visit.

October

On the coast, sea and water temperatures remain in the 20s but rainfall increases. Rafting comes to an end. The autumn leaves put on a show in Biogradska Gora National Park.

November

Wrap up warm and bring a raincoat. November is the wettest month and temperatures drop to the low teens, with average lows falling below freezing level in the mountains.

December

Rainfall remains high. On the coast, many businesses remain completely closed. Towards the end of the month you might get some days on the ski slopes.

Itineraries

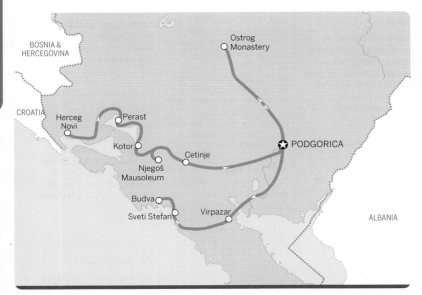

 A Taste of Montenegro

This 325km trip zigzags from the coast to Montenegro's heartland then back to the beaches again, taking in some of the country's most emblematic sights. It requires a car.

Start in **Herceg Novi** and slowly wind your way towards **Kotor**, allowing at least an hour in **Perast** en route. All three are ancient bayside towns filled with old churches and marbled squares. The next morning, take the dazzling drive to the historic Montenegrin capital **Cetinje** through Lovćen National Park, stopping to visit the **Njegoš Mausoleum** on the way. Explore Cetinje's museums and galleries by day, its lively cafe-bars by night.

Next day, head up to the dramatically positioned **Ostrog Monastery** before sweeping south to **Podgorica** to roam the small capital and sample its up-and-coming bar scene. On day four, continue to **Virpazar** for a chilled-out two-hour cruise on Lake Skadar. Carry on down to **Sveti Stefan**, check into somewhere with an island view and head to the beach. Spend your last day in **Budva**, splitting your time between exploring the Old Town and lazing on the sand.

The Full Monte

Most of Montenegro's big-hitting beauty spots are covered in this almost-800km itinerary.

Base yourself in **Herceg Novi** and take a boat or kayak trip to Rose, Mamula Island, the Blue Grotto and the beaches of the Luštica Peninsula. Stop at Morinj and Risan on your way to **Perast**, and don't miss the boat trip to Gospa od Škrpjela island. Continue to **Kotor** and use the walled town as a base to visit Dobrota, Prčanj and Stoliv. Then head through Lovćen National Park to **Cetinje**, making time for a quick tour of **Lipa Cave** before stopping in **Ostrog Monastery**. Carry on north through the Piva Canyon to **Šćepan Polje**, the main staging point for rafting trips down the Tara River. Stay the night at one of the rafting camps, and take on the river on a half-day trip. Hop back in the car and take the scenic road east from Plužine through Durmitor National Park to **Žabljak**. Allow some time to enjoy the park and, at a minimum, make sure you hike around the Black Lake.

Follow the road along the Tara River to the isolated Dobrilovina Monastery then continue on to **Biogradska Gora National Park** – you can stay in the cabins here or continue on to the upmarket hotels in **Kolašin**. Stop at the **Morača Monastery** on your way to **Podgorica**, then hang out in the capital for a day. Continue down to **Virpazar** for a morning's cruise on Lake Skadar. Skirt the Rumija Mountains until the road shies away from the Albanian border and hooks down to the buzzy beachside town of **Ulcinj**. Be sure to visit Velika Plaža before continuing back up the coast. Stop to check out the charming ruins of **Stari Bar** before you get to the beach town of **Petrovac**. Continue along the coast, stopping at the beaches of **Sveti Stefan** and **Pržno** before finishing up in **Budva**, with its walled Old Town and busy promenade.

If you're travelling by bus, you'll need to pare back the itinerary a little. From Kotor, the easiest way to Cetinje, Ostrog or rafting is on a day tour. Swap the Plužine–Žabljak road for a Nikšić–Žabljak bus. To get from Žabljak to Kolašin, you'll need to go via Pljevlja or Podgorica. From Virpazar, take a train to Bar followed by a bus to Ulcinj.

LARA-SH/SHUTTERSTOCK ©

Top: Petrovac (p76)

Bottom: Roman mosaics (p43), Risan

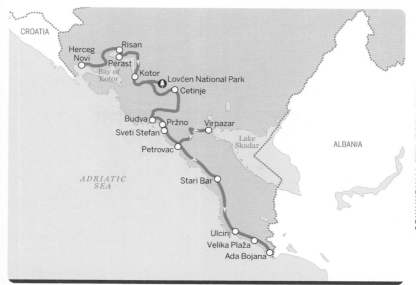

The Coast

Spend a day in **Herceg Novi** and consider a kayak tour or a boat trip to the beaches on the Luštica Peninsula. The following day, make your way slowly to Kotor, stopping to view the Roman mosaics at **Risan** and the baroque beauty of **Perast**. Base yourself in **Kotor** on day three; climb the fortifications, hike the Vrmac Ridge, explore neighbouring coastal villages or just hang out in the fascinating Old Town.

If you've got a car, take the serpentine road up to **Lovćen National Park**, then explore the museums and galleries of **Cetinje** before heading to **Budva** for the night. If you're travelling by bus, head straight to Budva and save Cetinje for another day.

For the following two days, base yourself anywhere on the stretch of coast between Budva and Petrovac. Budva is the easiest place to arrange a day tour to Ostrog Monastery and Lake Skadar, or a rafting trip on the Tara River, while **Petrovac** is more family-friendly, with a relaxed vibe and great beaches nearby. Close neighbours **Pržno** and **Sveti Stefan** also have excellent accommodation options, great restaurants and striking coastal views.

No matter where you put down roots, make sure you take the walk through the woods from Sveti Stefan to Pržno. A car or bike will get you to hidden bays such as Drobni Pijesak and Rijeka Reževići, and there are several monasteries to explore, including Podmaine and Podostrog, near Budva, and Reževići and Gradište, near Petrovac.

Continue south until you get to the Sozina tunnel near Sutomore, and drive through it to **Virpazar**, gateway to Lake Skadar, to take a boat cruise and enjoy a village-style meal in one of Montenegro's top restaurants. Retrace your steps back to the coast, and head southeast to visit the ruins of **Stari Bar** on your way to **Ulcinj**. The atmosphere of this largely Albanian town is quite different from anywhere else in Montenegro and there's a palpable buzz on the streets at night. The succession of rocky coves heading east from the crowded town beach are great for snorkelling. Nearby is the 12km continuous stretch of sand known as **Velika Plaža** and just across the Bojana River there's a further 3km of beach on the nudist island **Ada Bojana**.

 The Hidden North

This mountainous 650km loop includes visits to isolated monasteries and ample opportunities for wilderness hiking. You won't be able to tackle this route in winter, as snows close the Plužine–Žabljak road, and rafting stops in October.

Spend the morning exploring the nation's capital and biggest city, **Podgorica**, and then head through Danilovgrad to the extraordinary **Ostrog Monastery**. Continue on through Nikšić before reaching **Piva Monastery**, with its sumptuous frescoes, and the start of the Piva Canyon. From here the road passes through numerous tunnels cut into the canyon walls until you reach the Bosnian border at **Šćepan Polje**, the main rafting base. Check yourself into one of the rafting camps for the night.

Start day two with rafting on the Tara River, then drive back through the canyon as far as Plužine. From here, take the scenic mountain road through Durmitor National Park to **Žabljak**. Spend the rest of this and the next day hitting the park's hiking tracks.

On day four, drive east to the Tara Bridge and head north to **Pljevlja** to visit Montenegro's most beautiful mosque and a picturesque Orthodox monastery. Double back to the Tara Bridge and continue southeast along the river road. Consider making Eko-Oaza Tear of Europe your pit stop for this leg; from here you can walk to the secluded **Dobrilovina Monastery** and to a swimming hole on the river.

Continue to **Mojkovac** and then head north around the Bjelasica Massif and back down through Berane to Plav. Base yourself nearby for a day's hiking in **Prokletije National Park**; make sure you fit in a quick visit to the old Ottoman town of **Gusinje**. The following day, take the awe-inspiring back road through Andrijevica to **Kolašin**, Montenegro's best-developed mountain resort. Spend the rest of the day tackling the tracks through **Biogradska Gora National Park**.

The road back to Podgorica follows the Morača Canyon. At the start of the canyon, call in to admire the exquisite frescoes and icons at peaceful **Morača Monastery**.

Cycling, Kotor (p46)

Plan Your Trip

Outdoor Activities

Montenegro's diverse landscape lends itself to so much more than simply lazing on the country's beautiful beaches. Five national parks beckon, taunting nature buffs and adrenaline addicts with all the adventurous activities that such mighty mountains, rivers and lakes can inspire. And when nature calls, why resist?

Need to Know

When to Go

The best time for a well-rounded roster of adventures is May and early June, when the melting ice adds thrills to a rafting trip and the wildflowers are bursting into bloom.

Sea and air temperatures are highest in July and August, but you'll be battling the crowds on the beaches and there are sometimes wildfires during particularly hot summers. Otherwise, it's a good time to be in the mountains.

September and October are also good options, especially if you like your hikes accompanied by a blazing backdrop of autumn colour.

Ski buffs should head north between January and March.

What to Pack

You'll need a pair of sturdy hiking boots and you should consider packing a compass or GPS device, first-aid kit and a torch (flashlight). If you're a serious rock climber or mountaineer, it's best to bring any specialist gear you might need with you.

On the Water

Rafting

This is Montenegro's premier active drawcard. Commercial rafting is well established on the Tara River and once you've experienced the spectacular canyon you'll understand why. The season runs between April and October.

Kayaking

The Bay of Kotor and Lake Skadar are both brilliant places for a paddle, and several operators specialise in day tours. Very experienced white-water kayakers can take on the rapids of some of Montenegro's rivers, but you're best to take local advice first as some stretches are dangerous.

Diving

Not all the landscape, wildlife and history is above ground. Montenegro's azure waters hide caves, shelves, springs and thousands of years' worth of shipwrecks – those Ulcinj pirates were busy chaps and WWII added to the collection. Visibility ranges from 10m to 25m but is usually around 15m. The main fauna you're likely to spot are swarms of young dentex, gilthead bream and the occasional lobster or sea turtle.

The best times to dive are from the middle of May until September, when the surface water is up to 25°C, dropping to 16°C under 30m (you'll need a 7mm neoprene wetsuit). You'll find diving operators in Budva, Pržno and Ulcinj.

Kitesurfing

At the far south of the coast, the Velika Plaža and Ada Bojana area has taken off as one of the Mediterranean's kitesurfing hubs. It's a great place to learn the sport.

On Land

Hiking

Thanks to the enthusiastic members of mountain clubs all over the country, Montenegro has an excellent network of hiking tracks – although they're not all well maintained or well marked.

Whether you're armed with a tent or just planning a day walk, be well prepared for sudden changes in temperature and storms, and note that water supplies can be limited.

The main difficulty serious walkers and mountaineers will face is access to accommodation on longer expeditions. Mountain huts are available in some places but it can be difficult for the independent traveller to access them. Adventure-focused travel agencies can help with this, and can also arrange experienced guides from the local club. Montenegro's Mountaineering Association (www.pscg.me) can also help.

Some of the best short hikes include the easy circuits of Biogradska Gora's **Lake Biograd** and Durmitor's Black Lake (p117), and the Vrmac Ridge in the Bay of Kotor. Hard-core hikers should consider tackling the Peaks of the Balkans trail (Prokletije Mountains) or the 180km Coastal Mountain Traversal (p41).

Canyoning

Montenegro is run through with countless canyons, and organised expeditions up, down and through them are becoming more popular. Nevidio (p119), just south of Durmitor National Park, is one of the most visited; active tours of Sopot (p41) near Herceg Novi, Škurda (p50) above Kotor, and Rikavac and Medjurečje (p81) near Bar are also available. Of these, only Rikavac is suitable for kids; for the rest, a modicum of physical fitness is required, as are strong swimming skills.

If you're an experienced canyoner looking to choose your own adventure, get in touch with the crew at Extreme Canyoning (www.extremecanyoning.com); the website also has a full list of canyons in Montenegro and neighbouring Serbia.

Cycling

With so many mountains in Montenegro, it's no surprise that mountain biking is on the agenda. The National Tourist Office (www.montenegro.travel) has developed five 'top trails', outlined in a Wilderness Biking pamphlet (available from tourist offices). Montenegro Biking (www.pedalaj.me) is an independent affiliation of bike enthusiasts; their website has a wealth of information on Montenegrin trails and tours.

Diving in the Adriatic Sea

Montenegro Bed and Bike (www.bedandbike.me) is an accommodation network of cyclist-orientated hotels, hostels and eco-villages.

For a single day's cycling, consider the Vrmac Ridge (starting near Kotor), the loop track from Cetinje through Lovćen

PLAN YOUR TRIP OUTDOOR ACTIVITIES

EXPERT HELP

Rafting, kayaking, canyoning and skiing can be easily organised when you get to Montenegro, but arranging mountain guides, access to huts, specialist equipment and logistical support for more difficult expeditions can be a nightmare. If you're planning an action-intensive holiday, it is well worth engaging the services of one of the agencies that specialise in such things. Options include the following:

➡ Black Mountain (p40)

➡ Montenegro Adventures (p103)

➡ Undiscovered Montenegro (p170)

➡ Explorer Tourist Agency (p114)

➡ Anitra Travel Agency (p108)

➡ Summit Travel Agency (p119)

➡ Active Travels Montenegro (p40)

➡ Montenegro+ (p59)

Parasailing, Budva (p66)

National Park or the loop from Virpazar through Crmnica field.

Skiing

Montenegro's ski season lasts from roughly January to March, with the peak time being around New Year. The best-equipped ski resort is near Kolašin, but the most reliable skiing is in Durmitor National Park, where there are slopes close to Žabljak with options for beginners or serious skiers. There are also small ski centres near Nikšić and Rožaje in the east. Cross-country skiing can be undertaken in Lovćen and Durmitor National Parks.

In the Air
Paragliding & Parasailing

Montenegro has plenty of precipices from which you can hurl yourself and while hang-gliding is yet to take off, paragliding is starting to soar. If you want the feeling of flying without having to jump off anything, you might like to try the less vertigo-inducing option of parasailing. Both activities are offered from near Bečići.

Regions at a Glance

Bay of Kotor

Vistas of the Bay

Whether gazing at it from water level or from high above on the Lovćen road, the bay's mountain ramparts and inky waters will take your breath away.

Echoes of Venice

Built to last out of gleaming stone, the Bay of Kotor's numerous palaces and churches owe much to the influence of its one-time taskmaster to the north. Nowhere is this more apparent than in Perast, a little town bathed in the baroque.

Coastal Cuisine

The seafood dishes of the coast represent the best of the country's traditional cuisines. Try specialities such as grilled squid, fish soup, squid-ink risotto or simply grilled fish, drizzled with olive oil, parsley and garlic.

p36

Adriatic Coast

Beach Life

Clear waters, mountain backdrops and a sunny summer conspire to bring the Mediterranean fantasy into reality. Rows of umbrellas and recliners blanket the busier beaches, but you can escape the tourist hordes in secluded spots such as Kraljičina Plaža and Drobni Pijesak.

Walled Towns

From the marbled streets of Budva's Old Town, to the cobbled lanes of Ulcinj's, to the ruins of Stari Bar, the coast's walled towns will transport you through time.

Party Central

Come summer, Budva becomes Montenegro's party capital. Up to 5000 people regularly dance the night away at the open-air Top Hill nightclub, while down by the water, a string of alfresco bars and clubs pulls punters day and night.

p64

Central Montenegro

National Parks

From the depths of Lake Skadar to the heights of Lovćen, central Montenegro's national parks protect a broad range of habitats. Birdwatchers will find plenty to twitch about, especially around Skadar, which is categorised as a wetland of international importance.

The Royal Capital

Much of Montenegro's history, culture and national identity is tied to Cetinje, its former capital. That story is told through the town's historic buildings and an array of museums.

Spiritual Outposts

The monastic life is integral to the Serbian Orthodox faith, and this region is blessed with the country's most significant shrine, Ostrog Monastery. Almost as affecting are the tiny island monasteries scattered around Lake Skadar.

p91

Northern Mountains

Mountain Majesty

Large areas of rugged wilderness blanket this region, from Durmitor in the northwest to Prokletije in the southeast and Bjelasica in between. It's an extraordinary landscape that never fails to astound.

Outdoor Adventures

Durmitor is the activity capital of Montenegro. The big three are rafting, hiking and skiing, but there's also the potential for rock climbing, canyoning and mountaineering.

Frescoes & Icons

Not only does Morača Monastery have an exquisite setting, it contains an extraordinary wealth of religious art. Morača may be the most beautiful of Montenegro's monasteries, but Piva, Dobrilovina and Pljevlja's Holy Trinity are no slackers either.

p111

Dubrovnik (Croatia)

The City & the Sea

Gazing down upon the spectacularly beautiful old town provides such a thrill that the town's most popular attractions provide opportunities to do just that. Circle the city walls for an intimate perspective or take the cable car up Mt Srđ for the bird's-eye view.

Stone & Marble

Wandering amid the honey-coloured stone buildings of the old town is like walking through a textbook on the history of European architecture. Everywhere you look there are impressive Romanesque, Gothic, baroque and Renaissance structures – still standing and still in use, despite the wartime battering.

Museums

Learn about the Republic of Ragusa in the Rector's Palace or brush up on more recent events at the Homeland War Museum and War Photo Limited.

p127

On the Road

Dubrovnik
(Croatia) ◉
p127

Central
Montenegro
p91

Northern
Mountains
p111

Bay of
Kotor
p36

Adriatic
Coast
p64

Bay of Kotor

Best Places to Eat

➜ Ribarsko Selo (p63)

➜ Konoba Ćatovića Mlini (p43)

➜ Galion (p51)

➜ Konoba Školji (p45)

Best Places to Sleep

➜ Hotel Aurora (p40)

➜ Hotel Hippocampus (p50)

➜ Klinci Village Resort (p63)

➜ Regent Porto Montenegro (p60)

➜ Old Town Hostel (p50)

➜ Camp Full Monte (p42)

Why Go?

Gorgeous, breathtaking, majestic, divine; however hefty your thesaurus, the brain-blowing beauty of the Bay of Kotor will leave you struggling for superlatives. Hemmed in by commanding cliffs and shape-shifting between rippling gulfs and sparkling straits, the cobalt cove even manages to defy geographic description: is it a fjord? A submerged canyon? It seems there's only one way to define Boka Kotorska: unmissable.

Scattered with photogenic medieval towns admiring their reflections in peacock-blue inlets, the compact bay – or simply the 'Boka', as it's known in local parlance – is stitched together by a series of scenic, serpentine roads, making it easy to explore. As if determined to prove the 'good things come in small packages' adage, the region crams in everything from island monasteries and show-stopping citadels to adventure sports and extraordinary eateries, where waterfront views induce as much drooling as the fresh seafood. Whatever your bliss, you'll find it in the Boka.

When to Go

➜ May is dry, with mild temperatures and fragrant Mediterranean foliage in bloom.

➜ June is the best month, with temperatures in the high 20s, low rainfall and off-peak prices.

➜ July and August are the hottest and driest months – but also the busiest and most expensive.

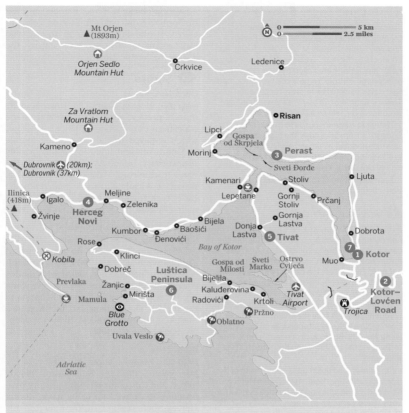

Bay of Kotor Highlights

1 **Kotor's Old Town** (p46) Randomly roaming the atmospheric laneways until you're at least a little lost.

2 **Back road to Mt Lovćen** (p51) Winding your way to dizzying views on the snaking back road from Kotor to Lovćen National Park.

3 **Perast** (p44) Admiring the baroque beauty of historic palazzos and churches.

4 **Herceg Novi** (p38) Cooling off in the shade with a drink on Trg Herceg Stjepana.

5 **Tivat** (p57) Seeing how the other half lives

in glitzy, glamorous Porto Montenegro.

6 **Luštica Peninsula** (p61) Losing yourself within the olive groves in the remote byways.

7 **Kayaking** (p49) Paddling your way to island fortresses, remote beaches and sea caves on a day tour.

Climate

The weather in the outer section of the bay isn't markedly different from the pleasant Mediterranean climate of the coast. Southwest-facing Tivat has a reputation for being one of the sunniest spots. Cloud often drapes the high cliffs of the inner bay.

Crkvice in the Orjen massif above Risan is said to have the highest rainfall in Europe, averaging 5300mL per annum. The record was in 1937 when it hit 8065mL. Luckily, the karstic nature of the terrain causes the water to disappear into the limestone rather than flooding the towns below.

ℹ Getting There & Away

Jadranski Put (Adriatic highway) connects the Bay of Kotor to Dubrovnik and to Budva. A highway leaves the bay at Lipci, near Risan, and connects to the main Trebinje–Nikšić highway. Kotor and Cetinje are linked by a narrow and precipitous – but extremely scenic – back road that dates back to the Austrian occupation. There's an ambitious plan – as yet unfulfilled – to connect the two by a 15km cable car.

There are frequent buses to Budva and Podgorica from all around the bay, with some services heading as far as Sarajevo and Belgrade. Buses head between Kotor and Dubrovnik six times a day, via Herceg Novi.

Tivat Airport welcomes domestic and international flights.

ℹ Getting Around

A road wends its way around the entire coast, narrowing considerably between Kotor and the car ferry and on the Luštica Peninsula. From Kotor the main road takes a tunnel and comes out near Tivat Airport. A car ferry crosses back and forth between Kamenari and Lepetane at the bay's narrowest point.

There are three main bus routes in the Boka. Frequent services take the coastal road from Herceg Novi to Kotor, stopping at all the villages along the way. Buses also connect Herceg Novi to Tivat via the car ferry and Kotor to Tivat via the tunnel.

In summer, taxi boats are a useful form of transportation, particularly between Herceg Novi and the beaches on the Luštica Peninsula. They're easy enough to find in the busy marinas in July and August but more difficult at other times.

Herceg Novi

🖉 031 / POP 11,100

Standing at the entrance to the Bay of Kotor like an eager host, Herceg Novi (Херцег Нови) welcomes visitors with bright bouquets, sparkling seas and almost-constant sunshine. Can't find the party? Look down; it's all happening a few dozen wonky steps below the main highway. The Old Town's shiny squares, elegant churches and formidable fortresses echo with the clatter of cafes and bars. Further down, pebbly beaches and concrete terraces offer access to the bay's best – and cleanest – swimming. Follow the pedestrian-only promenade and you'll hit Igalo, famed for its therapeutic mud.

'Novi' means 'new', and while this is indeed one of the newer towns on the bay, it's no spring chicken; it was founded in 1382 by Bosnia's King Tvrtko I. 'Herceg' refers to Herceg (Duke) Stjepan Vukčić Kosača, who fortified the town in the 15th century; the remaining fortifications are a little younger.

◉ Sights

Ulica Njegoševa   STREET

(Map p39) Herceg Novi's Old Town is at its most impressive when approached from the pedestrian-only section of Ulica Njegoševa, which is paved in the same shiny marble as Dubrovnik and lined in elegant, mainly 19th-century buildings. The street terminates in cafe-ringed Trg Nikole Đurkovića, where steps lead up to an elegant crenulated 1667 clock tower (Map p39) FREE above the main city gate.

Archangel Michael's Church   CHURCH

(Crkva svetog Arhanđela Mihaila; Map p39; ⊘ 7.45am-midnight Jun-Aug, to 9pm Sep-May) Built between 1883 and 1905, this beautifully proportioned, domed, Serbian Orthodox church sits at the centre of gleaming white Trg Herceg Stejpana (known as Belavista to the locals). The archangel is pictured in a mosaic in the lunette above the door, under an elegant rose window.

Kanli Kula   FORTRESS

(Map p39; I Bokeške brigade bb; adult/child €2/ free; ⊘ 9am-9pm) Kanli Kula means 'bloody tower', and this notorious 16th-century prison more than lived up to its name during Herceg Novi's years of Turkish rule (roughly 1482–1687); in the dungeon below the lower set of flagpoles, you can see where doomed inmates carved into the walls. The huge fort is a far more pleasant place these days, offering stupendous views over the town from its sturdy fortifications. During summer it often hosts musical and theatrical performances.

Forte Mare   FORTRESS

(Map p39; Save Kovačevića bb; €2; ⊘ 9am-8pm) The bastion at the town's seaward edge was built between the 14th and 17th centuries but owes its current look to an Austrian makeover in 1833. It's now used for film screenings on summer nights. Downstairs, a 15-minute video tells the story of Ottoman admiral Barbarossa wresting the fort from the Spanish in the 1539 Siege of Castelnuovo.

In the sea below, you can see the ruins of the Citadela (Map p39), a Venetian-built fort that was the victim of a major earthquake that hit the coast in 1979.

Herceg Novi

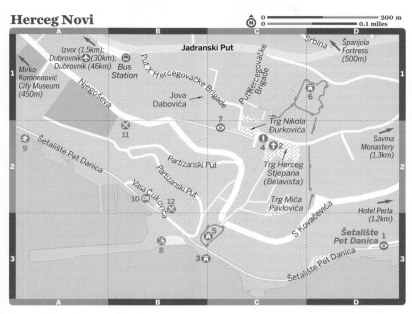

Herceg Novi

★ **Šetalište Pet Danica**   WATERFRONT
(Map p39) Named after five young women named Danica who died during WWII, this pedestrian promenade stretches along the waterfront for more than 5km from Igalo to Meljine. It's lined with summer bars, shops, concrete swimming platforms and the odd rocky cove; in places it ducks in and out of tunnels carved through headlands. The strip follows the route of a former train line that once linked the coast to Sarajevo.

Mirko Komnenović City Museum   MUSEUM
(Gradski muzej; ☏ 031-340 265; www.rastko.rs/rastko-bo/muzej; Mirka Komnenovića 9; adult/child €3/1; ☺ 8am-8pm Mon-Sat May-Sep, 9am-5pm Mon-Sat Oct-Apr) Apart from the building itself (a fabulous bougainvillea-shrouded baroque palace with sea views), the highlight of this little museum is its impressive collection of religious icons. Displays detail Herceg Novi's complicated history, along with archaeological relics and folk costumes. It's named after the former mayor, who donated the building.

Savina Monastery   CHRISTIAN MONASTERY
(Manastir Savina; Braće Grakalić bb; ☺ 6am-8pm) Named after Sava, founder of the Serbian Orthodox Church, this peaceful monastery enjoys wonderful coastal views from its location on the town's eastern slopes. It's dominated by the elegant 18th-century **Church of the Dormition** (Crkva uspenja Bogorodice; literally 'the falling into sleep of the Mother of God'), carved from Croatian pinkish stone. Inside there's a beautiful gilded iconostasis. The smaller church beside it

has the same name but is considerably older (possibly 14th century) and has the remains of frescoes.

The monastery grounds also include a vineyard, part of the Savina Winery (www. castelsavina.me); the wine is sold at the monastery shop.

Savina is well signposted from the large roundabout on the highway at Meljine.

🏃 Activities

Herceg Novi is arguably the country's best base for arranging active pursuits, with a diverse network of professional, customer-focused, environmentally aware businesses offering a huge variety of options.

Kayak Herceg Novi　　　　　KAYAKING
(Map p39; ☑ 067-531 366; www.kayak-hercegnovi. com; Zalo Beach; hire per 1/4/8hr from €7/25/35; ⊙ May-Oct) Don't just admire the beautiful bay from the Old Town and along the promenade: hop aboard a kayak and explore it! In addition to rentals, this outfit also runs guided kayaking tours (half-/full day from €30/50) to Rose, Dobreč, Igalo and Mamula Island.

Yachting Club 32　　　　　BOATING
(Map p39; ☑ 069-263 888; Šetalište Pet Danica 32) Hires jet skis (€45 per 30 minutes), pedal boats (€5 per hour) and mountain bikes (€3/10 per hour/day), and organises sailing classes and boat trips. If all that sunshine has tuckered you out, it's a top spot to kick back with a drink and do some water-watching.

Adriatic Blue　　　　　DIVING
(☑ 069-833 043; www.divingmontenegro.com) This friendly group explores the wrecks, underwater caves and islands of Boka Bay. Intro dives (€50), two-tank dives (€70) and PADI courses (from €300) include all gear and boat transfers.

ⓘ CYCLE THE SHORELINE

Cyclists should consider leaving the highway at Igalo and pedalling along the waterfront. In summer you'll be slowed by foot traffic but it's a much flatter, safer and more picturesque route than the highway. Apart from a few stretches where you'll be forced back on to the main road, you can travel most of the way to Kamenari alongside the water.

Active Travels Montenegro　　ADVENTURE
(☑ 068-658 285; www.activetravelsmontenegro. com) Local guys with excellent English lead rafting, coasteering, hiking and canyoning trips, vineyard visits and sightseeing tours.

★ Black Mountain　　　　ADVENTURE
(☑ 067-076 676; www.montenegroholiday.com) 🖉 An excellent full-service agency that can arrange pretty much anything, anywhere in the country, including mountain biking, diving, rafting, hiking, canyoning, boat trips and wine tasting. It can take care of the basics too, such as accommodation, car hire and transfers.

✹ Festivals & Events

Mimosa Festival　　　PARADE, MUSIC
(www.hercegfest.co.me; ⊙ Feb) A mash of yellow blooms, marching majorettes, concerts and sports events.

🛌 Sleeping

For all its popularity, Herceg Novi is poorly served by hotels, with only a few decent options. Private accommodation is a better bet.

Stanica Hotel Aurora　BOUTIQUE HOTEL €€
(Map p39; ☑ 067-552 319; www.aurorahotel.me; Šetalište Pet Danica 42; d/apt €70/100; ❈ 🛜) Famous (and famously quirky) Serbian director Emir Kusturica is to thank for converting Herceg Novi's former train station into this seaside inn. The rooms and apartments are characterful (ask for one with a sea view), and it's located in the thick of the action. There's a good but noisy on-site bar and restaurant, and – of course – a small cinema.

Hotel Perla　　　　　HOTEL €€
(☑ 031-345 700; www.perla.me; Šetalište Pet Danica 98; r/apt from €74/230; 🅿❈🛜) It's a 15-minute stroll from the centre but if it's beach you're after, Perla's position is perfect. The helpful staff speak excellent English and the front rooms of this medium-sized modern block have private terraces and sea views. Bikes are available for hire and there's a great kids' playground by the beach.

🍴 Eating & Drinking

★ Konoba Feral　　　MEDITERRANEAN €€
(Map p39; ☑ 031-322 232; www.konobaferal.com; Vasa Ćukovića 4; mains €8-20; ⊙ 8am-midnight; 🛜) A *feral* is a ship's lantern, so it's seafood, not unruly animals, that takes pride of place on the menu. The grilled squid and homemade seafood tagliatelle are excellent, and

the wine list includes vintages from the Savina Monastery (p39). This charming place is consistently ranked as the best in town; book ahead if you want to sit on the terrace.

Gradska Kafana　　　　　MEDITERRANEAN €€
(Map p39; 📱031-324 067; www.gradskakafana. me; Njegoševa 31; mains €7-22; ⏰7am-midnight; 🛜) Austrian-era elegance infuses this venerable cafe-restaurant, but sophisticated dishes, such as grilled prawns in a honey-and-orange sauce, prove that it's not stuck in the past. It's also a lovely spot to soak in the sea views over coffee and cake.

ⓘ Getting There & Around

BOAT

Taxi boats ply the coast during summer, charging about €10 for a trip to the beaches on the Luštica Peninsula or €15 to the Blue Cave. You'll sometimes get a better rate in Igalo where there's more competition.

BUS

Buses stop at the **station** (Map p39; 📱031-321 225; Dr J Bijelići 1; ⏰6am-midnight) just above the Old Town. There are frequent buses to Kotor (€4, one hour), which stop at all of the small towns around the bay. Buses to Budva (€6) either go via Kotor or on the ferry through Tivat (€3), which is usually quicker depending on the queues. Frequent services head to Cetinje (€8, 2½ hours) and Podgorica (€10, three hours).

International destinations include Dubrovnik, Trebinje, Sarajevo, Belgrade and Skopje.

CAR

A tortuous, often gridlocked, one-way system runs through the town. Street parks are divided into two zones charged at either 50c or 80c per hour, or €5 per day; purchase tickets from newsagents or kiosks, circle the time and date, and display them on your dashboard. You can also pay by SMS: follow the directions on the signs.

TAXI

Taxi More (📱19730; www.taximore.com; minimum fare €1.30, per km 90c) Advertises set fares to Dubrovnik Airport (€60), Tivat (€45), Kotor (€50), Budva (€60) and Podgorica Airport (€110). You'll pay extra if there are queues for the Kamenari car ferry.

Around Herceg Novi

Herceg Novi's coastal sprawl starts at Igalo to the west, where the muddy silt from the sea floor is said to have therapeutic qualities. Heading east along the bay, you'll pass

ⓘ STEP BY STEP
....

Herceg Novi is extremely hilly and the fastest way from the highway to the beach is via one of the numerous sets of steps. Charming as the stairways (stepenište) are, they make Herceg Novi one of the most challenging towns in Montenegro for the mobility-impaired.

beachside communities at Zelenika, Kumbor, Đenovići, Baošići and the industrial town of Bijela before reaching Kamenari, where a ferry plies the waters to and from Lepetane.

⊙ Sights

Mt Orjen　　　　　　　　　　MOUNTAIN
Hulking Mt Orjen (1893m) separates Herceg Novi from Hercegovina and is higher than the more famous Mt Lovćen. It's a popular spot for hiking and mountain biking (bring plenty of water). A hiking trail commences near the bus station at Herceg Novi (look for the red and white markings); heading towards Kotor, take the first road to the left, followed quickly by a right turn. This is the start of the mammoth Coastal Mountain Traversal (Primorska planinarska transverzala; PPT) hiking path, which goes on to Lovćen, the shores of Lake Skadar, Mt Rumija and Bar.

There are more than 60km of marked tracks on the mountain. A relatively easy 16km round-trip hike goes from Herceg Novi to the small Sv Ilija church; follow the coast to Igalo and take the signposted trail.

For six months of the year, there is snow on Mt Orjen; even on a summer's day you should be prepared for a storm.

Planinarski Klub Subra (www.pksubra.me; guide per day from €70), the local mountaineering club, operates two huts on the mountain and can arrange guides.

🏃 Activities

Sopot Canyon　　　　　　ADVENTURE SPORTS
Not far from Herceg Novi, this little-visited canyon was opened for organised expeditions with Active Travels Montenegro. Five-hour canyoning trips (€115) include hiking through water, swimming and abseiling down waterfalls (15m to 65m). For confident swimmers aged 16 and up.

ⓘ KAMENARI–LEPETANE CAR FERRY

The Bay of Kotor is a very peculiar shape. The entrance is guarded by two peninsulas that shelter the first section of the bay incorporating Herceg Novi and Tivat. The waters then narrow into a thin channel before the spectacular inner bay opens up. **Car ferries** (☎031-673 522; www.ferry.co.me; car/motorcycle/bicycle/passenger €4.50/2/1/free; ⊘24hr) wend their way across the narrowest point (the Verige Strait) from Kamenari (15km east of Herceg Novi) to Lepetane (5km north of Tivat). They depart roughly every 15 minutes (hourly after 10pm) and the journey only takes about five minutes.

The alternative, the coastal road along the bay to Kotor, is truly spectacular and should be travelled at least once, whether by car or bus. The distance between Herceg Novi and Kotor is only 43km, but it can easily take an hour, longer if you get stuck behind a truck on the narrow winding road.

There's no doubt that the ferry is quicker for Tivat or Budva, but in the height of summer there can be horrendous queues, sometimes stretching for kilometres. For Kotor, the benefit is more marginal. If there are no queues and you've already travelled the scenic route, you might consider catching the ferry and heading to Kotor via the tunnel south of the town. You're unlikely to gain more than about 10 minutes but you will save on petrol. Buses from Herceg Novi to Budva take both routes.

Long-held plans for a bridge spanning the Verige Strait may be edging closer to fruition. If completed, the four-lane cable-stayed Verige Bridge (981m) would cross between the two current ferry points, and significantly reduce traffic around the bay. Watch this space...

🛏 Sleeping

Camp Full Monte   CAMPGROUND €
(☎067-899 208; www.full-monte.com; Malta-Prijevor Put bb; campsites per person €12, tent rental 3-night minimum €20-25, glamping per person week/fortnight €280/550; ⊘May-Sep) 🌿 Hidden in the mountains near the Croatian border (check online for driving instructions), this campground offers solar-generated hot water, odourless composting toilets and heaps of seclusion. In case the name didn't give it away, clothing is optional. There's a fully equipped kitchen, and meals can be arranged. Customised glamping holidays are available, and include accommodation in a 'mansion' tent.

Igalo Spa   HOTEL €€
(☎031-658 555; www.igalospa.com; Sava Ilića 5, Igalo; r €41-53, ste from €60) More than just a Yugoslavia-era behemoth, this is also a health clinic, where guests can take advantage of the curative powers of Igalo's famous therapeutic mud (among other treatments). While the rooms haven't been as well cared for as visitors' health, caring staff, top views and the old-school bowling alley are top notch. Half- and full-board rates are also available.

Palmon Bay Hotel and Spa   RESORT €€€
(☎031-332 442; www.palmonbayspa.com; Sava Ilića 7, Igalo; d €150-240, ste €440; P❄🛜🏊) This sparkling new upscale resort is gorgeous inside and out. Looming from manicured grounds over a pretty pebbled beach, the hotel houses modern, clean rooms (some with exceptional views), four restaurants and a beautifully designed indoor pool/spa area. As befitting Igalo's reputation as a healing centre, the resort has numerous treatments, massages and saunas for guests to choose from.

🍴 Eating

Restoran Olimpija   SEAFOOD, MONTENEGRIN €€
(☎031-580 235; Kumbor; mains €4-15; ⊘8am-11pm) The locals love this family-run place for its stupendous mama-cooked meals, down-home atmosphere and enormous portion sizes. *Meso ispod sača* (meat cooked under a metal lid with hot coals on top) is the speciality here, though the flavourful fish soup is more than worth loosening your belt for.

Leut   SEAFOOD €€
(Braće Pedišić 59-61, Meljine; mains €6.50-20) You'll need to make an effort to find this local favourite, but the pay-off comes in the form of excellent Bokelj-style seafood served on a large terrace facing the water. To get here, follow the sign to Savina at the giant Meljine roundabout and then take the first left.

ℹ️ Getting There & Around

To truly explore this area, it's best to have your own wheels, though there are tons of buses running between Herceg Novi and Igalo (€1.50, 10 minutes) and in the other direction through all the villages en route to Kamenari (€2, 30 minutes).

The ferry between Kamenari and Lepetane runs 24 hours a day.

Morinj

📋 032 / POP 230

Secluded in the first bend of the inner bay, the fishing village of Morinj (Морињ) is divided into *gornji* (upper) and *donji* (lower) sections, like many of the coastal villages. The silver dome of St Petka Church (Crkva Sv Petke) sparkles above, but the main attraction here is the pretty beach. It's a sheltered nook so you may see algae in places, but the water's mainly clear and the views down the bay are amazing.

Morinj is a peaceful place now, but between 1991 and 1992, 300 Croatian POWs and civilians were incarcerated at a prison camp here.

⊙ Sights

Lipci Prehistoric Drawings   ARCHAEOLOGICAL SITE

You'd never know it – thanks to a distinct (and puzzling) lack of hype – but 3km up the road from Morinj, a quick hike will bring you to the Balkans' most comprehensive collection of prehistoric drawings. Created in the 8th century BC, the drawings – which include mystical animal and sun symbols – have been largely left alone: there's no signage bar a token street sign, no admission fee and no fences. If you're the Indiana Jones type, this one's for you.

To get here, head up the small single-lane road leading uphill after the lone Lipci road sign. Where the asphalt ends, follow the arrow up a rocky path (keep going past the cave) until you reach a cliff face. Look up. See paintings. Commence goosebumps.

🛏️ Sleeping & Eating

Autocamp Naluka   CAMPGROUND €

(📞 069-346 346; www.naluka.montenegro.com; campsites per adult/child €5/1, per tent/car/campervan €4/3.50/10; ☉May-Sep) Pitch your tent under the mandarin and olive trees and next to the stream that bubbles out of a spring at a constant 10°C – the water's too cold for mosquitoes but perfect for keeping your beer cold! There are only squat toilets but the site is kept immaculate by its English-speaking owner.

★**Konoba Ćatovića Mlini**   SEAFOOD €€€

(📞 032-373 030; www.catovica-mlini.com; mains €12-25; ☉11am-11pm) This rustic former mill masquerades as a humble *konoba* (simple family-run establishment), but they doth protest too much: this is one of Montenegro's best restaurants. Watch the geese waddle while you sample the magical bread and olive oil, which appears unbidden at the table. Fish is the focus, but give the traditional Njeguši specialities a go. Whatever you order, you will dream – while drooling – of it for years to come.

ℹ️ Getting There & Away

Morinj is a 30-minute bus ride from either Herceg Novi or Kotor.

Risan

📋 032 / POP 2040

While sunseekers still head to its small beaches, Risan (Рисан) has a rundown feel, not helped by the port and large (now-abandoned) hotel hogging its sea frontage. But Montenegro is booming, and with the explosion of mega-resorts, one can't help but believe Risan's ramshackle days are numbered.

It wouldn't be the first time Risan has risen from a slump. This is the oldest town on the bay, dating to at least the 3rd century BC when it was a fortified Illyrian town. After the Romans took over, the town exploded to a population of about 10,000, and its seaside was lined with sumptuous mansions.

Apart from the town's famous mosaics, not much remains from Risan's glory days, but those with a taste for history should take a stroll up Gabela, an atmospheric lane with interesting patterned cobbling dating from the Ottoman occupation.

⊙ Sights

Mosaics   RUINS

(€2; ☉8am-5pm) In 1930 the foundations of a grand villa were discovered in Risan, complete with wonderfully preserved Roman mosaics from the 2nd century AD. The building's not much to look at from the outside, but within, you'll find a dining-room floor decorated with flowers, herbs, grapevines and squid, while other rooms have intricate geometric patterns. Best of all is the bedroom, with its glorious depiction of Hypnos, the Greek god of sleep, reclining on a pillow.

🛏 Sleeping & Eating

Risan is a good option for those with wheels who are keen to explore the region without the price tag of the more popular towns. Private apartments are your best bet. Many advertise online, or look for signs reading 'sobe' (rooms).

Apartmani Risan APARTMENT €
(📞 032-371 077; www.apartmani-risan.com; Stara Slanica bb; apt from €35; 🅿 ❄ 🛜) Perched up a precarious hill, the two great-value apartments here offer majestic views over the sea and to the brooding mountains beyond. Both apartments have plenty of space and good facilities; the larger one has a sleeping loft. The owners – Sasha and Radan – live on-site, and are happy to be as hands-on (or off) as you'd like.

Restoran Risan SEAFOOD, MONTENEGRIN €€
(📞 032-371 805; mains €5-17; ⏱ 7am-11pm) Looking across the bay from Risan's main drag, the town's eponymous restaurant ladles out large portions of fresh seafood (including scrumptious local mussels) and heartier fare (it's renowned for its beef stroganoff).

❶ Getting There & Away

Buses running between Herceg Novi (30 minutes, €2.50) and Kotor (20 minutes, €2) stop in Risan.

Just out of Risan, a road climbs up, up, up to Nikšić and Žabljak, branching out west to Trebinje in Herzegovina.

Perast

📞 032 / POP 270

Looking like a chunk of Venice that has floated down the Adriatic and anchored itself onto the Bay of Kotor, Perast (Пераст) hums with melancholy memories of the days when it was rich and powerful. Despite having only one main street, this tiny town boasts 16 churches and 17 formerly grand palazzi. While some are just enigmatic ruins sprouting bougainvillea and wild fig, others are caught up in the whirlwind of renovation that has hit the town.

The town slopes down from the highway to a narrow waterfront road (Obala Marka Martinovića) that runs along its length. At its heart is St Nicholas' Church, set on a small square lined with date palms and the bronze busts of famous citizens.

Perast's most famous landmarks aren't on land at all: two peculiarly picturesque islands with equally peculiar histories.

◎ Sights

★ **Gospa od Škrpjela** ISLAND
(Our-Lady-of-the-Rock Island; ⏱ church 9am-7pm Jul & Aug, to 5pm Apr-Jun & Sep-Nov, to 3pm Dec-Mar) This picturesque island was artificially created (on 22 July 1452, to be precise) around a rock where an image of the Madonna was found; every year on that same day, the locals row over with stones to continue the task. In summer, boats line up on the Perast waterfront to ferry people there and back (€5 return); off-season, you may need to ask around.

The magnificent **church** at its centre was erected in 1630 and has sumptuous Venetian paintings, hundreds of silver votive tablets and a small museum (€1.50). The most unusual – and famous – exhibit is an embroidered icon of the Madonna and Child partly made with the hair of its maker.

Sveti Djordje ISLAND
(St George's Island) Sveti Djordje, rising from a natural reef, is the smaller of Perast's two islands. It houses a Benedictine monastery shaded by cypresses and a large cemetery, earning it the local nickname 'Island of the Dead'. Legend has it that the island is cursed...but it looks pretty heavenly to us. The island can only be admired from afar; visitors aren't encouraged.

St Nicholas' Church CHURCH
(Crkva Sv Nikole; Obala Marka Martinovića bb; treasury €1; ⏱ 8am-6pm) This large church has never been completed, and given that it was commenced in the 17th century and the bay's Catholic community has declined markedly since then, one suspects it never will be. Its treasury contains beautifully embroidered vestments and the remains of various saints. Climb the imposing 55m bell tower (€1) for impressive views over the bay.

Perast Museum MUSEUM
(Muzej grada Perasta; 📞 032-373 519; www.muzej perast.me; Obala Marka Martinovića bb; adult/child €4/1; ⏱ 9am-9pm May-Oct, to 3pm Nov-Apr) The Renaissance-baroque Bujović Palace, dating from 1694, has been lovingly preserved and converted into a museum showcasing the

town's proud seafaring history. It's worth visiting, less for the portraits of ships and bewhiskered gents, and more for the building itself – and for the wondrous photo opportunities afforded by its balcony.

✯✯ Festivals & Events

Fašinada RELIGIOUS, SPORTS
(www.fasinada-cup.com; ⊘ 22 Jul) In this traditional annual event, male descendants of Perast's leading families row a convoy of decorated and roped-together boats to deposit stones on Gospa od Škrpjela island. It's now accompanied by a two-day yachting regatta, the Fašinada Cup, with participants racing to Tivat and back.

⌱ Sleeping

Bogišić Rooms & Apartments APARTMENT €
(☑ 067-440 062; www.bogisicroomsapartment. com; Obala Marka Martinovića bb; s/apt €25/70; ⊘ May-Oct; ✻ ⚘) This welcoming place offers great value for money and a big serve of genuine Montenegrin hospitality. The rooms aren't massive, but they're comfortable, cute and right on the waterfront, and they have kitchenettes.

Palace Jelena BOUTIQUE HOTEL €€€
(☑ 032-373 549; www.palacejelena-perast.com; Obala Marka Martinovića bb; r €80-140; ✻ ⚘) This quaint, family-run hotel isn't suffering from delusions of grandeur; its four atmospheric rooms and lovely restaurant are actually located within a palace (the Lučić-Kolović-Matikola Palace to be precise). It's so close to the shore that you can hear waves lapping from your room. All rooms have gorgeous sea and island views; the most expensive has a balcony.

Hotel Conte APARTMENT €€
(☑ 032-373 687; www.hotelconte.me; Obala Marka Martinovića bb; r/apt from €95/160; ✻ ⚘) Conte is not so much a hotel as a series of deluxe studio to two-bedroom apartments in historic buildings scattered around St Nicholas' Church. The sense of age resonating from the stone walls is palpable, even with the distinctly nontraditional addition of a Jacuzzi and sauna in the flashest apartment. It's worth paying extra for a sea view.

✗ Eating & Drinking

Konoba Školji MONTENEGRIN, SEAFOOD €€
(☑ 069-419 745; www.skolji.com; Obala Marka Martinovića bb; mains €8-24; ⊘ 10am-midnight; ⚘) This appealing traditional restaurant is all about the thrill of the grill: fresh seafood and falling-off-the-bone meats are barbecued to perfection in full view of salivating diners. Thankfully they're not shy with the portion sizes; the delightful/maddening smell of the cooking and the sea air will have you ravenous by the time your meal arrives. The pasta is good, too.

★ Restaurant Conte SEAFOOD €€€
(☑ 032-373 722; www.hotelconte.me; Obala Marka Martinovića bb; mains €10-25; ⊘ 8am-midnight; ⚘) If you don't fall in love here – with Perast, with your dining partner, with a random waiter – consider your heart stone; with its island views, table-top flowers and superfresh oysters, this place is ridiculously romantic. You'll be presented with platters of whole fish to select from; the chosen one will return, cooked and silver-served, to your table.

Beach Bar Pirates BAR
(www.facebook.com/BeachBarPirates; Obala Marka Martinovića bb; ⊘ 8am-9pm Jun-Sep) Tucked under the road on the Risan edge of Perast, this little beach bar serves beers, cocktails and coffees to the beautiful board-shorts-and-bikinis brigade. It often hosts live music acts, DJs and beach parties – and it's the best spot in Perast for a swim.

ⓘ Information

There are no banks or ATMs in Perast (though credit cards are accepted almost everywhere).

ⓘ Getting There & Away

➜ Paid parking is available on either approach to town (per day €2) but, in summer, it's in hot demand.

➜ Car access into the town itself is restricted.

➜ There's no bus station but buses to and from Kotor (€1.50, 25 minutes) stop at least every 30 minutes on the main road at the top of town.

➜ Water taxis zoom around the bay during summer and call into all ports, including Perast.

➜ Regular taxis from Kotor to Perast cost around €15.

Dobrota

☑ 032 / POP 8170
Dobrota (Доброта) is effectively a residential suburb of Kotor, starting north of Kotor's Old Town and stretching along the shoreline for 5km. Despite the close proximity to its famous neighbour, it retains a distinctive feel.

While Kotor looks inwards from its walls, Dobrota gazes out to sea.

Foreign investors have renovated many of the decaying palazzos, some of which are much grander than those you'll find in Perast or Kotor. Soak it all up with an evening sashay along the elegant paved boardwalk tracing the water's edge.

◉ Sights

St Eustace's Church CHURCH
(Crkva Sv Eustahija) Cavernous St Eustace's dates from 1773 but has a 19th-century steeple and a little walled graveyard. It houses a valuable collection of paintings, including by Bellini and baroque master Carlo Dolci. Opening hours are iffy: you may be able to get in on Sundays.

Žuta Plaža BEACH
Dobrota is effectively Kotor's beach suburb. Private swimming platforms take up much of the waterline, but this pebbly stretch closest to Kotor is open to everybody. It's a beautiful spot for a swim, with the sheer mountain walls looming above, but it should be noted that there have been problems with water quality here.

🛏 Sleeping

Dobrota is a perfect base for exploring Kotor at arm's length from the noise and flurry of the Old Town. During summer, there are hundreds of private rooms and apartments available. Seek them out online or ask around; whomever you ask will invariably have a cousin (or a cousin's cousin) with accommodation to rent.

Montenegro Hostel 4U HOSTEL €
(☑067-675 070; Donji put bb; dm €10-13; ❋ 🛜) This buzzy hostel may be away from the clamour of the Old Town, but that doesn't mean sleep will come easy. If drinking games, nightly knees-ups and beach parties are your thing, you're unlikely to be interested in catching any zzzzs anyway. The fun-loving staff here somehow find the time to keep the place spotless.

★ Palazzo Radomiri HOTEL €€€
(☑032-333 176; www.palazzoradomiri.com; Dobrota 220; s/d/ste from €160/180/250; ⊙Apr-Oct; P ❋ 🛜 ⛱) This honey-coloured early-18th-century palazzo on the Dobrota waterfront, 4km north of Kotor's Old Town, has been transformed into a first-rate boutique hotel. Some rooms are bigger and

grander than others, but all 10 have sea views and luxurious furnishings. Guests can avail themselves of a small workout area, sauna, pool, private jetty, bar and restaurant.

✖ Eating

Caffe del Mare INTERNATIONAL €
(☑067-279 189; Donji put bb; mains €4.80-12; ⊙8am-11pm) Pasta, burgers, pizzas; they've got all the classics here and do them remarkably well (the spicy Diavolo pizza is bliss for those with a taste for the hot stuff). Best of all, it does free deliveries all over Dobrota and Kotor for those nights you can't face another restaurant.

Restoran Stari Mlini SEAFOOD €€€
(☑032-333 555; www.starimlini.com; Ljuta bb; mains €10-22) It's well worth making the trip to Ljuta, just north of Dobrota, to this magical restaurant set in and around an 18th-century flour mill by the edge of the bay. It's pricier than most and the service is variable, but the food is excellent and the setting wonderfully romantic.

ℹ Information

Kotor Health Centre (Dom zdravlja Kotor; ☑032-334 533; www.dzkotor.me; Jadranski Put bb) Kotor's main clinic.

ℹ Getting There & Away

A one-way road runs along the waterfront heading south towards Kotor. This road can either be accessed from Jadranski Put at the top end or from a side road about halfway along. Expect an extremely slow crawl along here in summer.

Kotor

☑032 / POP 13,000
Wedged between brooding mountains and a moody corner of the bay, achingly atmospheric Kotor (Котор) is perfectly at one with its setting. Hemmed in by staunch walls snaking improbably up the surrounding slopes, the town is a medieval maze of museums, churches, cafe-strewn squares, and Venetian palaces and pillories. It's a dramatic and delightful place where the past coexists with the present; its cobblestones ring with the sound of children racing to school in centuries-old buildings, lines of laundry flutter from wrought-iron balconies, and hundreds of cats – the descendants of seafaring felines – loll in marble laneways. Come nightfall, Kotor's spectacularly lit-up

walls glow as serenely as a halo. Behind the bulwarks, the streets buzz with bars, live music – from soul to serenades – and castle-top clubbing.

Budva's got the beaches, and nearby Dubrovnik's got the bling, but for romance, ambience and living history, this Old Town outflanks them all.

History

It's thought that Kotor began as Acruvium, part of the Roman province of Dalmatia. Its present look owes much to nearly 400 years of Venetian rule, when it was known as Cattaro. In 1813 it briefly joined with Montenegro for the first time, but the Great Powers decided to hand it back to Austria, where it remained until after WWI. There's a strong history of Catholic and Orthodox cooperation in the area.

◉ Sights

The best thing to do in Kotor is to let yourself get lost and found again in the maze of winding streets. You'll soon know every nook and cranny, but there are plenty of old churches to pop into, palaces to ogle, and many coffees and/or vinos to be drunk in the shady squares.

Sea Gate   GATE
(Vrata od Mora; Map p48) The main entrance to the town was constructed in 1555 when it was under Venetian rule (1420–1797). Look out for the winged lion of St Mark, Venice's symbol, which is displayed prominently on the walls here and in several other spots around the town. Above the gate, the date of the city's liberation from the Nazis is remembered with a communist star and a quote from Tito. An enormous (and inexplicable) bench outside the entrance makes for amusing snaps.

As you pass through the gate, look for the 15th-century stone relief of the Madonna and Child flanked by St Tryphon and St Bernard.

★ Kotor City Walls   FORTRESS
(Bedemi grada Kotora; Map p48; €8; ⊙24hr, fees apply 8am-8pm May-Sep) Kotor's fortifications started to head up St John's Hill in the 9th century and by the 14th century a protective loop was completed, which was added to right up until the 19th century. The energetic can make a 1200m ascent up the fortifications via 1350 steps to a height of 260m above sea level; the views from St John's

Fortress, at the top, are glorious. There are entry points near the River Gate and behind Trg od Salate.

St Tryphon's Cathedral   CATHEDRAL
(Katedrale Sv Tripuna; Map p48; Trg Sv Tripuna; church & museum €2.50; ⊙9am-8pm Apr-Oct, to 5pm Nov, Dec & Mar, to 1pm Jan & Feb) Kotor's most impressive building, this Catholic cathedral was consecrated in 1166 but reconstructed after several earthquakes. When the entire frontage was destroyed in 1667, the baroque bell towers were added; the left one remains unfinished. The cathedral's gently hued interior is a masterpiece of Romanesque architecture: slender Corinthian columns alternate with pillars of pink stone, thrusting upwards to support a series of vaulted roofs. Look for the remains of Byzantine-style frescoes in the arches.

Maritime Museum of
Montenegro   MUSEUM
(Pomorski muzej Crne Gore; Map p48; ☎032-304 720; www.museummaritimum.com; Trg Bokeljske Mornarice; adult/child €4/1; ⊙9am-8pm Mon-Sat, 10am-4pm Sun Jul & Aug, 8am-6pm Mon-Sat, 9am-1pm Sun May, Jun & Sep, 9am-5pm Mon-Fri, to noon Sat & Sun Oct-Apr) Kotor's proud history as a naval power is celebrated in three storeys of displays housed in a wonderful early-18th-century palace. An audio guide helps explain the collection of photographs, paintings, uniforms, exquisitely decorated weapons and models of ships.

St Nicholas' Church   CHURCH
(Crkva Sv Nikole; Map p48; Trg Sv Luke) Breathe in the smell of incense and beeswax in this Orthodox church, built in 1909 and adorned with four huge canvases depicting the gospel writers, a gift from Russia in 1998. The silence, the iconostasis with its silver bas-relief panels, the dark wood against bare grey walls, the filtered light through the dome and the simple stained glass conspire to create a mystical atmosphere.

St Luke's Church   CHURCH
(Crkva Sv Luke; Map p48; Trg Sv Luke) Sweet little St Luke's speaks volumes about the history of Croat–Serb relations in Kotor. It was constructed in 1195 as a Catholic church, but from 1657 until 1812 Catholic and Orthodox altars stood side by side, with each faith taking turns to hold services here. It was then gifted to the Orthodox Church.

Fragments of 12th-century frescoes still survive, along with two wonderfully painted

48

Kotor

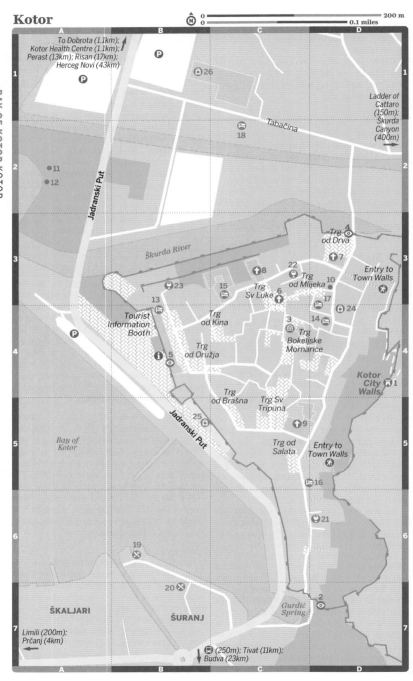

Kotor

iconostases: a 17th-century one in the main church and one from the 18th century in the side chapel of St Spiridon, another saint venerated by both faiths.

St Mary's Collegiate Church CHURCH
(Crkva Sv Marije Koleđate; Map p48; Trg od Drva) Built in 1221 on the site of a 6th-century basilica, this Catholic church is distinguished by impressive 20th-century bronze doors covered in bas-reliefs, the remains of frescoes, a particularly gruesome larger-than-life crucifix, and a glass coffin containing the body of Blessed Osanna of Cattaro (1493–1565). She was what is known as an anchoress, choosing to be walled into a small cell attached to a church so as to devote her life to prayer.

🏃 Activities & Tours

Various tour boats leave from opposite the Old Town to explore the bay; expect to pay upwards of €15 for a day tour. If you're keen to potter around the Boka on a boat of your own, you'll be disappointed unless you have a boat licence. Most hire companies supply skippers and cater firmly to the top end.

Ladder of Cattaro HIKING
FREE The truly vigorous can climb the ancient caravan trail known as the Ladder of Cattaro, which starts near the Škurda River and zigzags up the mountain to join the Coastal Mountain Traversal in Lovćen National Park. The usual requirements of water/sturdy shoes/strong lungs apply.

Adventure Montenegro OUTDOORS
(☑ 069-049 733; www.adventuremontenegro.com; Trg od Mlijeka) Rent a kayak and explore the bay on your own terms (single/double kayak €20/25 per day). There are also three-hour kayaking tours (€35), guided full-day hikes up Mt Lovćen (€50), rafting on the Tara River (€80), five-hour speedboat tours of the bay (€280 for up to six people) and a range of sightseeing tours for cruise-boat passengers.

Kotor Open Tour BUS
(☑ 067-333 977; www.hoponhopoff.me; adult/child €20/10; ☉ departs every 30min 9am-5pm) On sunny days during summer, these open-top, hop-on-hop-off sightseeing buses ply the busy road between Kotor, Perast and Risan, showing off the hotspots and providing histories and explanations via multilanguage audio guides. The ticket lasts all day and includes a Kotor walking tour and admission to museums in Perast and Risan. At peak times the traffic can crawl.

Kotor Bay Tours TOURS
(☑ 069-152 015; www.kotorbaytours.com; Park Slobode) This well-organised group offers tons of tours and activities, from sunset hikes up the Ladder of Cattaro (€50, three hours) to various boat, kayak and cycle trips. Gourmands won't want to miss their 'All about Mussels' tour (€50), which combines a Kotor and Perast tour with hours of eating and drinking at a local mussel farm.

Montenegro Submarine
BOATING

(Map p48; ☏ 069-576 355; www.montenegro submarine.me; Park Slobode; ☺9am-8pm Mar-Nov) Want to find out if Kotor Bay is as beautiful down below as it is on top? Hop aboard this really-quite-adorable bright-red semi-submersible (adult/child €12/8) and find out; there's above-water seating as well. The company also offers speedboat tours to Perast and Gospa od Škrpjela island (€20/10) and to the Blue Cave (€30/15).

Škurda Canyon
ADVENTURE SPORTS

The much-photographed St John's Hill hides a secret in the form of this rugged canyon. In addition to the splendid views of the Old Town, the canyon – about an hour's clamber from Kotor – is riddled with sheer, smooth drops, tunnels and waterfalls. Canyoning trips (average €80) are run by Kotor Bay Tours (p49) and Montenegro+ (p59).

🎉 Festivals & Events

Camellia Day
CULTURAL

(☺mid-Mar) A celebration of the bloom that enlivens many Kotor gardens in mid-March. Includes the Camellia Ball, where a prominent local woman is chosen as the Lady of the Camellia.

Summer Carnival
CARNIVAL

(☺Aug) A condensed version of the main (pre-Lent) carnival staged at a more tourist-friendly time.

Kotor Art
PERFORMING ARTS

(www.kotorart.me; ☺late Jun–mid-Aug) Kotor's summer arts festival acts as an umbrella for several established events, including the Children's Theatre Festival (Kotorski festival pozorišta za djecu; www.kotorskifestival.me; ☺early Jul), Don Branko's Music Days (featuring international artists performing classical music in Kotor's squares and churches), Perast's Klapa Festival, and assorted workshops, lectures and touring productions.

Traditional Winter Carnival
CARNIVAL

(☺Feb) Carrying on the Venetian Renaissance tradition with two weeks of masked balls, parades and performances in the lead-up to Lent.

Boka Night
CULTURAL

(☺mid-Aug) Decorated boats light up the bay, fireworks explode in the sky and the populace parties like there's no tomorrow.

🛏 Sleeping

Although the Stari Grad (Old Town) is a charming place to stay, you'd better pack earplugs. In summer, the bars blast music onto the streets until 1am every night, rubbish collectors clank around at 6am and the chattering starts by the cafes by 8am. Enquire about private accommodation at the tourist information booth (p52).

★ Old Town Hostel
HOSTEL €€

(Map p48; ☏ 032-325 317; www.hostel-kotor. me; 29 Novembar bb; dm from €14, r €75, without bathroom €60; ❀ 🛜 ☳) If the ghosts of the Bisanti family had any concerns when their 13th-century palazzo was converted into a hostel, they must be overjoyed now. Sympathetic renovations have brought the place to life, and the ancient stone walls echo with the cheerful chatter of happy travellers. A second building, directly across the road, has modern rooms and a small pool.

★ Palazzo Drusko
BOUTIQUE HOTEL €€€

(Map p48; ☏ 067-333 172; www.palazzodrusko. me; near Trg od Mlijeka; s/d from €69/139; ❀ 🛜) Loaded with character and filled with antiques, this venerable 600-year-old palazzo is a memorable place to stay, right in the heart of the Old Town. Thoughtful extras include water jugs loaded with lemon and mint, a guest kitchen, 3D TVs and old-fashioned radios rigged to play Montenegrin music.

Hotel Marija
HOTEL €€

(Map p48; ☏ 032-325 062; www.hotelmarija.me; Stari Grad; r €65-130; ❀) This charming little hotel occupies a beautiful palazzo in the centre of the Old Town and although the decor of the rooms is a little old-fashioned, it's very comfortable, clean and has a romantic feel, despite its dated furnishings. One room has a balcony for those Juliet moments. The location is unbeatable, but be warned: the walls aren't soundproofed.

Tianis
APARTMENT €€

(Map p48; ☏ 032-302 178; www.tianis.net; Tabačina 569; r/apt from €77/83; 🅿 ❀ 🛜) Well located without being in the midst of the melee, this friendly establishment has a clutch of clean, comfortable apartments of varying sizes, some of which have magical views across the Škurda River to the Old Town from their terraces.

BACK ROAD TO MT LOVĆEN

The journey from Kotor to Mt Lovćen, the ancient core of the country, is one of Montenegro's great drives. Take the road heading towards the Tivat tunnel and turn right just past the graveyard. After 5km, follow the sign to Cetinje on your left opposite the fort. From here, there's 17km of good but narrow road snaking up 25 hairpin turns, each one revealing a vista more spectacular than the last. Take your time and keep your wits about you; you'll need to pull over and be prepared to reverse if you meet oncoming traffic. From the top, the views stretch over the entire bay to the Adriatic. At the entrance to Lovćen National Park you can continue straight ahead through Njeguši for the shortest route to Cetinje or turn right and continue on the scenic road through the park.

Hotel Hippocampus   BOUTIQUE HOTEL €€€
(Map p48; ☑068-889 862; www.hotelhippocampus.com; near Trg od Mlijeka; r/ste from €165/180; ❋☎) The hippocampus is the part of the brain responsible for memories, and you'll have plenty of those after a stay at this gorgeous hotel. The owner is an architect, and it shows: every inch of the place is elegant, interesting and evocative. They haven't placed style over substance, though: the beds are comfortable, the rooms spacious and the staff attentive.

Hotel Cattaro   BOUTIQUE HOTEL €€€
(Map p48; ☑032-311 000; www.cattarohotel.com; Trg od Oružja; r/ste from €157/232; ❋☎) Perched up in the town walls, Cattaro looks down over the bay and Old Town, offering a vista that's tough to beat. The rooms area are spacious and elegant but don't let in a lot of light. The popular Citadela bar is attached to the hotel, and Kotor's king of clubs – Maximus – is a stagger away. Thankfully, rooms are soundproofed.

🍴 Eating

There are dozens of restaurants, bakeries and takeaway joints on Kotor's cobbled lanes. Most restaurants stick to the tried-and-true Montenegrin seafood theme. For the sweet-toothed, cherry-filled strudel is a speciality of the region.

Self-caterers can stock up at the **market** (Gradska pijaca; Map p48; Jadranski Put; ☉7am-2pm) under the town walls, or at the big supermarket within the **Kamelija** (Map p48; ☑032-335 380; www.kamelija.me; Trg Mata Petrovića; ☉9am-11pm; ☎) shopping centre.

Konoba Galerija   MONTENEGRIN, SEAFOOD €€
(Map p48; ☑032-322 125; www.restorangalerija.com; Šuranj bb; mains €9-22; ☉11am-11pm) This bustling place on the waterfront excels in both meat and seafood, as well as fast and attentive service (along the coast, you'll find these things are often mutually exclusive). Try the prawns or mixed seafood in *buzara* sauce, a deceptively simple – yet sublime – blend of olive oil, wine, garlic and mild spices.

Galion   SEAFOOD €€€
(Map p48; ☑032-325 054; Šuranj bb; meals €12-22; ☉noon-midnight; ☎) With an achingly romantic setting, extremely upmarket Galion gazes directly at the Old Town across the millionaire yachts in the marina. Fresh fish is the focus, but you'll also find steaks, risotto and pasta. It usually closes in winter.

🍷 Drinking & Nightlife

Kotor is full of cafe-bars that spill onto its squares and fill them with the buzz of conversation. Take your pick.

Bokun   WINE BAR
(Map p48; www.facebook.com/BOKUNWINEBAR; near Trg Sv Luke; ☉8am-1am May-Oct, to 11pm Nov-Apr; ☎) This evocative little nook is an ideal place to sample local wines (and perfectly paired meats and cheeses), all to the accompaniment of live music on weekends (think jazz, soul and samba).

Bandiera   BAR
(Map p48; www.facebook.com/bandiera.kotor; 29 Novembar bb; ☉8am-1am; ☎) This cluttered, cavernous old-school bar is a top hang-out, where laid-back conversations and rock music take precedence over texting and techno.

Maximus   CLUB
(Map p48; ☑067-217 101; www.discomaximus.me; near Trg od Oružja; free-€5; ☉11pm-5am Thu-Sat, nightly in summer) Montenegro's most pumping club comes into its own in summer, hosting big-name international DJs and local starlets. It's set up in the baffling

Balkan style, with little high tables covering the dance floor.

🛍️ Shopping

There are almost as many antique and souvenir shops as there are cats in the Stari Grad.

Cats of Kotor
GIFTS & SOUVENIRS

(Map p48; ☑069-249 783; www.catsofkotor.com; near Trg od Mlijeka; ☺9am-9pm) Though you can't bundle them into your backpack (tempting as it may be), you can bring home the cats of Kotor in the form of beautiful, locally made handicrafts with a feline flavour. Part gallery, part boutique, this quirky shop sells everything from cat-themed jewellery and clothes to original artworks.

ℹ️ Information

The post office and a choice of ATMs are on the main square, Trg od Oružja. There's a medical clinic (p46) in Dobrota.

Tourist Information Booth (Map p48; ☑032-325 951; www.tokotor.me; Jadranski Put; ☺8am-8pm Apr-Oct, to 6pm Nov-Mar) Stocks free maps and brochures, and can help with contacts for private accommodation.

ℹ️ Getting There & Away

➡ The main road to Tivat and Budva turns off the waterfront road at a baffling intersection south of the Stari Grad and heads through a long tunnel.

➡ The **bus station** (☑032-325 809; www.autobuskastanicakotor.me; Škaljari bb; ☺6am-8pm) is to the south of town, just off the road leading to the tunnel. Buses to Herceg Novi (€4, one hour), Tivat (€1.50, 20 minutes), Budva (€4, 40 minutes), Cetinje (€5, 1½ hours) and Podgorica (€7.50, 2¼ hours) are at least hourly. International destinations include Dubrovnik, Mostar, Belgrade, Tirana and Vienna.

➡ A taxi to Tivat Airport should cost around €10.

Prčanj

☑032 / POP 1200

A formerly prosperous maritime town, Prčanj (Прчањ) has lots of old stone buildings, a couple of restaurants, a bakery, a minimarket, a post office and Catholic churches that come in a choice of small, medium and XXL.

👁️ Sights

St Nicholas' Church
CHURCH

(Crkva Sv Nikole) Built in the baroque style in 1735, this medium-sized church has a Franciscan monastery attached, although the last monks left in 1908. The church was badly damaged in the 1979 earthquake but wasn't fully restored until 2011. It contains a grand Venetian-built high altar containing an oil painting of St Nicholas flanked by wooden carvings of St Peter and St Paul.

Church of the Birth of the Blessed Virgin Mary
CHURCH

(Crkva Rođenja Blažene Djevice Marije; ☺7-9pm Mon-Sat, 9-11am Sun) Even the name of this whopping church is outsized. It's said to be the biggest religious building on the Adriatic coast and it certainly dominates this little town in a God-is-watching-you kind of way. It was begun in 1789 but not completed until 1908, when Catholics were in the majority in Prčanj.

St John the Baptist's Church
CHURCH

(Crkva Sv Ivana Krstitelja) Simple, solid and semi-derelict, this tiny church dates from 1221 or 1397, depending on which resource you believe.

🛏️ Sleeping & Eating

The hotels have good-quality restaurants with the obligatory bay views. The waterfront is dotted with local eateries selling grilled meats and fish.

Hotel Splendido
HOTEL €€€

(☑032-301 700; www.splendido-hotel.com; Jadranska Magistrala; r €100-130, apt €130-180; P❄@🛜🏊) Splendido is magnifico. Completely gutted and fitted with comfortable modern rooms, this large stone palazzo still surveys the bay as solidly as it's ever done, although there's now a blissful terrace and swimming pool separating it from the water's edge. Its restaurant, Tramontana, is excellent and open to nonguests.

ℹ️ Getting There & Away

Heading north along the bay from Kotor to Prčanj, the road narrows to a single lane despite it being two-way, which makes for lots of fun and plenty of honking when a bus meets a truck coming in the opposite direction. Prčanj is 5km from Kotor.

Continued on p57

ALEXAFELICE/SHUTTERSTOCK ©

Naturally Gifted

When you're this little it's easy to be overlooked, so Montenegro overcompensates by being rammed full of extraordinary sights. The coastline is so beautiful that not even the mountains can resist dipping their toes in the clear waters.

Contents

➡ **Sundrenched Coast**

➡ **Mountain Majesty**

Above Biogradska Gora National Park (p115)

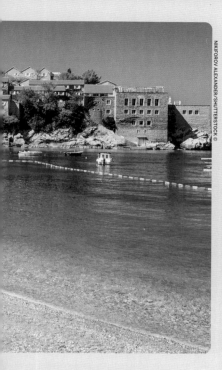

NIKIFOROV ALEXANDER/SHUTTERSTOCK ©

Sundrenched Coast

Lord Byron described this coastline as 'the most beautiful encounter between the land and the sea'. Wherever you choose to splash about in the crystalline waters, chances are there will be a mountainous backdrop proving the great Romantic poet right.

Bay of Kotor

The combination of Mediterranean vegetation, historic towns, cute-as-a-button villages and rugged mountains plunging to an opalescent sea makes the Bay of Kotor pretty hard to beat. More fragrant than the ground floor of a department store, the Bay is subtly infused with the scent of wild herbs, perfumed flowers and aromatic trees.

It's little wonder that the inner part of the bay was the first site in Montenegro to be inscribed on the Unesco World Heritage list – recognising both its natural and cultural value.

1. Sveti Stefan (p74) **2.** View of the Bay of Kotor (p36) and Kotor Old Town (p46) **3.** Medieval ruins, Budva (p66)

Walled Towns

For centuries the people of the coast have protected their towns with stone walls, creating a picturesque counterpoint to the natural beauty surrounding them.

At Budva and Ulcinj the ancient fortifications jut out over the azure blue of the Adriatic. Kotor's walls arch high up on the cliffs behind the town. At night they are spectacularly illuminated, forming a halo from their reflections in the still, dark waters of the bay.

Most striking of all is Sveti Stefan, a picture-perfect island village anchored to the coast by the narrowest of causeways. While off-limits to the general public it has survived its transformation into a luxury resort with all of its historic charm intact.

Durmitor National Park (p116)

Mountain Majesty

Much of Montenegro's surface looks like it's been dug up by a giant puppy out of freshly laid concrete. Montenegro's mountains push up behind each other, filling most of the land, with only a scattering of sparkling lakes and deeply cut river canyons to give them breathing space.

Durmitor National Park

A lunar landscape of craggy peaks gives way to high plains and twinkling glacial lakes known as 'mountain eyes' – this is the second of Montenegro's World Heritage Sites. The Tara River slices deeply through the Durmitor range, providing one of the world's most dramatic rafting routes and the nation's most popular active attraction. Savin Kuk never quite sheds its cap of snow and in the winter its 3.5km run is adored by enthusiastic skiers and snowboarders.

Biogradska Gora National Park

If you're on the hunt for wood nymphs or satyrs, the 1600 hectares of virgin forest at the heart of the Bjelasica Mountains would be a good place to start.

Mountaintop Monuments

Seemingly sprouting out of the surrounding cliffs, gleaming white Ostrog Monastery is the country's spiritual heart for its Orthodox population and a popular pilgrimage site. At the top of one of Mt Lovćen's highest peaks stands the Njegoš Mausoleum. This tomb for a national hero echoes the grandeur of the black mountain itself, through imposing sculpture, solemn architecture and awe-inspiring views.

Continued from p52

Stoliv

032 / POP 350

Donji Stoliv (Lower Stoliv; Столив) is a pleasant seaside village with a huddle of stone houses surmounted by a grand church, 9.5km from Kotor. It's worth stopping here to take the idyllic but steep half-hour's walk through the olive and chestnut trees to the upper village, **Gornji Stoliv**. Most of the families who lived here for centuries have now left, with only a few houses remaining in use and the rest in varying states of picturesque ruin. A church dedicated to the prophet Elijah (Crkva Sv Ilije), dating from 1553, keeps a lonely vigil. At 250m, the views over the bay to Perast are sublime.

Down in Donji Stoliv, several houses offer camping in July and August under their fig and olive trees for around €10 for two people with a car and tent. Facilities are basic (squat toilets with a basket for toilet paper) and water supplies sometimes run out. Keep an eye out for signs reading *auto kamp*. If you prefer to be out of the elements, ask around for private rooms *(sobe)* to let.

During summer, buses to and from Kotor stop at Stoliv.

Lastva

032 / POP 750

Lastva (Ластва) is a divided village, and the *gornja* (upper) section has been actively promoted to tourists for its rustic ambience. There's a decent road for starters, leading 3km up the hill. **Gornja Lastva** doesn't offer the same off-the-beaten-track satisfaction as Stoliv, but it's nice to see that this village has been kept alive, with kids darting about and old ladies dressed in black pottering about gathering wild herbs.

The best time to visit is the first Saturday in August, when a village fair is held.

☉ Sights

St Mary's Church　　　　　　　CHURCH
(Crkva Sv Marije) If you're lucky, the parish priest will be around to unlock this 15th-century village church, which reputedly has some accomplished Italian paintings inside.

🛏 Sleeping & Eating

Eco Hotel Carrubba　　BOUTIQUE HOTEL €€€
(☏032-540 153; www.septemberhotels.com; Donja Lastva; r from €130) Enjoy dreamy views from the terraces of this elegant 19th-century building, a mere step from the sea. It's a good option if you wish to be near Tivat while enjoying a tranquil remove. The attached restaurant is no slouch in the seafood department.

Waikiki Restaurant &
Beach Club　　　　　　INTERNATIONAL €€
(☏069-141 710; www.waikikibeach-tivat.com; Donja Lastva; mains €7-20; ☉7am-1am) Sprawling, sunny and scene-y, this complex tends more towards Tivat (or its namesake) than Donja Lastva. The seafood restaurant here is excellent; the very swimmable private beach, cocktail bar, sunbed service, squeal-inducing kids' playground and typically Mediterranean beach posturing offer good reasons to make a day of it.

❶ Information

Tourist Office (☉8am-noon & 5-8pm Mon-Sat, 8am-noon Sun)

❶ Getting There & Away

From Stoliv, the road rounds the tip of the Vrmac Peninsula and passes the ferry terminal at Lepetane before popping out in the front section of the bay; Lastva is another 2km up the road.

Tivat

032 / POP 9370

Bobbing super yachts, a posh promenade and rows of swanky apartment blocks: visitors to Tivat (Тиват) could be forgiven for wondering if they're in Monaco or Montenegro. The erstwhile-mediocre seaside town has undergone a major makeover – courtesy of the multimillion-dollar redevelopment of its old naval base into a first-class marina – and while it bears no resemblance to anywhere else in the country, Tivat is now attracting the uberwealthy (and less-loaded rubberneckers) in droves.

The town has a reputation as being one of the sunniest spots in the Bay of Kotor. While Tivat will never rival Kotor for charm, it makes a pleasant stop on a trip around the bay, and is a useful base for exploring the Vrmac and Luštica Peninsulas.

Tivat

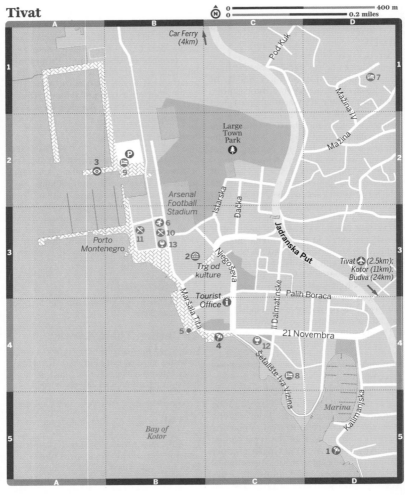

⊙ Sights

Porto Montenegro   MARINA
(Map p58; www.portomontenegro.com) Single-handedly responsible for Tivat's transformation, this surreal 24-hectare town-within-a-town occupies the former Arsenal shipyard and naval base. Primped, preening and planned right down to the last polished pebble, the almost impossibly glamorous complex includes upmarket apartment buildings, a 'lifestyle village' of fancy boutiques, bars, restaurants and leisure facilities, a museum, a resort-style hotel and berths for 450 yachts (with a total of 850 berths planned by completion).

Porto is a phased development – construction is ongoing – but the works don't detract from the surreal feeling of finding yourself in a place usually reserved for those of otherworldly wealth.

Unsurprisingly, the project hasn't been without controversy: 3500 locals took to the streets to protest the sale of the shipyard – a state asset – to foreign investors (an international consortium of the exceedingly rich led by the Canadian businessman, the late Peter

Tivat

Munk, who sold the complex to the government of Dubai in 2016) and the loss of 480 jobs. Yet many naysayers have been silenced by the improvements that are evident in the town.

The complex is open to the public and it's a pleasant place to stroll and ogle opulent yachts – if you're not prone to fits of rage at the injustices of contemporary economics. Kids will love the playground shaped like a pirate ship near the maritime museum.

The success of such a venture relies partially on enticing yacht crews to dock here for the winter, so bars, restaurants and activity providers operate year-round (unlike along most of the Montenegrin coast). Prices are generally geared more towards crew members than oligarchs and so, while expensive for Montenegro, they are reasonable by European standards. It appears the strategy is having no small amount of success: the marina was named Superyacht Marina of the Year (2015) by the international Yacht Harbour Association.

Buća-Luković
Museum & Gallery   MUSEUM
(Muzej i galerija Buća-Luković; Map p58; ☑032-674 591; www.czktivat.me; Trg od kulture; ⊙8am-2pm & 5-10pm Mon-Fri, 5-10pm Sat & Sun) FREE Aristocratic families from the inner bay once built their summer residences at Tivat to take advantage of its sunnier outlook. One of the few survivors is this 500-year-old fortified enclosure with its own Catholic chapel, which once belonged to Kotor's Buća family. The solid stone defensive tower houses a collection of Roman bits and bobs; next door is a well-presented ethnographical museum with fishing and farming artefacts. Head upstairs for beautiful jewellery and folk costumes.

The gallery focuses on modern painting and sculpture, and often hosts exhibitions.

Town Beach   BEACH
(Gradska plaža; Map p58; 21 Novembra bb) You're better off heading to the Luštica Peninsula for a proper swim, but Tivat does offer a couple of options if you're desperate for a dip. Town Beach is a long concrete platform with a 20m pebbly section right by the main promenade.

There's another pebbly beach, **Belani** (Plaža Belane; Map p58; Kalimanjska bb), just past the marina.

⃗ Activities

Montenegro+   OUTDOORS
(Map p58; ☑069-190 190; www.montenegroplus.me; ⊙9am-7pm) This well-organised group has active pursuits around Tivat covered. It rents stand-up paddleboards (half-/full day €25/35), kayaks (€50 per day) and mountain bikes (€25 per day), and offers guided kayaking, hiking and cycling trips, along with diving, canyoning and snowshoeing.

Pura Vida   SPA
(Map p58; ☑032-540 356; www.puravida-spa.com; Obala bb, Porto Montenegro; massages from €30; ⊙7.30am-10pm Mon-Fri, 10am-8pm Sat & Sun) Of course Porto has a day spa, offering all the plucking, pummelling and pampering treatments you'd expect from a luxury resort.

Montenegro Cruising   CRUISE
(Map p58; ☑068-330 231; www.montenegrocruising.com; cruises €12; ⊙May-Sep) Offers daily cruises departing at 9am during the tourist season on boats named *Vesna,* stopping at Žanjic beach, Herceg Novi, Perast's islands and Kotor; the boat returns to Tivat at 6pm. Budva-based travel agents commonly sell this cruise inclusive of bus transfers (€20), with their clients finishing the cruise at Kotor.

🛏 Sleeping

Hostel Anton
HOSTEL €

(Map p58; ☑ 069-261 182; www.hostelanton.com; Mažina IV bb; dm/r €18/38; P 🛜) This hilltop backpackers is a hostel of the old-school: family-run, oddball art on the walls, instruments waiting to be picked up, and a communal vibe. If glam is your bag, keep moving; amenities are functional but far from flash.

Hotel Palma
HOTEL €€€

(Map p58; ☑ 032-671 393; www.hotelpalma. me; Šetalište Kapetana Iva Vizina 8; s/d/ste from €83/110/250; P ✳ 🛜) The Palma ticks all the seaside-holiday boxes: it's got a private beach, a restaurant, ocean views, comfortable beds and amiable staff. It's not quite Porto Montenegro...but then again, nor are the prices.

Regent Porto Montenegro
HOTEL €€€

(Map p58; ☑ 032-660 660; www.regenthotels.com; Porto Montenegro; r/ste from €407/619; ✳ 🛜 🏊) Divided into the Italianate 'Venezia' wing and the more contemporary-looking 'Aqua' wing, the Regent is a luxurious place for a splurge. The room decor is remarkably restrained; the designers have left the balcony views to speak for themselves. Facilities – including multiple restaurants and bars, a 20m infinity pool and a first-class spa – are as chic as you'd expect.

🍴 Eating

You'll find Tivat's finest restaurants at Porto Montenegro. It's also a great place to check out if you're hankering after something other than the usual seafood or Montenegrin mixed grills, with multicultural eateries lining the marina.

Self-caterers will find gourmet goods at the excellent Bonella (Map p58; www.bonella greenbazaar.me; Porto Montenegro; snacks 60c-€1.50; ⏰ 8am-10pm) supermarket.

★ One
ITALIAN €€€

(Map p58; ☑ 067-486 045; www.facebook.com/ jettyone; Porto Montenegro; mains €10-22; ⏰ 8.30am-midnight) This singular brasserie has one of the most expensive views in the country, gazing over trillions of euros' worth of megayachts. The service is a match for the lovely location and the menu is as jet-setting as the clientele – flitting between French, Russian, Indian and American but excelling in Italian. It also does excellent Western-style breakfasts (from €6).

🍷 Drinking & Nightlife

★ Black Sheep
PUB

(Map p58; ☑ 068-900 013; www.facebook.com/ tbsgastropub; Ribarski Put bb; ⏰ 8am-1am; 🛜) This wonderful little gastropub swims against Montenegro's tsunami of wines and *rakija* (fruit brandy), serving up lashings of craft beer and cool cocktails. Hip, happening and occasionally hectic (weekends go off with live music and DJs), a night out here is as far from yachtie yahooing as you can get.

Clubhouse
BAR

(Map p58; ☑ 032-662 722; www.facebook.com/ TheClubhousePortoMontenegro; Porto Montenegro; ⏰ 9am-1am; 🛜) Doing its very best to keep the yacht crews entertained, this lively bar with an upmarket beach-shack vibe hosts live music and kooky themed nights, and screens international football and rugby matches. There's a good selection of imported beer, and visiting Antipodeans can drown their homesickness in Aussie shiraz.

🔒 Shopping

As might be expected of a place designed with the mega-wealthy in mind, Porto Montenegro is busting at the designer seams with luxury-brand boutiques and speciality shops including an English-language bookstore.

ℹ Information

Tourist Office (Map p58; ☑ 032-671 324; www. tivat.travel; Palih Boraca 8; ⏰ 7am-8pm Mon-Fri, 8am-3pm Sat & Sun May-Sep, 8am-3pm Mon-Sat Oct-Apr) Accommodation contacts and information about local sights and walks.

ℹ Getting There & Around

AIR

Tivat Airport (p172) is 3km south of town and 8km through the tunnel from Kotor. The only year-round flights are to Belgrade and Moscow, but dozens of destinations are added in the tourist season.

Taxis charge around €7 for Tivat, €10 for Kotor and €20 for Budva. You'll find car-hire counters at the airport.

BICYCLE

Mountain bikes can be rented through Montenegro+ (p59).

BUS

Buses to Kotor (€1.50, 20 minutes) stop outside a silver kiosk on Palih Boraca. The main bus station is inconveniently located halfway between

MAMULA ISLAND

Lapped on all sides by the sparkling Adriatic and dominated by a photogenic Austro-Hungarian fortress, Mamula Island is one of the most stunning spots in the bay. But its beauty is a haunted one; in 1942 the fortress was commandeered as a concentration camp by Mussolini's fascists, holding an estimated 2000 mostly local prisoners, of whom more than 130 were tortured or starved to death. While such grim reminders of man's inhumanity to man are usually left to rot or turned into memorials, no such future awaits Mamula: the former death camp is set to be transformed into an elite resort.

Approved by the Montenegrin government in 2016, construction of the luxury hotel – complete with marina, nightclub and spa – has unsurprisingly provoked intense outrage, particularly among families of those killed or interned at Mamula. So too has advertising for the project, which billed the future resort as being steeped in a 'party ambience'. Promises of a museum and memorial honouring the victims have done little to appease the rage.

Tivat and the airport. From there, buses head to Herceg Novi (€3, one hour), Budva (€4, 30 minutes), Cetinje (€5, 1¼ hours) and Podgorica (€6, two hours) at least hourly.

CAR

Tivat sits on the western side of the Vrmac Peninsula, which juts out into the Bay of Kotor and divides it in two. The quickest route to Kotor is to take the main road southeast in the direction of Budva, turn left at the major intersection past the airport and take the tunnel. The alternative is the narrow coastal road. For Herceg Novi, take the ferry from Lepetane, 5km northwest of town.

Around Tivat

Tivat town may be a mecca for the moneyed, but its surrounds are rich in natural and historic attractions. Three unspoiled islands, each with its own unusual tale to tell, are within easy reach of Tivat and all make for a pleasant day of exploring.

◉ Sights

Ostrvo Cvijeća   ISLAND

(Island of Flowers) The overly poetically named Ostrvo Cvijeća is accessed by an unlikely looking road that heads behind the airport and through a rundown area where a former tourist complex shelters people displaced by the region's most recent wars. At the very end of the potholed road is **St Michael the Archangel's Monastery** (Manastir Sv Arhanđela Mihaila). This is the area's most historically significant site. The sweet little 19th-century **Holy Trinity Church** (Crkva Sv Trojice) stands nearby, shaded by trees and protected by stone walls.

The remains of Roman mosaics have been discovered here, along with the ruins of a 9th-century church and Benedictine monastery. From the early 13th century, St Michael's was the seat of the Orthodox bishop of Zeta until it was destroyed by the Venetians in 1452.

Sveti Marko   ISLAND

(St Mark's Island) The larger of two islands stretching out in a line from Ostrvo Cvijeća, the heavily forested Sveti Marko (St Mark) has run wonderfully wild since its stint as a Club Med came to an end with the Yugoslav wars. Plans for the construction of a six-star resort come and go; for now, it lies green, glorious and abandoned.

You can get to the island on a taxi boat from Tivat or Herceg Novi.

Gospa od Milosti   ISLAND

(Our-Lady-of-Mercy Island) The diminutive Gospa od Milosti was once the residence of Kotor's Catholic bishops and is now a convent. A wooden statue of the Madonna kept in the church is said to have miraculous powers. Pop over for a look on a taxi boat from Tivat or Herceg Novi.

ⓘ Getting There & Around

Sveti Marko and Gospa od Milosti can be reached via water taxi – or by hitching a ride with a friendly yachtie – from either Tivat or Herceg Novi.

Luštica Peninsula

Reaching out to form the southern headland of the Bay of Kotor, the lovely Luštica Peninsula (Луштица) hides secluded beaches and a dusting of idyllic villages scattered among the olive groves of its remote southern edge. If you want to enjoy this magical area while it's still relatively untouched, you'd better get in quick: developers are snapping up Luštica in droves.

The first section of the peninsula facing Tivat is already quite developed, with works on five-star resorts under way around Radovići and Pržno. At **Krtoli** the pebbly beaches look over the green swathe of St Mark's Island and the picturesque Our-Lady-of-Mercy Island, which are immediately offshore. If you're looking for a spot to chill out and relax by the water, you could do a lot worse. This area is cheaper and less frantic than most of the coast and some excellent midsized apartment hotels have sprung up. Further west, **Bjelila** is a cute little fishing village comprising a cluster of old stone houses dipping their feet in the water.

Continuing along the peninsula, the houses stop, the road gets narrower and the scenery gets greener and prettier. Climbing up the ridge on the way to Rose, a panorama of the bay opens up before you. If you're in the mood for a leisurely drive with a high probability of getting at least temporarily lost, continue on the narrow back roads from Rose that meander through the bucolic olive groves of the southern half of the peninsula. If you see signs for Radovići, you're still heading in the right direction.

Along the southern coastline is a string of clean beaches that are popular with day trippers travelling from Herceg Novi by taxi boat.

◉ Sights

Blue Grotto
CAVE

(Plava Špilja) A popular cruise stop, the Blue Grotto gets its name from the mesmerising effect of the light reflecting through the clear water. Boats head into the 9m-high cave and allow you an opportunity for an iridescent swim. Most boat and kayak tour operators in the region offer trips out here; opt for one that arrives early, before the crowds descend.

Uvala Veslo
BEACH

It's rougher and rockier than most other peninsula beaches, but with super-clear water and steep rugged drop-offs, this secluded bay offers adventure galore for strong swimmers keen on snorkelling and cliff jumping. It's not one for the kids, but those seeking splendid isolation might just find their paradise here. There's a little signposted campground in an olive grove nearby.

Žanjic
BEACH

Sitting in a sheltered cove below the olive groves, Žanjic's 300m-long white pebbly beach, restaurants and bars attract up to 1000 people a day in the height of summer. Come by car or water taxi or paddle over in a kayak.

Mirišta
BEACH

This beach may be smaller than neighbouring Žanjic, but it's every bit as popular. The Austro-Hungarian Arza fortress lies abandoned (for how long remains to be seen along this development-crazed coastline) at the tip of Mirišta; it's not in the best condition and safety isn't guaranteed, but if you simply can't help yourself, it's there for the exploring.

There's an excellent seafood **restaurant** (☑ 069-515 485; www.restoranmirista.com; Mirišta; mains €8-22) right on the beach.

Plavi Horizont
BEACH

(Blue Horizon) Located in the little town of Pržno (not to be confused with the other Pržno near Sveti Stefan), Plavi Horizont is – for now – a definite candidate for the title of Montenegro's best beach; a gorgeous scallop of white sand, it sits within a green horseshoe of scrub, pines and olive trees. Alas, its days as relatively unspoiled paradise are numbered: at the time of research, construction of the Qatari-owned Beyond Horizon five-star resort was about to get under way.

Dobreč
BEACH

Blue-flagged Dobreč is reported to have some of the cleanest waters in Montenegro and is only accessible by sea – usually by taxi boat from Herceg Novi, though tours with Kayak Herceg Novi (p40) also stop in here. Make a day of it, as there's a good restaurant, hammocks to laze in and a little water park for the kids.

Rose
VILLAGE

At the peninsula's very tip you'll find this sleepy fishing village (pronounced with two syllables: ro-seh), a blissful stand of stone houses gazing at Herceg Novi across the sparkling waters of the bay. Outside summer, village life winds down to near inertia, but from May to September a handful of waterside eateries open their doors to day trippers. If you fancy staying over, ask a local about private accommodation.

Rose is easily reached by taxi boat from Herceg Novi (€10 to €15). Kayak Herceg Novi (p40) stops here on its guided paddle tours or you can hire a kayak and go it alone; it takes about 30 minutes each way.

Oblatno · BEACH
It was inevitable that the virtually untouched paradise of green headlands and blue waters at Trašte Bay would attract the attention of developers. It's now home to the chic Almara Beach Club (www.almara.me), with a restaurant, day beds, DJs and live music – attracting a young crowd of sunseekers and partygoers. Five minutes away, work on the Luštica Bay development – an entirely new town complete with seven hotels, countless private residences, a golf course and marina – is well under way.

🛏 Sleeping

Forte Rose · B&B €€
(☑ 067-377 311; www.forterose.me; Rose; apt from €90; P ✳ 🛜) This charming old stone fortress still serves a protective purpose; a stay here guards against the intrusion of rude reality. It's a world unto itself with a private beach, top restaurant and discreet, personal service. The apartments aren't huge, but they're clean and the sea views are outlandish. Chartered tours of nearby hotspots are available on the owners' yacht.

Apartments Briv · APARTMENT €€
(☑ 032-680 110; Obala Đuraševića bb, Krtoli; apt from €80; P ✳ @) Step down from the sun deck of this modern block and straight into the water. There are 24 attractive apartments of differing sizes and configurations on offer. Try for the ones on the ground floor that have large terraces facing the water. You can rent a jet ski or borrow a kayak to paddle out to the islands.

Klinci Village Resort · B&B €€€
(☑ 063-200 050; www.klincivillageresort.me; Klinci; apt from €115; P ✳ 🛜 ⚓) Tucked away on a 300-year-old olive farm with views to the Adriatic, this gorgeous B&B is one of Montenegro's most romantic getaways. The spick-and-span one- and two-bedroom apartments are divided between three old stone cottages; all have balconies, kitchens and tons of space. The sense of privacy and intimacy here is palpable; the staff are there when you need them, invisible when you don't. There's an exceptional restaurant attached.

Klinci village is 3km from Rose.

🍴 Eating

Ribarsko Selo · SEAFOOD €€
(Fishing Village; ☑ 069-149 119; www.ribarskoselo.com; Žanjic; mains €8-26; ⊘ 9am-1am; 🛜) Wherever you're staying and whatever you're doing, make a stop at Ribarsko Selo a priority. Less a mere eatery than an all-encompassing experience, this fantastic new waterfront 'village' has no menu, basing its daily meals on whatever the local fishermen bring in (and whatever organic veggies the chefs have picked from their garden).

The owners have made this a destination in its own right: there are day beds by the beach, kayaks for rent, massages available and impeccable accommodation (apartments €280, bungalows €110 to €150) for those needing to sleep off their meals (or are rightfully entranced by the unbeatable location and dégagé ambience).

Vino Santo · SEAFOOD €€€
(☑ 067-851 662; www.vinosanto.me; Obala Đuraševića bb, Krtoli; mains €9-22; ⊘ noon-midnight) If different-restaurant-same-menu fatigue is starting to set in, the deceptively humble-looking Vino Santo offers the antidote. The traditional seafood favourites are all present and accounted for, but acclaimed chef and author Dragan Peričić adds a creative French twist in the delivery. The bayside views are almost as sublime as the food.

Adriatic Coast

Best Places to Eat

➡ Konoba Zago (p74)

➡ Miško (p89)

➡ Kaldrma (p84)

➡ Grill Bistro Parma (p70)

➡ Mercur (p70)

➡ Paštrovića Dvori (p76)

Best Places to Sleep

➡ Hostel Pirate (p87)

➡ Aman Sveti Stefan (p75)

➡ Avala Resort & Villas (p69)

➡ Hotel Poseidon (p70)

➡ Palata Venezija (p87)

➡ Le Petit Chateau (p81)

Why Go?

Beautiful places often get slugged with the tedious tagline, 'The pearl of...', and the southern coastline of Montenegro is no exception: in this case, it's '...the Adriatic'. But this 80km stretch is less milky dewdrop than eye-popping opal; the malachite greens of the looming mountains and the intense blues of the reflecting waters are dazzling enough to cause hallucinations.

Budva – the so-called 'Montenegrin Miami' – is the country's most-visited destination, thanks to its alluring Old Town, buzzy bars and a bevy of Blue Flag beaches. Nearby, elegant Sveti Stefan offers million-dollar ogling, while Bečići, Pržno and Petrovac burst at the seams with sun-seeking families come summertime. Further south, the evocative cliffside ruins of Stari Bar provide a peep into the past, while Eastern-flavoured Ulcinj is the gateway to a 12km succession of sandy beaches running to the Albanian border; perhaps surprisingly, you'll find Montenegro's best nudist beach here.

When to Go

➡ Enjoy the beaches and balmy weather in May and June before the crowds descend.

➡ July and August see soaring temperatures, crowded beaches, peak prices – but this is the best time to party.

➡ In September and October you may get some rain, but the air and water temperatures are still warm.

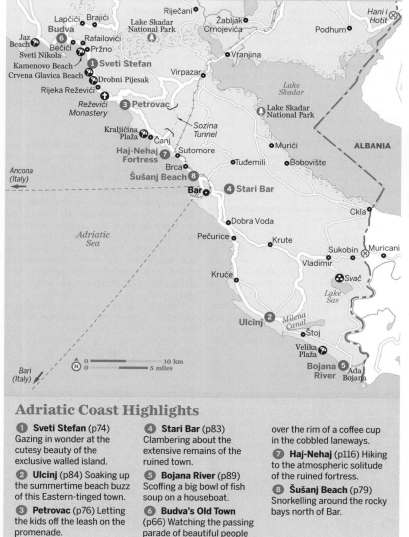

Adriatic Coast Highlights

1 **Sveti Stefan** (p74)
Gazing in wonder at the cutesy beauty of the exclusive walled island.

2 **Ulcinj** (p84) Soaking up the summertime beach buzz of this Eastern-tinged town.

3 **Petrovac** (p76) Letting the kids off the leash on the promenade.

4 **Stari Bar** (p83)
Clambering about the extensive remains of the ruined town.

5 **Bojana River** (p89)
Scoffing a big bowl of fish soup on a houseboat.

6 **Budva's Old Town** (p66) Watching the passing parade of beautiful people

over the rim of a coffee cup in the cobbled laneways.

7 **Haj-Nehaj** (p116) Hiking to the atmospheric solitude of the ruined fortress.

8 **Šušanj Beach** (p79)
Snorkelling around the rocky bays north of Bar.

Climate

'Gorgeously Mediterranean' is the best way to describe it. Ulcinj is said to be one of the sunniest spots on the Adriatic, notching up 218 sunny days a year.

🛈 Getting There & Away

Budva is connected to the Bay of Kotor by the Jadranski Put (Adriatic highway; also known as 'Jadranska magistrala'). The main route to Cetinje and Podgorica leaves Jadranski Put between Budva and Bečići, and climbs steeply into the mountains. Petrovac is connected to Podgorica via a highway leading through Virpazar and the western edge of Lake Skadar. This route can also be reached by a tunnel starting near Sutomore, north of Bar (toll €3.50). A scenic back road links Ulcinj to the southern edge of Montenegro's section of Lake Skadar.

Regular buses connect all the coastal towns with the Bay of Kotor and Podgorica. A railway line links Bar with the centre of the country, including Lake Skadar and Podgorica. There are ferries from Bar to Italy and bus connections to Albania from Ulcinj.

ⓘ Getting Around

Jadranski Put is the main road connecting all coastal towns and is well served by buses. In summer, taxi boats are a useful option for short trips between beaches.

Budva

♩033 / POP 13,400

Budva (Будва) is the poster child of Montenegrin tourism. Easily the country's most-visited destination, it attracts hordes of holidaymakers intent on exploring its atmospheric Stari Grad, sunning themselves on the bonny beaches of the Budva Riviera and partying until dawn; with scores of buzzy bars and clanging clubs, it's not nicknamed 'the Montenegrin Miami' for nothing.

Though Budva has been settled since the 5th century BC, you'll be hard-pressed finding much – outside of the Old Town – that isn't shiny and relatively new. Development has run rampant here, and not all of it appears to be particularly well thought out. In the height of the season, Budva's sands are blanketed with package holidaymakers from Russia and Ukraine, while the nouveau riche park their multimillion-dollar yachts in the town's guarded marina. That said, Budva has a hectic charm all of its own.

⊙ Sights

◉ Stari Grad

Budva's best feature and star attraction is the **Stari Grad** (Old Town) – a mini-Dubrovnik with marbled streets and Venetian walls rising from the clear waters below. You can still see the remains of Venice's emblem, the winged lion of St Mark, over the **main gate** (Map p68). Much of the Old Town was ruined by two earthquakes in 1979, but it has since been completely rebuilt and now houses more shops, bars and restaurants than residences. At its seaward end, the **Citadela** (Map p68; €3.50; ⊘9am-midnight May-Oct, to 5pm Nov-Apr) offers striking views, a small museum and a library full of rare tomes and maps. In the square in front of the citadel is a cluster of interesting churches. Nearby is the entry to the **town walls** (Bedemi grada; Map p68; €2; ⊘10am-8pm).

Trg između crkava   SQUARE
(Map p68) Literally the 'square between the churches', this open area below the citadel provides a visual reminder of the once-cosy relationship between Orthodox and Catholic Christians in this area.

Beautiful frescoes cover the walls and ceiling of **Holy Trinity Church** (Crkva Sv Trojice; Map p68; ⊘8am-10pm Jun-Sep, 8am-noon & 4-7pm Oct-May), in the centre of the square. Constructed in 1804 out of stripes of pink and honey-coloured stone, this Orthodox church is the only one of the square's interesting cluster of churches that is regularly open.

The largest of the churches is Catholic **St John the Baptist's Church** (Crkva Sv Ivana Krstitelja; Map p68), which was built towards the end of the 12th century and served as a cathedral until 1828 (Budva is now part of the diocese of Kotor). Parts of it possibly date from as early as the 9th century, and the last earthquake revealed the foundations of its predecessor, a 5th-century basilica, beside it. A side chapel houses the *Madonna of Budva* – a 12th-century icon venerated by Catholic and Orthodox Budvans alike. There's also a colourful mosaic by Ivo Dulčić behind the altar. Opening hours are sporadic.

Built into the city walls are two tiny churches, which are rarely open. Budva's oldest remaining church is Catholic **St Mary's in Punta** (Crkva Sv Marije; Map p68), dating from 840. Immediately next to it is **St Sava's Church** (Crkva Sv Save; Map p68), named after the founder of the Serbian Orthodox Church; it once had both Orthodox and Catholic altars.

Budva Museum   MUSEUM
(Muzej Budve; Map p68; ♩033-453 308; Petra I Petrovića 11; adult/child €3/1.50; ⊘8am-9pm Tue-Fri, 3-9pm Sat & Sun) This archaeological and ethnographic museum shows off Budva's ancient and complicated history – dating back to at least 500 BC – over four floors

Budva

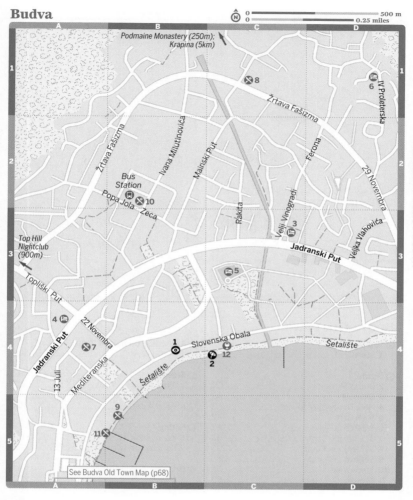

Budva

⊙ Sights
1 Slovenska Obala	B4
2 Slovenska Plaža	C4

🛏 Sleeping
3 Hotel Kangaroo	C3
4 Hotel Lučić	A4
5 Hotel Slovenska Plaža	C3
6 Saki Apartmani	D1

✖ Eating
7 Green Market	A4
8 Grill Bistro Parma	C1
9 Jadran kod Krsta	B5
10 Mercur Cafe	B2
11 Porto	B5

🍷 Drinking & Nightlife
12 Torch	C4

of exhibits. There's an impressive collection of Greek and Roman jewellery, ceramics, mosaics and glassware (how it survived in a town so prone to earthquakes and war is

Budva Old Town

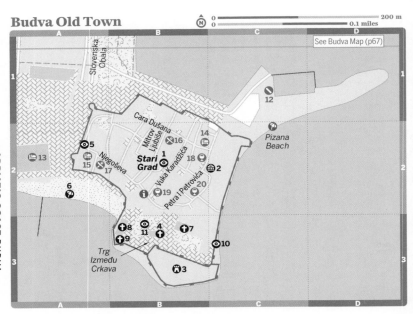

Budva Old Town

anyone's guess), as well as a 5th-century BC helmet with holes in the back, which suggest that the former owner had at least one very bad day.

Ričardova Glava
BEACH

(Richard's Head; Map p68) Immediately south of the Old Town, this little beach has the ancient walls as an impressive backdrop. Wander around the headland and you'll come to a statue of a naked dancer, one of Budva's most-photographed landmarks. Carry on and you'll find the quiet, double-bayed

Mogren Beach. There's a spot near here where the fearless or foolhardy leap from the cliffs into the waters below.

◎ Rest of Budva

Slovenska Plaža
BEACH

(Map p67) After the marina, the long sweep of Budva's main beach commences, heralded by blaring local pop and endless rows of sun umbrellas and loungers (available for hire at about €3 each). If you can't get your head around this typically Mediterranean concept, there's no charge for spreading out your towel on the patches of beach set aside for the purpose.

Slovenska Obala   WATERFRONT
(Map p67) In summer, Budva's main beachside promenade morphs into a bustling, hustling strip of fast-food outlets, beach bars in the guise of pirate ships and famous landmarks, travel agencies hawking tours, market stalls and a fun fair.

Podmaine Monastery   CHRISTIAN MONASTERY
(www.manastirpodmaine.org) On the surprisingly peaceful northern slopes of town, this Serbian Orthodox monastery features the same stripes of pink and honey-coloured stone as the Stari Grad's Holy Trinity Church. Interesting frescoes inside the church include a Judgement Day scene showing the fate to befall the damned (look for the communist officer with the red star on his military uniform), including being eaten alive by fish and what appears to be a chicken.

From here, a walking track leads up the mountains for 2km to the fortified **Podostrog Monastery**. It was here that Njegoš wrote *The Mountain Wreath* and also here that his predecessor Danilo is said to have instigated the savage events that inspired it.

🏃 Activities & Tours

Travel agencies on Slovenska Obala peddle every kind of day tour, including Ostrog and Cetinje (€15), the Bay of Kotor (€17) and Dubrovnik (€28). You can hire a kayak (€5 per hour) or paddle boat (€6 per hour) from Mogren Beach. A huge range of boats with skippers are available for hire from the marina. A midsized launch might charge €400 for a day's fishing, while a flash one could be €1200 or more.

For underwater thrills, contact **Budva Diving** (Map p68; ☑ 068-060 416; www.budva diving.com; Dukley Marina Open Swimming Pool; incl equipment from €40).

🎊 Festivals & Events

Carnival of Budva   CULTURAL
Venetian-masked high jinks in April or early May.

Theatre City   PERFORMING ARTS
(☑ 033-402 935; www.gradteatar.me; ⊘ Jul-Aug) Renowned arts festival happening largely in and around the Old Town for seven weeks.

Sea Dance Festival   MUSIC
(www.seadancefestival.me; ⊘ Aug-Sep) Three huge days of international music acts on Buljarica Beach (p77).

🛏 Sleeping

Budva has a few good hostels and top-end hotels, and lots of rental apartments. The tourist office (p72) can provide you with information on renting private rooms.

🛏 Stari Grad

Freedom Hostel   HOSTEL €
(Map p68; ☑ 067-837 110; www.fb.com/freedom hostelbudva; Cara Dušana 21; dm/tw from €21/55; ⊘ Feb-Oct; ❄ 🛜) In a quieter section of the Old Town, this beloved, sociable hostel has tidy little rooms scattered between three buildings. The terraces and small courtyard are popular spots for impromptu guitar-led singalongs.

Hotel Astoria   BOUTIQUE HOTEL €€€
(Map p68; ☑ 033-451 110; www.astoriamontene gro.com; Njegoševa 4; s/d/ste from €90/110/130; ❄ 🛜) Water shimmers down the corridor wall as you enter this chic boutique hotel hidden in the Old Town's fortifications. The rooms are on the small side but they're beautifully furnished; the sea-view suite is spectacular. To top it all off, the wonderful roof terrace is home to Budva's most magnificent dining space, La Bocca.

Avala Resort & Villas   RESORT €€€
(Map p68; www.avalaresort.com; Mediteranska 2; d/villa/ste from €225/316/360; 🅿 ❄ 🛜 🏊) Stunning, breathtaking, luxurious: and that's just the views from the sea-facing rooms. This modern resort is a decadent delight, with a prime location right on Ričardova Glava, and an array of simple yet elegant rooms and sumptuous suites to choose from. The eye-smartingly blue outdoor pool makes direct eye contact with the Old Town and Sveti Nikola; you'd better waterproof your camera, as this is prime selfie-scenery.

🛏 Rest of Budva

Saki Apartmani   APARTMENT €€
(Map p67; ☑ 068-453 535; www.facebook.com/ SakiHostelBudva; IV Proleterska bb; dm €19, apt from €59; 🅿 ❄ 🛜 🏊) Not quite a hostel and not quite an apartment hotel, this friendly family-run block on the outskirts of town

offers elements of both. Individual beds are rented, hostel-style, in a rambling set of rooms. Private apartments have large balconies, but beds have been crammed in where kitchens might otherwise be. Grape and kiwifruit vines shade the pleasant communal terrace.

Hotel Lučić HOTEL €€
(Map p67; ☑033-403 320; www.hotellucic.com; Jadranski Put 37; d/apt from €70/110; P❋🛜) The Lučić is fairly generic, but who needs zany themed rooms when your digs are clean, comfortable, spacious and central? The staff here are helpful, and the restaurant isn't shy with serving sizes. It's about 400m from both the beach and the Old Town.

Hotel Kangaroo HOTEL €€
(Map p67; ☑033-458 653; www.hotelkangaroo.me; Velji Vinogradi bb; s/d €40/65; P❋@🛜) Bounce into a large clean room with a desk and terrace at this minimal-frills midsized hotel that's a hop, skip and jump from the beach. The owners once lived in Australia, which explains the name and the large 3D mural of Captain Cook's *Endeavour* in the popular restaurant below.

Hotel Poseidon HOTEL €€€
(☑033-463 134; www.poseidon-jaz.com; Jaz Beach; r from €112; ☾Jun-Oct; P❋🛜) This glorious seaside hotel has been sitting by the sands of Jaz Beach since 1967, and while the clean, spacious rooms don't show their age, the excellent service certainly echoes decades of experience. The views from every room – many of which have kitchens – are picture-perfect, and the hotel has its own small slice of private beach.

Hotel Slovenska Plaža RESORT €€€
(Map p67; ☑033-451 654; www.hgbudvanskariv ijera.com; 1 Trg Slobode; d/ste from €105/130; ☾May-Oct) With more than a thousand rooms, two pools, 11 tennis courts, four restaurants, salons, a cinema, galleries and markets on-site, this recently renovated resort is less a hotel than a rambling, raucous village (or – with its nightly entertainment schedules and karaoke parties – a beached cruise ship). Fans of Yugoslav architecture will find its spacious socialism-meets-Spanish-Mission aesthetic fascinating. Some facilities are also open to nonguests.

 Eating

For cheap fast food and delicious gelato, you need only stroll along Slovenska Obala. Self-caterers will find plenty of supermarkets around Budva, or check out the **green market** (Zelena pijaca; Map p67; 22 Novembra bb; ☾6am-8pm Mon-Sat, to 1pm Sun) for fresh produce and domestic cheese, meats and fish.

Stari Grad

Konoba Portun MONTENEGRIN, SEAFOOD €€€
(Map p68; ☑068-412 536; Mitrov Ljubiše 5; mains €12-21; ☾1pm-midnight; 🛜) Hidden within the Old Town's tiny lanes, this atmospheric eatery has only three outdoor tables and a handful inside; it feels like you're eating in a long-lost relative's home. The traditional dishes are beautifully presented. Don't miss out on the house speciality, *hobotnica ispod sača* (octopus cooked under a metal lid with hot coals). The grilled squid is excellent too.

Konoba Stari Grad SEAFOOD €€
(Map p68; ☑033-454 443; www.konobastarigrad.me; Njegoševa 14; mains €10-20; ☾10am-11pm) With an attractive stone-walled interior and a sunny terrace sandwiched between the Stari Grad's walls and beach, this *konoba* (family-run establishment) isn't short on atmosphere. It's a touch touristy, but the seafood's very good and there's live music most nights.

Rest of Budva

Mercur Cafe EUROPEAN €
(Map p67; ☑067-570 483; Trg sunca 7; mains €2-7; ☾5.30am-11pm) Bus stations and good nosh are usually mutually exclusive territories, but this relaxed restaurant is the exception to the rule. For starters, it sits in a gorgeous green oasis populated by peacocks, chickens and fluffy bunnies; there's also a play space. The menu includes sandwiches, grilled meat, pizza, pasta and cake.

Grill Bistro Parma MONTENEGRIN €€
(Map p67; ☑069-028 076; Mainski Put 70; mains €3-10; ☾24hr) A good grill *(roštilj)* is easy to find in meat-loving Montenegro, but if you're looking for one that's great, get your carnivorous self to Parma post-haste. Everything from *ćevapi* (spicy sausages) to chicken is barbecued to perfection here; their *punjena*

DON'T MISS

SEA DANCE FESTIVAL

Ever since the Rolling Stones served up satisfaction to a 40,000-strong crowd in 2007, Jaz Beach has become renowned as one of Europe's best open-air music venues. Though Mick, Keef and co were followed by the big-name likes of Madonna and Lenny Kravitz, it's the annual Sea Dance festival (p69) that's kept the sands of Jaz tamped down by hundreds of thousands of boogieing feet.

A rip-roaring three-day celebration of electronic and alternative music, Sea Dance was established in 2014 as an extension of Serbia's award-winning EXIT festival for revellers reluctant to end the party. Since then, Sea Dance has attracted 300,000 merrymakers (and counting), and has been named 'Best medium-sized European festival'. Previous acts include Jamiroquai, Underworld, Prodigy, Skrillex and Montenegro's favourite musical maverick, Rambo Amadeus.

Most festivalgoers camp on-site, though Jaz is within walking distance of Budva if sandy sleeps aren't your thing (be sure to book far, far ahead). If you're keen to make a dancey, delirious week of it, EXIT organisers run transfers between the festivals; check online at www.exitfest.org for details.

pljeskavica (stuffed spicy hamburger) will inspire daydreams and drooling for months after your meal. Portions are massive. The restaurant is friendly and often packed; they also do deliveries.

⭐**Jadran kod Krsta** MONTENEGRIN, SEAFOOD **€€**
(Map p67; ☑069-030 180; www.restaurantjadran.com; Slovenska obala bb; mains €7-20; ☺7am-1am; 🛜) With candlelit tables directly over the water, this extremely popular, long-standing restaurant offers all the usual seafood suspects along with classic Montenegrin dishes from the interior. It may seem incongruous, but there's a rip-roaring bikers' bar out the back.

Porto MONTENEGRIN, SEAFOOD **€€**
(Map p67; ☑069-025 850; www.restoranporto.com; Marina, Šetalište bb; mains €8-23; ☺10am-midnight) A little bridge arches over a fish pond and into this romantic restaurant, where jocular bow-tied waiters flit about with plates laden with fresh seafood. The food's excellent and the wine list offers plenty of choice from around the region.

 Drinking & Nightlife

 Stari Grad

Greco BAR
(Map p68; Njegoševa 17; ☺10pm-2am) On summer nights, the little square that Greco shares with its neighbour/rival Jef is packed from wall to wall with revellers.

⭐**Casper** BAR
(Map p68; www.facebook.com/casper.bar.budva; Petra I Petrovića bb; ☺10am-2am; 🛜) Chill out with a craft beer, cocktail or fair-trade, organic coffee under the pine tree of this picturesque Old Town cafe-bar. It regularly hosts live jazz gigs, and DJs kick off in July and August, spinning everything from soul to house.

Prince PUB
(Map p68; Vranjak bb; ☺8am-midnight; 🛜) If you're hankering for something slightly more stout than Montenegro's light lagers, pop down to this friendly little hang-out. It bills itself as an 'English pub', and while the inside is indeed dim and cosy, you'd never mistake its sunny, mega-Mediterranean outdoor area for anything you'd find in Blighty. Yes, there's football on the telly.

Rest of Budva

Top Hill CLUB
(☑067-478 888; www.tophill.me; Topliški Put bb; ☺hours vary Jun-Aug) The top cat of Montenegro's summer party scene attracts up to 5000 revellers to its open-air club atop Topliš Hill, offering them top-notch sound and lighting, sea views, big-name touring DJs and performances by local pop stars.

Torch BAR
(Map p67; ☑033-683 683; www.budvabeach.com; Slovenksa obala bb; ☺8am-1am summer; 🛜) It's totally scene-y, but Torch is a fun, over-the-top outdoor party palace that epitomises summertime Mediterranean madness.

Pool parties, sun-lounge cocktails, water pipes and light noshing are the order of the day.

ⓘ Information

Budva Health Centre (Dom zdravlja Budva; Map p67; ☎ 033-427 200; www.dialysiscenter. me; Popa Jola Zeca bb; ⊙7am-9pm) Includes an emergency clinic and a pharmacy.

Tourist Office (Map p68; ☎ 033-452 750; www.budva.travel; Njegoševa 28; ⊙9am-9pm Mon-Sat & 3-9pm Sun Jun-Aug, 9am-8pm Mon-Sat Sep-May) Small but helpful office in the old town.

ⓘ Getting There & Around

BUS

➡ The **bus station** (Map p67; ☎ 033-456 000; Popa Jola Zeca bb) has regular services to Kotor (€4, 40 minutes), Tivat (€4, 30 minutes), Ulcinj (€7, two hours), Cetinje (€4, 40 minutes) and Podgorica (€6, 1½ hours).

➡ International destinations include Dubrovnik, Zagreb, Sarajevo, Belgrade and Tirana.

➡ In summer you can flag down the Mediteran Express from the bus stops on Jadranski Put to head to Jaz Beach (€1.50, at least hourly), Ploče Beach (€2, at least hourly) or Sveti Stefan (€1.50, every 10 minutes).

CAR

There are plenty of well-marked parking areas; expect to pay about €5 per day or around €2 per hour. Tow trucks earn steady business from the Mediteranska shopping strip.

Meridian Rentacar (Map p67; ☎ 033-454 105; www.meridian-rentacar.com; Popa Jola Zeca 7) offers one-day hire from €26. For something a bit zippier, **Rent A Scooter Montenegro** (☎ 068-201 095; www.facebook.com/scooter-budva; Jadranski Put bb) has mopeds from €23 per day.

TAXI

Taxis are in ready supply in Budva, but many of those that hang around the nightspots in the early hours are prone to overcharging. You're better off calling a reputable company. Otherwise check that the taxi has a meter and what rate it charges; €4 per kilometre is *not* the going rate.

Eco Taxi (☎19567; www.taxibudva.com)

Terrae-Taxi (☎19717; www.terraecar. com) Advertises set fares to the following airports: Tivat (€15), Podgorica (€40) and Dubrovnik (€90).

Around Budva

◉ Sights

Jaz Beach   BEACH
The blue waters and broad sands of Jaz Beach look spectacular when viewed from high up on the Tivat road. While it's not built-up like Budva and Bečići, the beach is still lined with loungers, sun umbrellas and noisy beach bars; head down to the Budva end of the beach for a little more seclusion.

Sveti Nikola   ISLAND
Known locally as 'Hawaii', Sveti Nikola is Montenegro's largest island, stretching to nearly 2km. Fallow deer wander about on this uninhabited green spot, which is only a nautical mile away from Budva or Bečići Beach. Its rocky beaches make it a popular destination in summer when taxi boats regularly ferry sunseekers to and fro; those leaving from Slovenska Plaža charge about €3 per person each way (charter your own for €15 to €20).

Krapina   VILLAGE
(☎ 033-402 522) It's easy to be seduced by Budva's Old Town treats and beach scene, but if the smell of suntan lotion is getting a bit cloying, head for the hills and the lovely oasis of Krapina. Just 6km from town, this clean, green escape offers a sweet taste of village life that's great fun for the whole family; there are donkeys and rabbits for the littlies to cuddle, a zipline (€5) over a canyon for the older kids and a gorgeous waterfall-splashed natural pool for everyone to swim in. The delightful restaurant (mains €5 to €18) serves fish straight from its own farm; you can snooze it off on one of the lawn lounges.

Krapina is a 6km winding and well-signposted drive from Budva.

Bečići & Rafailovići
☎033

Welcome to the Benidorm of Montenegro! Like the Spanish tourist town, Bečići (Бечићи) has been completely swallowed by large resort complexes, complete with swimming pools, nightclubs and casinos. If the primary objective of your trip is to flit between the pool, pokies and sand, cocktail in hand, this is the place to do it. Just don't expect any actual engagement with Montenegrin culture.

Bečići and its neighbour Rafailovići (Рафаиловићи) share a 1950m-long sandy beach immediately east of Budva. In 1935 it won a Parisian prize and was named the most beautiful beach in Europe, although it's unlikely to win that prize today. It does, however, have a Blue Flag rating for cleanliness and water quality.

Rafailovići is equally built-up but retains the vaguest remnants of a village feel. Older-style apartment hotels hug the cliffs and restaurants line the shore. It's a popular spot for families, but at high tide there's hardly any beach.

🏃 Activities

During summer there's usually someone hiring jet skis, pedal boats, banana boats and kayaks from the beach, and taxi boats ply the shore for the trip to Sveti Nikola. If you fancy a spot of parasailing you'll need to keep your eyes open to watch where the boats dock. A short ride costs around €25. If the kids are getting restless, there's a large water park attached to the **Hotel Mediteran** (☑ 033-424 383; www.mediteran.me; Jadranski Put; r €95-280; P ❄ 🛜 🏊).

🛌 Sleeping & Eating

Hotel Aleksandar   BOUTIQUE HOTEL €€
(☑ 033-560 290; www.hotel-aleksandar.me; Rafailovići; d €85-95, ste €270-350; P ❄ 🛜 🏊) Elegant and surprisingly understated, this new designer hotel is a delight. It's already winning die-hard devotees, thanks to an exceptionally accommodating staff, posh restaurant–wine bar and prime location smack on the beach. The rooms are sparkling and large. It also has a detox centre attached, which may come in handy for those getting a little too fond of the local *rakija* (fruit brandy).

Hotel Obala   HOTEL €€
(☑ 033-471 045; www.hotelobala.me; Rafailovići; d/ste from €80/160; P ❄ 🛜) The Obala may not have the razzamatazz of its flashier neighbours, but this clean, understated, beachfront hotel is run by some of the friendliest people you'll meet along the coast. If the hotel is full, they also have apartments and rooms in other locations around Rafailovići.

Hotel Splendid   RESORT €€€
(☑ 033-773 777; www.montenegrostars.com; Jadranski Put, Bečići; s €244-290, d €490-580; P ❄ @ 🛜 🏊) The rooms are luxurious, but the real star of this mammoth resort is the pool complex. Three outdoor pools (there's another one inside) swirl around palm trees and manicured slices of lawn leading down to the large chunk of beach that the hotel consumes. There's also a kids' club, lavish health and beauty spa, and various spots to eat and drink.

In a smart – or cynical – move, the Splendid's attached Casino Royale was named after the James Bond film of the same name, which was purportedly filmed in nearby Petrovac. It wasn't, but that hasn't stopped punters looking to soak up a bit of 007's luck on the tables (or, ahem, otherwise).

Porat   SEAFOOD €€
(☑ 069-028 279; Rafailovići; mains €7-23; ☉ 8am-1am) Romantic (but sans soppiness) and nautical (without the naff), this excellent restaurant has 'atmosphere' down pat. Sitting on the promenade, Porat has been in continuous business since 1980, and the experience shows in their attentive staff and top-notch fish dishes. They also have a superb wine list.

ⓘ Getting There & Away

Regular buses run between Budva and Bečići (50c) or Rafailovići (€1).

Pržno

☑ 033 / POP 320

Charming little Pržno (Пржно) offers a cramped, family-friendly, red-sand beach and a surprisingly good selection of restaurants. An enigmatic ruin rests on a craggy island offshore, and just enough old stone houses remain to counterbalance the large-scale resort at the northern end of the beach. The walk from here through the woods to Sveti Stefan is exceedingly beautiful.

⊙ Sights

Kamenovo   BEACH
If you're feeling the squeeze on Pržno's beach, take a wander up to lovely little Kamenovo. There are no hotels here and while you'll find a couple of beach bars and a handful of umbrella renters, it feels positively deserted

after the mayhem of nearby resort towns. It's 1km north of Pržno. Don't go barefoot: *kamen* means 'stone' and there are plenty around.

In late May every year, calm little Kamenovo gets all amped up for the Spring Break electronic music festival (www.spring breakmontenegro.me).

🏃 Activities

Pro Diving Montenegro — DIVING (📞 069-013 985; www.prodivingmontenegro.com; Hotel Maestral) This well-established outfit offers shore dives (€20) and diving trips to various wrecks (€45), caves (€40 to €100) and various reefs. PADI diving courses are €300.

🛌 Sleeping

Apartmani Kažanegra — APARTMENT €€ (📞 033-468 429; www.kazanegra.com; Obala 12; per person €50-60; P ❄ 🛜) This stone villa is as close as you can get to the beach without ending up with sandy toes. It houses a range of tidy one- and two-bedroom apartments with private terraces overlooking the sea.

Hotel Residence Miločer — HOTEL €€€ (📞 033-427 100; www.residencemontenegro.com; Jadranski Put; r €122, apt €140-208; P ❄ 🛜 🏊) Maybe it's because it's linked to an award-winning hospitality school that this hotel ticks all the right boxes. The decor's fresh and modern, there's secure parking, the breakfast buffets are excellent, and the staff aren't afraid to smile. The rooftop pool is tiny, but has brilliant views (and a cocktail bar).

Maestral Resort & Casino — RESORT €€€ (📞 033-410 100; www.maestral.info; s/d/apt from €150/200/250; P ❄ 🛜 🏊) The Maestral offers everything you'd expect from a large seaside resort: luxurious rooms (ask for one facing the sea), private beach, spa centre, plenty of pools, good restaurants and live entertainment in summer. The attentive staff somehow keep the whole place running like clockwork.

🍴 Eating

Konoba Zago — MONTENEGRIN, SEAFOOD €€€ (📞 033-468 463; www.zago-przno.com; Obala 5; mains €8-24; ⏰ 9am-midnight) 'If it ain't broke, why fix it?' seems to be the adage adhered to by the owners of Zago, one of Pržno's first restaurants, and still one of its best. The tra-ditional menu is as authentic as you can get (they make their own olive oil, catch their own fish and bake their own bread), as is the restaurant's setting in an old stone villa overlooking the Adriatic. They also have apartments to rent for those who can't get enough of the calm, far-from-the-madding-crowds location (or food).

Konoba Langust — SEAFOOD €€€ (📞 033-468 369; Obala 34; mains €9-22) This highly rated fish restaurant has been serving traditional seafood meals from its stretch of the Pržno promenade for more than 20 years. Take it from their many guests who have been returning here year after year: you can certainly find these dishes cheaper elsewhere, but you're unlikely to find them better.

ℹ️ Information

There's an ATM in the lobby of the large Maestral resort at the northern end of town.

The post office is at the southern end by the main bus stop and taxi stand.

ℹ️ Getting There & Away

Budva and Sveti Stefan are 10 minutes in either direction from Pržno. The Mediteran Express bus running between the two stops here (€1.50).

Sveti Stefan

📞 033 / POP 364

Of all the sights along the Adriatic shoreline, Sveti Stefan (Свети Стефан) is the most extraordinary. A fortified island village connected to the mainland by a narrow causeway, its photogenic jumble of 15th-century stone villas overlooks an impeccable pink-sand beach and tempting turquoise waters. The island was nationalised in the 1950s and is now part of the luxurious Aman resort, meaning it's off-limits to all but paying guests. But ogling comes for free; Sveti Stefan has unsurprisingly been named as Montenegro's most photographed site.

Sveti Stefan is also the name of the township that's sprung up onshore. From its steep slopes, you can admire the iconic island to your heart's content. On the downside, parking is difficult, there are lots of steps and there's little in the way of shops. Families will be delighted to discover an excellent (and free) playground near the Olive restaurant.

◉ Sights

Sveti Stefan Beach
BEACH

The main point of coming to Sveti Stefan is to spend as much time horizontal as possible, with occasional breaks for a cooling dip. The water here gets deep quickly, as if the surrounding mountains couldn't be bothered adjusting their slope. The sands are pinkish and pebbly, but it's difficult to care about a stray rock in your bathers when you've got a jaw-dropping view of the famous island to squint at from behind your sunnies.

The uncrowded beach on the Budva side of the causeway belongs to the resort. If you don't fancy shelling out €100 for the day-use fee (ie you're not completely insane), the deckchairs on the other side of the causeway get cheaper the further along the beach you go, and there's plenty of rocky – but free – space near the end.

Miločer Beach
BEACH

(King's Beach, Kraljeva Plaža) At the northern end of Sveti Stefan Beach, a path leads over a headland draped in pine and olive trees to the turquoise waters and pink sands of Miločer Beach. Set back from the tranquil bay and fronted by a loggia draped in sweet-scented wisteria is the Villa Miločer. This grand two-storey stone building was built in 1934 as the summer residence of the Karađorđević royal family, the Serbian monarchs who headed the first Yugoslavia.

The whole area is now part of the Aman resort and while you're welcome to walk through, access to the beach itself will cost you a hefty €120.

Crvena Glavica
BEACH

A short hike south of Sveti Stefan will bring you to this collection of small beaches with rocky red sand (*crvena glavica* means 'red head'). It's a steep and bumpy path, but if you're intent on seeking out some peace and quiet (or are a dedicated nudist), it's worth the journey.

Praskvica Monastery
CHRISTIAN MONASTERY

(Прасквица Манастир; Jadranska magistrala bb) Just off the highway in the hills slightly north of Sveti Stefan, this humble 600-year-old monastery, named after the peach-scented water of a brook that flows nearby, rests amid an ancient olive grove. It was an important political centre for the Paštrovići, a local tribe whose distinctive cultural traditions have survived along this section of the coast despite numerous foreign occupations. The monastery is well signposted from the main road and an easy walk from either Sveti Stefan or Pržno. It's a working monastery; visitors are welcome, but be sure to dress accordingly.

🛏 Sleeping

Crvena Glavica Auto Kamp
CAMPGROUND €

(☑ 033-468 070; campsites per adult/child/tent/car €2.50/1/3.50; ☉ Jun-Sep) You don't need to be a movie star or oligarch to enjoy those million-dollar views. Pitch your tent under the olive trees and stroll past the roving chickens down to the rocky but peaceful shoreline. The toilet block and outdoor showers are very basic.

★ Drago
B&B €€

(☑ 033-468 477; www.viladrago.com; Slobode 32; r/apt from €80/155; ※ 🞀) The only problem with Drago is that you may never want to leave your terrace; the views are *that* sublime. The super-comfy pillows and fully stocked bathrooms are a nice touch. Some rooms and both apartments have kitchens, but it's unlikely you'll use them; the on-site restaurant is excellent (mains €5 to €20), serving specialities from the local Paštrovići clan.

Apartments Dijana
APARTMENT €€

(☑ 069-256 101; www.dijana-montenegro.com; Slobode bb; apt from €75; P ※ 🞀 ☒) Be sure to book far, far ahead if you want to snag one of these comfortable, extremely clean apartments; word of Dijana's warm welcomes has got around, and it's a popular place. Most units have kitchens, balconies and impeccable views to the sea; the flower-strewn communal terrace makes for a beautiful spot to wind down with a vino or three.

Aman Sveti Stefan
RESORT €€€

(☑ 033-420 000; www.aman.com; ste from €1323; P ※ 🞀 ☒) This superlatives-defying resort is one-of-a-kind. Occupying the entire Sveti Stefan island, it offers 50 luxurious suites that showcase the stone walls and wooden beams of the ancient houses. Amazingly, there's still a village feel here, with cobbled lanes, churches and an open-air cafe on the piazza. Back on the shore, Villa Miločer has a further eight suites by the beach.

✗ Eating

Paštrovića Dvori MONTENEGRIN, SEAFOOD €€
(📞033-468 162; Blizikuće bb; mains €8-16; ⏰11am-10pm) With its authentic, homemade Paštrović cuisine, this happy, hospitable, family-run restaurant ought to be on every traveller's to-try list. It is less flash than most of the other choices in shiny Sveti Stefan (though it does tick the 'divine views' box), but therein lies its charm. The restaurant is well signposted from the main road, south of Sveti Stefan.

ℹ Information

There's an ATM by the strip of shops before the causeway.

ℹ Getting There & Away

➡ Mediteran Express buses head to and from Budva (€1.50, 20 minutes) every 10 minutes in summer and hourly in winter, stopping on the hill about halfway down to the beach.

➡ Sveti Stefan is all windy, narrow roads, which, of course, the locals tear down with gay abandon; visitors should exercise a touch more caution on the many blind bends.

Rijeka Reževići

📞033 / POP 40

The traditional Paštrović-style architecture of Rijeka Reževići (Ријека Ржевићи) differs from the rest of Montenegro, favouring rows of terrace houses with stone walls, small windows, single-pitched roofs and 'hog's back' curved terracotta tiles. This charming village offers some lovely examples and although gentrification is evident, the focus has been on restoration rather than demolition.

Rijeka Reževići is an easy 5km drive from Petrovac.

◉ Sights

Presjek BEACH
This quiet, boulder-strewn beach is great for snorkelling (bring your own gear) or simply slipping off and finding your own secluded swimming spot. Get here by following the footpath that starts at the car park below the village church and onwards through the woods.

Reževići Monastery CHRISTIAN MONASTERY
Hospitality has always been important at this atmospheric stone complex, just 2km south of Rijeka Reževići. Until the 19th century, the Paštrovići would leave a bottle of wine here for passers-by, one of whom in 1226 was King Stefan the First-Crowned of the Serbian Nemanjić dynasty, who founded the **Church of the Dormition** (Crkva Uspenja Bogorodice), the smaller church of the complex. There are fine frescoes covering the walls, though the frescoes in the larger **Church of the Holy Trinity** (Crkva Sv Trojice; 1770) – repainted in the 1970s – are more vivid.

Drobni Pijesak BEACH
Hidden in a secluded cove three minutes north of Rijeka Reževići, Drobni Pijesak is a 240m stretch of 'ground sand' (the literal translation of the name) surrounded by green hills and turquoise waters. Every year on 28 June, the elders of the 12 Paštrović clans hold the Bankada here, a community court with origins in the 16th century. Nowadays its main focus is the restoration and preservation of the tribe's traditions, environmental and cultural conservation and economic development. The day ends with a folk and arts festival.

🛏 Sleeping & Eating

Reževići Apartments APARTMENT €€
(📞033-468 181; www.rezevici-apartmani.com; Reževići Rijeka bb; d €50, apt €65-110; 🅿❄🛜🐾) If a day trip to Rijeka Reževići just isn't enough, you can drop your bags at this lovely family-run property overlooking the village and the sea. It's clean, quiet and a couple of minutes to the beach; the hosts have lavish hospitality down pat.

Balun SEAFOOD €€
(📞069-285 652; mains €9-20) This beachside restaurant is comparatively pricey, but it's highly rated by the locals. If you're on a budget but keen on million-dollar views, you can always just order a coffee and gaze over the oleanders to the clear waters below.

Petrovac

📞033 / POP 1400

The Romans had the right idea, building their summer villas on this lovely bay. If only the new crop of developers had a scrap of their classic good taste. Still, once you get down to the pretty beachside promenade where lush Mediterranean plants perfume the air and a 16th-century Venetian fortress

ČANJ & SUTOMORE

If you're on a budget, or simply have a yen for a seaside holiday that's more splash, less flash, give Budva the bump and head south to Čanj or Sutomore. Located roughly mid-way between Petrovac and Bar, the two beach towns attract hordes of Montenegrin and Serbian families and young 'uns intent on spending their summers swimming, sunning and staggering between beach bars and nightclubs. Neither spot is particularly upmarket, but the beaches are beautiful with water clear enough for snorkelling, and both towns have a carefree nostalgic feel. The best beach in the region is the pink-sanded **Kraljičina Plaža**, just around the headland from Čanj. It can only be reached by boat; you'll find them running from Čanj in the peak season, or from Bar for as little as €3.

There are plenty of hotels in Sutomore – none of them is exceptional, but they are cheap – and a few in Čanj. In both towns, you'll find a plethora of *sobe* (rooms) or *apartmani* signs; many also advertise online. Private apartments hover around the €30 to €40 range, while a double room in a beachfront hotel goes from €35 up.

guards a tiny stone harbour, the aberrations up the hill are barely visible. This is one of the best places on the coast for families: the accommodation is reasonably priced, the water is clear and kids roam the esplanade at night with impunity.

Petrovac (Петровац) enjoyed a few minutes of Hollywood fame in 2006 when the town was billed as the location for the Casino Royale in the James Bond film of the same name. Tourists and developers arrived in droves; many of them still haven't discovered that all 'Petrovac' scenes were actually filmed in the Czech Republic.

⊙ Sights

In July and August you'll be lucky to find an inch of space on the fine reddish pebbles of the **town beach**, but wander south and there's cypress- and oleander-lined **Lučice Beach**, with a kids' waterslide on its far end. Continue over the leafy headland for another 30 minutes and the 2.4km-long sweep of **Buljarica Beach** comes into view, most of which is blissfully undeveloped – at least for now.

The small **Katič** and **Sveta Nedjelja** (Holy Sunday) islets just offshore can be visited by kayak or by arranging a lift from Petrovac's small harbour.

Kastio   FORTRESS
Clamber up the steps of this small Venetian fortress for photogenic views of the beach and the dramatic diagonal stratification of the limestone cliffs melting into the turquoise water below. An interesting socialist-realist bas-relief remembering the 'socialist revolution' is partly obscured in the foliage. The entrance is by the small Petrovac harbour.

Roman Mosaics   RUINS
(Kasnoantički mozaik) Apart from the beaches, Petrovac's most interesting attraction is also its least heralded. In 1902 the foundations of a Roman building complete with mosaics, probably dating from the 4th century AD, were discovered in an olive grove and here they remain in a precarious state of preservation. A glass shed covers a section of mosaic roughly 10m by 15m; it's invariably locked but you can peer through the windows. Around the shed, extensive brick foundations can be seen.

The site is a little tricky to find: take the path leading through private land opposite the 500-year-old **St Thomas' Church** then make your way through the olive grove to the dig site; you'll need to watch your footing.

The site has the potential to be a huge drawcard for Petrovac; whether this is ever acted upon remains to be seen.

Gradište Monastery   CHRISTIAN MONASTERY
Perched on a hill overlooking Buljarica Beach, Gradište Monastery is a tranquil collection of stone buildings facing onto a central courtyard. The monastery was first mentioned in documents from 1305, although it's believed to date from 1116. Like many Montenegrin monasteries, it's had a rough time over the years at the hands of invading armies and has been rebuilt several times.

The three churches on the site are renowned for their frescoes, some of which date back to 1620.

Taking the main road south of Petrovac, turn left after the tunnel and take the steep road up to the monastery (park at the bottom if you're not sure if your car is up to it).

🏃 Activities

Petrovac Kayak Club   KAYAKING
(☑ 068-613 622; www.montekayak.com; 46 Nika Anđusa) This friendly group offers guided kayaking trips, including two-hour journeys to Katič and Sveta Nedjelja islands (from €20) and full-day customised paddles (from €80). Kayak hire is available for those who want to go it alone (30 minutes/one hour/half-day/full day from €7/10/24/40). They can also organise kayak fishing trips (from €30).

✨ Festivals & Events

Petrovac Night   MUSIC, FOOD
(☉ late Aug) Free fish, wine and beer, majorette parades, performances by Eurovision contestants... Who could ask for anything more?

🛏 Sleeping

For private accommodation in and around Petrovac, try **Mornar Travel Agency** (☑ 033-461 410; www.mornartravel.me).

Rakočević Apartments   APARTMENT €
(☑ 067-626 795; www.rakocevic-apartments.com; apt from €30-80) These apartments offer possibly the best high-season value in Petrovac.

The 10 apartments in two locations (in the centre beside the promenade, or by the bus station near the top of town) range in size from studios to family-size units. If ubertrendy digs are what you're after, look elsewhere (and pay more), but if comfortable, clean and well appointed floats your boat, book now.

Camping Maslina   CAMPGROUND €
(☑ 033-461 215; www.campingmaslina.com; Buljarica bb; campsites per adult/child/tent/car/caravan €3.50/1.50/3/3/5; P 🛜) As Montenegrin campsites go, this is one of the best, with more than 100 camping spots under centuries-old olive trees, working wi-fi and a tidy ablutions block with proper sit-down toilets and solar-powered hot water. You'll find it just off the road to Buljarica Beach.

Hotel Đurić   HOTEL €€
(☑ 033-461 814; www.hoteldjuric.com; Brežine bb; d/ste/apt from €80/100/180; ☉ May-Sep; ❄🛜🏊) There's a vaguely Spanish Mission feel to this smart boutique hotel. All rooms have kitchen facilities and there's a restaurant at the back under a canopy of kiwi-fruit and grape vines.

Vile Olivia   RESORT €€€
(☑ 033-461 194; www.vileoliva.com; d from €150, apt from €210) Set on a large olive grove and just metres from the beach, Petrovac's largest hotel complex is a favourite with families for its kids' club, shady playground, two pools and nightly traditional entertainment

---

WORTH A TRIP

HAJ-NEHAJ FORTRESS

If you spent your youth playing Dungeons and Dragons or you just like poking around old ruins, the lonely battlements of Haj-Nehaj Fortress should be added to your itinerary. Haj-Nehaj was built in the 15th century by the Venetians to defend their southern border from the Ottoman Turks, whose conquests had brought them as far as the river that runs into Šušanj Beach in modern Bar.

To get here from Bar, follow the highway north for 6.5km and turn left where the fortress is signposted. At the intersection of the first sealed road to the right, a rough unsealed road heads hard right through the houses. Walk straight up this road with the castle directly in front of you and turn right at the end into a rough car park. Look for the start of the track among the bushes on the slope. From here it's a steep but attractive walk through the pines for 30 minutes on a stony path that's often hard to distinguish.

When the gate finally does come into view, the fortifications rise so precipitously from the stone that you'll be left wondering how it was ever built. Once you're inside, there are extensive ruins to explore, rising charismatically from a blanket of wild sage and flowers. At the very top, looking over Bar, is the shell of the 13th-century **St Demetrius' Church** (Crkva Sv Dimitrija), easily recognised by its vaulted roof and stone altar. It predates the fort itself and once had separate Catholic and Orthodox altars.

programs. The staff here are professional, and the buffet restaurant is up to scratch. Rooms and apartments are fairly generic but very spacious and clean; all have balconies.

✗ Eating

The esplanade is lined with fast-food joints, ice-cream stands, restaurants and cafe-bars. In the midst of it all, you'll find some excellent full-service restaurants.

The **Voli** (Nika Anđusa 22; ⊙6am-11pm) supermarket has everything for self-caterers. It's attached to a small fresh-produce market.

Oskar   SEAFOOD €€

(mains €5-17) There are loads of seafood joints to choose from along the esplanade, and pretty much all of them are good. Oskar takes it up a notch, with consistently brisk service, ginormous portions of fresh seafood, and a lively ambience courtesy of a buzzy crowd. As per its location, the views are sensational.

Balkan   MONTENEGRIN €€

(☑068-540569; Nika Andjusa 18; ⊙7am-midnight) One street behind the main seaside drag, Balkan is a cosy, traditional place that – for families, anyway – makes up for its lack of ocean views with a good playground. They do offer seafood, but Balkan is best for its heaped servings of beautifully barbecued meats.

Konoba Bonaca   MONTENEGRIN, SEAFOOD €€

(☑069-084 735; Barski Put bb; mains €6-17) Favoured by Petrovacians, this restaurant focuses mainly on seafood but the local cheeses and olives are also excellent. Grab a table under the grapevines on the terrace and make yourself comfortable; service isn't the speediest, but there's some prime people-watching and wine sipping to be done as you wait.

▼ Drinking & Nightlife

Terasa Castelo   BAR, CLUB

(terrace/club free/€2; ⊙8am-1am) Sip a cocktail and enjoy the romantic panorama over the parapets of the Venetian fortress. DJs spark up both on the terrace and downstairs in the club Castelo on summer nights. Whether you plan to stay for the late-night shenanigans or not, it's also a great place for a fine meal to match the view.

Ponta Beach Bar   BAR

(⊙8am-1am) With a sea-level terrace built into the stone at the south end of the beach, this is a great location for a sunset cocktail. Later on, local rock bands get the joint jumping.

❶ Information

Accident & Emergency Clinic (Zdravstvena stanica; ☑069-680 741) At the top of town; follow the road from the bus station.

❶ Getting There & Away

Petrovac's **bus station** (☑068-503 399) is near the top of town. There are regular services to Budva (€2.75, 30 minutes) and Bar (€3, 30 minutes), as well as Herceg Novi (€6, two hours, five daily), Kotor (€5, 1¼ hours, nine daily) and Ulcinj (€5, one hour, eight daily). International destinations include Dubrovnik (€20, 3½ hours, one daily) and Belgrade (€24, 10 hours, five daily).

Don Street Taxi Service (☑069-437 966; www.taxi-transfer.me) has metered cabs and advertises the following set fares: Tivat (€35), Budva (€15), Bar (€15), Ulcinj (€35) and Podgorica (€40).

Bar

☑030 / POP 17,000

Dominated by Montenegro's main port and a large industrial area, Bar (Бар) is unlikely to be anyone's holiday highlight, but it is a handy transport hub welcoming trains from Belgrade and ferries from Italy. Otherwise, the only real reason to come is to use the city as a base for visiting the fascinating ruins of Stari Bar (Old Bar) in the mountains behind.

Unlike the northern part of the coast, which remained largely under the rule of Venice and then Austria, the areas from Bar southwards spent 300 years under Turkish control. 'New' Bar itself – founded in 1908 – has a fairly modern feel to it, but once you start heading towards the Albanian border, you'll notice more mosques and Ottomanesque buildings.

◉ Sights

With a large industrial port and marina on its doorstep, Bar's **City Beach** (Map p80) is not the most appealing option for swimming. Heading north, **Šušanj Beach** (Map p80) is popular with Serbian holidaymakers. Beat the crowds in the succession of rocky coves that follow; they're perfect for

Bar

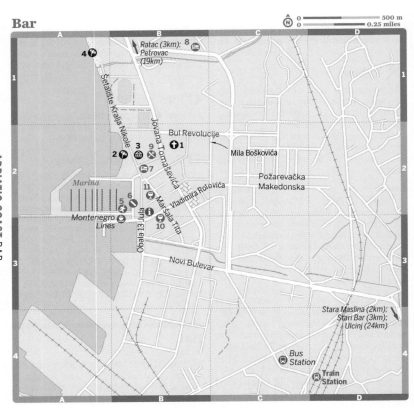

Bar

⊙ Sights
1	Church of St Jovan Vladimir	B2
2	City Beach	B2
3	King Nikola's Palace	B2
4	Šušanj Beach	A1

⊕ Activities, Courses & Tours
5	Montenegro Yacht Excursions	B2
6	Scuba Quest Diving Centre	B2

⊟ Sleeping
7	Le Petit Chateau	B2
8	Villa Jadran	B1

⊗ Eating
9	Knjaževu Baštu	B2

⊜ Drinking & Nightlife
10	Green Mill	B3
11	Salsa Familia	B2

snorkelling and sheltered swimming. If you're concerned about the Speedos chafing, you can go the full monty at a stony bay just before the rustic ruins of the 11th-century Benedictine monastery of the **Mother of God of Ratac** (Bogorodica Ratac). Destroyed by the Turks in 1571, the remains of its chapel now have a congregation consisting of wild figs and the occasional *baba* (grandma) in black.

King Nikola's Palace　　　　　MUSEUM
(Dvorac Kralja Nikole; Map p80; ☑ 030-314 079; Šetalište Kralje Nikole; adult/child €1.50/1; ☉ 8am-2pm & 5-11pm) Presenting an elegant facade to the water, King Nikola's Palace was built in 1885 and now houses a collection of antiquities, folk costumes and royal furniture.

Its shady gardens contain plants cultivated from seeds and cuttings collected from around the world by Montenegro's sailors.

Church of St Jovan Vladimir   CATHEDRAL
(Hram Sv Jovana Vladimira; Map p80; Bul Revolucije) This huge, modern, gold-topped cathedral can be seen from all across Bar. It's dedicated to Jovan Vladimir, the patron saint of Bar, who is considered to be the first Serbian saint.

🏃 Activities

Canyoning   ADVENTURE SPORTS
Just outside of Bar, two relatively unknown canyons have recently opened up for exploration with day trips run by Active Travels Montenegro (p40). Rikavac (€75) is a small canyon with a gentle three-hour program of hiking, abseiling and swimming suitable for beginners (including kids over eight); the remote Medjurečje canyon (€115) offers more hard-core adventure, with six hours of hiking through water, abseiling down waterfalls (15–30m) and plenty of sliding down the slippery canyon walls.

Scuba Quest Diving Centre   DIVING
(Map p80; 069-495 604; www.divemontenegro. com; Bar Marina; intro dive €60) Based in Bar,

this highly regarded group nevertheless covers the entire coast with an extensive choice of dive sites, which include wrecks, reefs and caves. Two-dive trips for certified divers are €60; PADI open-water courses are €300. They also rent snorkelling equipment (€5 per day) and can organise yacht charters (half-/full day €300/450).

Montenegro Yacht Excursions   BOATING
(Map p80; 067-109 109; www.utjeha.me; half-/ full-day cruise €380/760; ⊙May-Sep) These boat cruises take in some of the Adriatic's prime panoramas, including Sveta Nedjelja to the north and south to Ulcinj.

🛏 Sleeping & Eating

Given it's a major transport hub, it's surprisingly difficult to find decent accommodation in Bar, though the situation is slowly improving with a glut of private rentals appearing on the market. Hunt them down online or ask at the tourist office.

Le Petit Chateau   BOUTIQUE HOTEL €€
(Map p80; 030-314 400; Šetalište Kralja Nikole bb; d €90) This pretty little hotel is as cute – and almost as twee – as the name might suggest. Located in a beautifully restored, former royal residence within the walls of

---

WORTH A TRIP

BAR–BELGRADE TRAIN

Chugging over 435 bridges, into 254 tunnels and up steep, 1000m-plus mountains, a ride on the Bar–Belgrade train is no mere A-to-B commute. A marvel of engineering and one of Europe's most spectacular train trips, the railway runs through the heartlands of Montenegro and Serbia, taking in vistas and villages impossible to catch by car. Make sure your camera is charged; the journey from Serbia's landlocked capital to the Adriatic Sea twists and turns past massifs, monasteries, canyons, rivers and serene Lake Skadar. Those suffering vertigo may wish to avert their eyes during the crossing of the 500m-long Mala Rijeka bridge; swooning 200m above the river of the same name, the viaduct was – until 2001 – the highest railway bridge in the world.

The journey is more than just a series of scenic photo-ops: it's a social event. For 11 hours (or more, depending on border formalities), locals and travellers are banded together in close confines, with not much else to do but indulge in the Balkan propensity for banter. Combine the fact that there's no dining car with Slavic hospitality (and a tendency to pack way, way too much food...not to mention bottles of *rakija*), and voila! Instant party.

A major project of the former Yugoslavia, construction of the 476km line began in the 1950s, though it wasn't until 1976 that President Tito cut the ribbon. Josip Broz was such a fan of riding these rails that he had his own luxury train built, complete with sumptuous bedrooms, Turkish rugs and a full-sized bath-tub. To follow in his (somewhat less luxurious) footsteps, a 2nd-class ticket costs €21; trains run twice a day. Check with Montenegro Railways (www.cg-prevoz.me) for updated timetables and fares.

King Nikola's Palace, its handful of quaint but spacious rooms sit above an equally enchanting restaurant and bar. For ambience and location in Bar, this little house is unbeatable.

Villa Jadran   B&B €€
(Map p80; ☑ 030-350 330; www.vilajadran.net; Ilino bb; d/apt from €44/61; P ✴ 🛜) The rooms and apartments here may be humble, but for this price, they're a steal. The overall cleanliness and comfort don't suffer for the price, and you can expect a warmer welcome than what you'd get at many of the pricier places in town.

Knjaževu Baštu   MONTENEGRIN €€€
(Duke's Garden; Map p80; ☑ 030-312 601; www.knjazevabasta.com; King Nikola's Palace; mains €9-24; ⊙ 9am-11pm) While the regional specialities, service and exhaustive wine list here are indeed excellent, it's the palace location that makes Knjaževu Baštu so special. It's as lush and as opulent as you'd expect from such a regal setting, with tremendous chandeliers, luxurious furniture and – of course – divine views of the royal gardens.

🍷 Drinking & Nightlife

The one thing Bar isn't short of is bars. There are heaps of them along and just off Ulica Vladimira Rolovića.

Green Mill   BAR
(Map p80; Vladimira Rolovića bb) The 'best place to party in town' gong surely goes to Green Mill (and its friendly neighbour Bar Varadero), with exuberant crowds, thumping good-time music and occasional live acts. Nothing fancy, just tons of fun.

Salsa Familia   BAR
(Map p80; Maršala Tita bb; ⊙ 10am-midnight) Salsa in Crna Gora? Somehow, this unusual place works an absolute treat, with lively Cuban dance parties (and lessons), zingy cocktails and – perhaps strangest of all, for Montenegro – a nonsmoking interior. They also do food, and while Cuban food is not in abundance, the great pizzas and superb Russian *pelmeni* (dumplings) are worth a try. Great coffee too.

❶ Information

There are several banks with ATMs around Ulica Maršala Tita and Ulica Vladimira Rolovića.

Accident & Emergency Clinic (Map p80; ☑ 030-311 001; www.domzdravljabar.com; Jovana Tomaševića 42)

Tourist Information Centre (Map p80; ☑ 030-311 633; www.visitbar.org; Obala 13 Jula bb; ⊙ 8am-8pm Mon-Sat, to 2pm Sun Jul-Sep, 8am-4pm Mon-Fri Oct-Jun) Stocks city maps and useful brochures listing sights and private accommodation.

❶ Getting There & Away

BOAT

Ferries to Bari (deck/cabin/car from €48/67/78, nine hours) and Ancona (deck/cabin/car from €60/80/90, 16 hours) in Italy leave from the ferry terminal *(putnički terminal)* near the centre of town. You can book your **Montenegro Lines** (Map p80; ☑ 030-311 164; www.montenegrolines.net; deck/cabin/car tickets from €48/67/78) ferry tickets here, and there's a post office branch and an ATM.

In summer you can hail a taxi boat from the marina or beach for a short trip up the coast (from about €3 to €5).

BUS

The **bus station** (Map p80; ☑ 030-346 141; Beogradska bb) is adjacent to the train station, 1km southeast of the centre. Frequent buses head to Kotor (€6.50, two hours), Budva (€5, one hour), Ulcinj (€3, 30 minutes) and Podgorica (€4.50, 1¼ hours), and five daily go to Kolašin (€6.50, three hours).

Local buses stop in the centre on Ulica Jovana Tomaševića and head to Stari Bar and north along the coast as far as Čanj.

CAR

From Bar, the fastest route to Podgorica is via a toll road (€3.50 each way) and the 4km-long Sozina tunnel that leaves the highway just past Sutomore, northwest of Bar. The journey takes about 45 minutes.

Meridian Rentacar (Map p80; ☑ 069-318 666; www.meridian-rentacar.com; Jovana Tomaševića 30; per day from €37) has a branch in the centre of town.

TRAIN

The **train station** (Map p80; ☑ 030-301 622; www.zpcg.me; Beogradska bb) has services to Virpazar (€1.20, 25 minutes, seven daily), Podgorica (€2.40, one hour, 12 daily), Kolašin (€5.40, 2½ hours, four daily), Mojkovac (€6.20, 2¾ hours, five daily), Bijelo Polje (€7.20, 3¼ hours, five daily) and Belgrade (€21, 11 hours, two daily).

Stari Bar

📞 030 / POP 1870

The gloriously dilapidated Stari Bar (Стари Бар) – Bar's original settlement – teeters on a bluff at the foot of Mt Rumija, offering jaw-dropping views and enough enigmatic rubble to get even the dullest imagination running rampant. A steep, cobbled hill climbs past a cluster of old houses and shops to the fortified entrance, where a short dark passage leads to a large expanse of vine-clad ruins and abandoned streets overgrown with grass and wildflowers. Alas, visiting Stari Bar is – for now – not suitable for those in wheelchairs.

History

Discoveries of pottery and metal suggest that the Illyrians founded the city around 800 BC. In the 10th century, the Byzantine town was known as Antivarium as it is opposite the Italian city of Bari. It passed in and out of Slavic and Byzantine rule until the Venetians took it in 1443 (note the lion of St Mark in the entryway) and held it until it was taken by the Ottomans in 1571. Nearly all the 240 buildings now lie in ruins, mainly as a result of Montenegrin shelling when they captured the town in 1878. An explosion finished off the Franciscan Monastery in 1912 and the 1979 earthquake did still more damage.

◉ Sights

Stari Bar RUINS

(Old Bar; adult/child €2/1; ⏰8am-10pm) A small **museum** housed in a 17th-century customs building just inside Stari Bar's entrance explains the site and its history. From here, follow the green arrows around the major points of interest. In the western part of the town are the remains of the 13th-century **St Nicholas' Franciscan Monastery**, offering glimpses of Byzantine-style frescoes; it was converted to a mosque in 1595.

The northern corner has an 11th-century **fortress** with much-photographed views showcasing Stari Bar's isolated setting amid mountains and olive groves. Nearby are the foundations of **St George's Cathedral**. Originally a Romanesque church, it was converted into a mosque in the 17th century by the Turks, but the unlucky edifice was ruined after an accidental explosion of gunpowder.

If you're wondering why **St John's Church** is in such good nick, it's because it's been completely reconstructed by one of the families associated with the original church. One of the few other buildings to have an intact roof is **St Verenada's Church**, which contains a few photos from the greater Bar area. The 14th-century **St Catherine's Church**, in a tower above one of the lower gates, was being restored when we last visited.

Ottoman constructions include a solid and charming **Turkish bathhouse** from the 17th or 18th century, the **clock tower** (1752) and the 17th-century **aqueduct** that carried water from a spring 3km away; it was reconstructed after the 1979 earthquake.

Omerbašića Mosque MOSQUE

(Omerbašića džamija) Just outside Stari Bar's main gate, this simple construction (dating from 1662) has a square stone base and an elegant minaret enclosed by a stone wall. The domed structure near the entrance is the tomb of Dervish Hasan. Many of the Roma people who make a significant

---

WORTH A TRIP

THE OLD OLIVE TREE

There are more than 100,000 olive trees in the Bar area, many of which have seen more than a millennium. At Mirovica near Stari Bar is a living witness that has stood and mutely waved symbols of peace while the armies of consecutive empires have swept through the land. With 2000 birthdays under its belt, **stara maslina** (old olive tree; adult/child €1/50c) is possibly the oldest tree in continental Europe and one of the oldest of its species in the world.

A ring of white stone protects its personal space from tree-huggers and there's a nominal charge to visit, but it can be admired nearly as well from the road. Look for the signpost on the Bar–Ulcinj road; at the end of this road, look for the stone wall slightly to the right.

ADRIATIC COAST STARI BAR

proportion of Stari Bar's remaining population practise Islam.

🛏 Sleeping & Eating

Stari Bar has both an excellent new boutique hotel and a hostel. Some of the restaurants also offer rooms.

Kaldrma   MONTENEGRIN €€
(☑030-304 208; mains €5-13; ⊙10am-10pm; 🖋) 🍴 Located on the steep road leading to Stari Bar's main gate (the restaurant's name means 'cobblestone'), this wonderful little eatery manages to be simultaneously very traditional and slightly twee. The focus is on the cuisine of Stari Bar itself, including tender lamb dishes and tons of seasonal vegetarian/vegan options. The *japrak* (stuffed vine leaves) are made to a family recipe and absolutely must be tasted to be believed.

Sleep it all off in a sweet little room upstairs with mattresses laid on woven rugs (€20).

ℹ Getting There & Away

Stari Bar is 4km northeast of Bar, off the Ulcinj road. Buses marked Stari Bar depart from Ulica Jovana Tomaševića in the centre of 'new' Bar every hour (€1). *Apparently* every hour, that is: if you're in a rush, you can get a taxi for about €6.

Ulcinj

🗗 030 / POP 10,700

For a taste of Albania without actually crossing the border, head down to buzzy, beautiful Ulcinj (Улцињ). The population is 61% Albanian (68% Muslim), and in summertime it swells with Kosovar holidaymakers for the simple reason that it's a lot nicer than the Albanian seaside towns. The elegant minarets of numerous mosques give Ulcinj (Ulqin in Albanian) a distinctly Eastern feel, as does the lively music echoing out of the kebab stands around Mala Plaža (Small Beach). Ulcinj's ramshackle Old Town looms above the heaving beach and is a fantastic spot for people-watching without being surrounded by people.

◉ Sights

Mala Plaža (Map p86; Detarët e Ulqinit bb) is the town's main beach, but Ulcinj also has a series of little coves heading southeast along the coast. Each beach has a commercial licence, with seasonal beach bars and eateries. If you value your eardrums, avoid those with names like Ibiza and **Aquarius** (Map p86; Steva Đakonovića Čiče bb) and head somewhere like **Sapore di Mare** (Map p86; Steva Đakonovića Čiče bb), where you can either plant yourself on a concrete terrace or find

---

PIRATES OF THE MEDITERRANEAN

Listen up, me hearties, to a swashbuckling tale of murder, theft and slavery. Even before the Venetians took over in 1405, Ulcinj had a reputation as a pirate's lair. That didn't change when the Ottomans wrested control (nominally at least) in 1571. Quite the opposite, in fact. By the end of the 16th century, as many as 400 pirates, mainly from Malta, Tunisia and Algeria, made Ulcinj their main port of call – wreaking havoc on passing vessels and then returning to party up large on Mala Plaža.

Pirate captains became celebrities across the eastern Mediterranean, with stories of the Karamindžoja brothers, Lika Ceni, Ali Hodža and the like fuelling the imaginations of avid listeners. Spanish writer Cervantes was one victim; he's said to have spent five years in the vaults by the main square before being ransomed. Legend has it that he appropriated the town's name for his character Dulcinea in *Don Quixote*. Others were less lucky, including the pilgrims bound for Mecca robbed then drowned by Lika Ceni – an act that outraged the sultan and landed the pirate a hefty price on his head.

Along with their usual business of pirating, Ulcinj's crews had a lucrative sideline in slavery. Ulcinj became the centre of a thriving slave trade, with people (mainly from North Africa and some as young as two or three) paraded for sale on the town's main square. Ulcinj is perhaps the only place in the Western Balkans to have had a significant black minority.

THE MOSQUES OF ULCINJ

One of Ulcinj's most distinct features is its plethora of mosques. Most are fairly simple structures that are usually more interesting from the inside than out. An exception is the **Sailors' Mosque** (Xhamia e Detarëve, Džamija pomoraca; Map p86; Detarët e Ulqinit bb), an imposing stone structure right on the waterfront, which has some interesting frescoes inside. It was completed in 2012, replacing one (destroyed 1931) that predated the Ottomans and doubled as a lighthouse. Three minutes up the road, the 1719 **Pasha's Mosque** (Xhamija e Pashës, Pašina džamija; Map p86; Buda Tomovića bb) is an elegant complex with a *hammam* (Turkish bathhouse) attached.

The **Top-of-the-Market Mosque** (Xhamia e Kryepazarit, Džamija Vrhpazara; Map p86; Gjergj Kastrioti Skënderbeu bb) was built in 1749 at the intersection of the main streets. Within the same block but set slightly back from the road is the 1728 **Mezjah Mosque** (Xhamia në mezgjah, Džamija Namaždjah; Map p86; Hazif Ali Ulqinaku 71), Ulcinj's main Islamic place of worship. Further north, **Lamit Mosque** (Xhamia e Lamit, Džamija Ljamit; Map p86; Kadi Hysen Mujali bb) dates from 1689 but was substantially rebuilt after the 1979 earthquake. The ceiling has interesting green-painted geometric wood panelling.

Visiting Mosques

Unlike in some parts of the Islamic world, respectful non-Muslims are usually welcome to visit mosques in Montenegro, although some mosques don't allow women or have separate areas set aside for them (if you're unsure, ask for permission before entering). Mosques are primarily a place for prayer and most are kept purposefully plain so as not to distract the faithful – so there's usually not a lot to see inside anyway. The interiors of some are decorated with geometric patterns or Arabic calligraphy but the representation of people or animals is strictly forbidden. What they all have in common is a prayer niche aligned at the centre of the wall facing Mecca.

If you're keen to visit, a few simple protocols should be followed. Clothing should be loose and should cover the body: shorts, singlets, short skirts and tight jeans are a no-no and women will often cover their heads. Shoes must be removed and mobile phones switched off.

Devout Muslims are required to ritually cleanse themselves before entering for prayer, so there's usually a fountain or tap near the entrance. Non-Muslims aren't expected to do so. Don't distract anyone praying by wandering around or talking loudly inside the mosque – in fact, don't enter at all if group prayers or other community activities are taking place.

a patch of grass under the pines. **Ladies' Beach** (Map p86; Steva Đakonovića Čiče bb; €2), true to its name, has a strict women-only policy, while a section of the beach in front of the **Hotel Albatros** (Map p86; Steva Đakonovića Čiče bb) is clothing-optional. You can even take a dip at the very foot of the Old Town walls at **Sunset Beach** (☑069-889 209; www.facebook.com/SunsetBeachOldTown; Stari Grad bb; ☺9am-midnight Jun-Sep).

★**Old Town**   AREA
(Stari Grad; Map p86) The ancient walled town overlooking Mala Plaža is largely residential and somewhat dilapidated, a legacy of the 1979 earthquake. This is part of its charm – this Old Town really *does* feel old, with its uneven cobblestones and paucity of street lighting. Allow at least an hour to simply ramble around to your heart's content. Whatever else you find, spectacular views of Ulcinj and the beach below are guaranteed.

A steep slope leads to the upper gate, where just inside the walls there's a small **museum** (Muzej Ulcinj; Map p86; ☑030-421 419; www.ul-museum.me; adult/child €2/1; ☺8am-8pm Tue-Sun Jun-Sep, to 6pm Apr, May & Oct, 8.30am-3pm Nov-Mar) containing Roman and Ottoman artefacts and a relief map of the town. On the site is a 1510 church that was converted to a mosque in 1693; you can still see the ruined minaret.

Just outside the museum is a 17th-century **fountain** (Map p86) – these days, it's more

Ulcinj

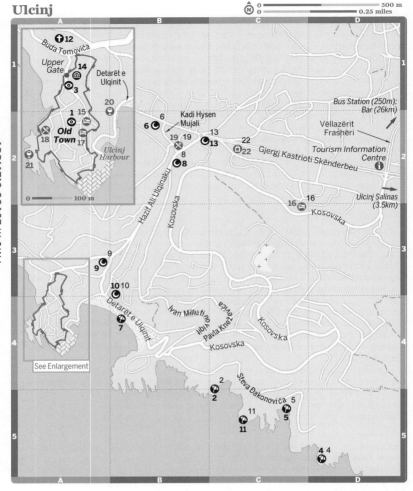

like a tap – with an Arabic inscription, a crescent moon and flowers carved into the stone.

There has been talk for time immemorial about installing an elevator from Ulcinj's little harbour up to the Old Town, so that everyone – rather than just able-bodied types – can enjoy its ambience. Locals have stopped holding their breath.

St Nicholas' Cathedral   CATHEDRAL
(Saborna Crkva svetog Nikole; Map p86; Buda Tomovića bb) Colourful frescoes fill this Serbian Orthodox cathedral, set among a pic-

turesque grove of gnarled olive trees just below the main gate to the Old Town. It's a relative newbie, having been built in 1890 shortly after the Ottomans were booted out, although it's believed to stand on the site of a 15th-century monastery.

🏃 Activities

Ulcinj Saltpans   BIRDWATCHING
(Ulcinjska solana; www.birdwatchingmn.org; Solanski Put bb) FREE If birds get you all aflutter, you've come to the right place. Founded in 1934 as a commercial salt works, this

Ulcinj

ADRIATIC COAST ULCINJ

1500-hectare private reserve attracts more than 250 species of migratory birds (half of the species registered in all of Europe), including Dalmatian pelicans, Eurasian spoonbills, various birds of prey and – believe it or not – flamingos. Contact the Tourism Information Centre (p88) to arrange a visit.

Commercial activities at the salt works ceased in 2013; when the seawater pumps stopped working, the artificially created salt pans were at risk of disappearing. Environmental groups and volunteers led the fight to save them and have them officially protected by the government. While their fate still hangs in the balance, the reserve does have a birdwatching tower, signposts and information boards.

The salt pans are located about 4km east of town. However, the site isn't well set up for visitors; if you turn up without making arrangements, and are prepared to brave the guard dogs at the gate, you may find someone to sign you in and grant you access.

🛏 Sleeping

Ulcinj has some excellent hotels, and a wonderful hostel and holiday park. Plus there's the usual range of private rooms and apartments on offer.

Olive Tree Holiday Park　　HOLIDAY PARK €
(Map p86; ☑069-060 026; http://olivetreehp. com; Ćazima Resulbegovića bb; tents €40; ⊙Jun-Sep; P🕸🛜🌊) The tents and bungalows may be new, but they're dotted across a

centuries-old olive grove that produces some of Montenegro's finest oil. It's an absolutely wonderful place to get away from the bustle of the beaches below. The pretty, raised tents come with either two singles or a queen bed, along with outdoor relaxing areas and barbecues.

★ Hostel Pirate　　HOSTEL €
(Map p86; ☑068-212 552; www.hostel-pirate.com; Nikole Djakonovića bb; dm/r with shared bathroom from €12/30; P🕸🛜) Just because it's Ulcinj's only hostel doesn't mean this jolly Pirate rests on its laurels. This is an immaculate, friendly, comfortable and flat-out-wonderful place that installs fierce love and loyalty in its guests. The hostel organises bike rentals, kayaking and boat trips. It also turns on free barbecue dinners fuelled by shots of equally gratis *rakija*.

Apartments Kalaja　　HOTEL €
(Map p86; ☑069-037 076; www.ulqin-kalaja.com; Stari Grad; d €33, apt €39-55; 🛜) The views are expansive, but expensive this friendly place is not. Perched up in Ulcinj's Stari Grad, Kalaja's nine decent – if unthrillingly furnished – rooms and apartments are housed in an old, rambling stone house that overlooks the sea and the gorgeous hodgepodge of Ulcinj city below. The excellent attached restaurant is open to – and whoppingly popular with – nonguests.

Palata Venezia　　HOTEL €€
(Map p86; ☑030-421 004; www.hotelpalata venezia.com; Stari Grad bb; r/apt from €90/110; 🕸🛜🌊) Situated within a centuries-old

ⓘ A SURFEIT OF STREET NAMES

You're unlikely to a find a single street sign in many Montenegrin towns but in Ulcinj, you'll sometimes find three different ones per street: a Montenegrin name, an Albanian version of the Yugoslav-era name, and a new Albanian name. Thus the main boulevard leading east–west at the top of town is either Maršala Tita or Gjergj Kastrioti Skënderbeu, and the main street heading down to the beach is either Ulica 26 Novembra or Rruga Hazif Ali Ulqinaku. We've used the names that were most prominently displayed at the time of research (usually the new Albanian names), but be aware that there is a push to return to the old names.

palazzo with ridiculously good views of Mala Plaža and out to sea, this gorgeously renovated place is the best choice for Old Town digs. While the attentive multilingual staff, excellent facilities, and large rooms and apartments are all very modern, the hotel is steeped in history: be sure to ask them to unlock the small museum.

✖ Eating

If you're keen to cook, hit the traditional **market** (Map p86; Gjergj Kastrioti Skënderbeu bb) at the top end of town. During summer, uncountable kebab stalls, *pekare* (bakeries) and other fast-food joints operate all along Mala Plaža.

Bazar　　　　　　　　　　PIZZERIA, SEAFOOD **€€**
(Map p86; Hazif Ali Ulqinaku bb; ⊙11.30am-midnight) This upstairs restaurant and pizzeria is a great people-watching perch when the streets below are heaving with tourists. It's the seafood that drags in the locals; the owners catch their own fish every morning. Be sure to try a plate of *lignje na žaru* (grilled squid), one of the restaurant's specialities.

★ Antigona　　　　　　　　　SEAFOOD **€€€**
(Map p86; ☑069-154 117; Stari Grad bb; mains €8-27; ⊙10am-midnight) Antigona's clifftop terrace offers perhaps the most romantic aspect of any restaurant in Ulcinj, and handsome waiters in bow ties only add to

the impression. The seafood is excellent too – but be sure to check the price and weight of the fish in advance if you wish to avoid any nasty surprises come bill time. It also rents rooms.

ⓨ Drinking & Nightlife

Provocateur　　　　　　　　　　　BAR
(Map p86; Detarët e Ulqinit bb; ⊙10am-2am summer) Part of a summertime strip of neon-lit doof-doof beachside bars, Provocateur is actually a lot more relaxed than it at first appears. It's an ideal spot to start your night and get the goss on where to head next.

ⓘ Information

Accident & Emergency Clinic (Map p86; ☑030-412 433; Majka Tereza bb) There's a pharmacy attached.

Tourism Information Centre (Map p86; ☑030-412 333; www.ulcinj.travel; Gjergj Kastrioti Skënderbeu bb; ⊙7am-10pm Jun-Aug, 8am-3pm Mon-Fri Sep-May) For information, maps, birdwatching arrangements and accommodation advice for Ulcinj, Velika Plaža and Ada Bojana.

ⓘ Getting There &Away

The **bus station** (☑030-413 225; www.busstationulcinj.com; Vëllazërit Frashëri bb; ⊙5am-10pm) is on the northeastern edge of town. Services head to Herceg Novi (€12, 3½ hours, daily), Kotor (€9, 2½ hours, daily), Budva (€7, two hours, nine daily) and Podgorica (€7, two hours, hourly). International destinations include Tirana, Pristina, Belgrade, Sarajevo and Zagreb.

Velika Plaža & Ada Bojana

The appropriately named Velika Plaža (Big Beach; Велика Плажа) starts 4km southeast of Ulcinj and stretches for 12 sandy kilometres. It's divided into sections with names such as Miami, Copacabana and Tropicana; these beaches don't always live up to their glamorous names, and the water is mostly too shallow for proper swimming, but it's hard not to have fun when everyone else is clearly having a ball.

The swimming is much better over the river at peculiar Ada Bojana (Ада Бојана). This island was formed around a shipwreck between two existing islands in the river mouth, which eventually gathered enough sediment to cover around 520 hectares and create 3km of beautiful sandy beach. During its Yugoslav heyday it became one of Europe's premier nudist resorts. If you'd prefer to keep your gear on, stick to the river mouth where there is a handful of hip beach bars.

◉ Sights

Milena Canal   CANAL

On the drive out to Velika Plaža, keep your eyes out for the murky Milena canal, where local fishermen use nets suspended from long willow rods attached to wooden stilt houses. The effect is remarkably redolent of Southeast Asia. There are more of these contraptions on the banks of the Bojana River at the other end of Velika Plaža.

🏃 Activities

This area is making a name for itself as a prime spot for water and wind sports, especially kitesurfing. There is a handful of well-rated outfits here, including **Kitesfera** (☑ 069-210 249; www.kitesfera.com) and **Kite Loop** (www.kiteloop.net).

Mountain Riders   HORSE RIDING

(www.mountainriders.me; 4hr ride €90; ☉ Oct-May) These four-hour guided horseback tours clip-clop along the entire length of Velika Plaža during the off-season (ie when there's nobody to trample). Suitable for beginners.

✯ Festivals & Events

Southern Soul Festival   MUSIC

(www.southernsoulfestival.me; ☉ late Jun-early Jul) Four days of soul, jazz, funk, house and disco on Velika Plaža's Copacabana Beach.

✖ Eating

Several memorable fish restaurants jut out over the Bojana River near the Ada Bojana bridge. The local speciality is *riblja čorba* (fish soup). Each of these restaurants is worth making the 14km drive from Ulcinj.

Miško   SEAFOOD €€

(☑ 069-022 868; www.facebook.com/Misko1953; Bojana River; mains €10-17; ☉ 11am-11pm; 🐾) The most upmarket of the Bojana River restaurants is focused completely on seafood, including octopus, shrimp, shellfish, a big selection of fresh fish, and, of course, delicious *riblja čorba* (fish soup). Its motto, with apologies to Julius Caesar, is: '*Veni, Vidi, Sjedi, Jedi*', which translates from a

ADRIATIC COAST VELIKA PLAŽA & ADA BOJANA

LAKE ŠAS

If you've got your own wheels and fancy getting well off the beaten track, this pretty area near the Albanian border makes a pleasant drive. Take the road leading northwest from Ulcinj. After 17km you'll reach the large village of **Vladimir**, where a marked turn-off to the right leads to the lake.

After 2km, you'll see to your right the ruins of the once-great Zetan city of **Svač** (Šas). Park here and cut across to the top-left corner of the rough football field, where you'll find the beginnings of a rocky path. Wear proper shoes; the track is rough and there are a lot of thorns. There's not much left of Svač apart from the shells of a couple of buildings, one of which was obviously a church. The town was razed by the Mongols in 1242 and the Ottomans in the 16th century, after which it was abandoned. It's now a rustic, beautiful spot, offering broad views over the plains towards the Rumija Mountains.

Jump back in the car and continue to follow the signs to the lake, which is 2.5km further on. Lake Šas (Šasko Jezero; Шаско Језеро) covers 364 hectares and is lined with a muddy border of reeds and water lilies; it's an important habitat for 240 species of bird. In winter it attracts both dedicated birdwatchers and Italian hunters.

Character-filled **Restaurant Shasi** (☑ 069-592 873; restorantshasi@gmail.com; mains €7-15; ☉ 9am-11pm) is a rambling stone complex built into a cliff by the lake. It's a lovely, quiet spot where the staff spring into action when you arrive and fish soup is served with delicious corn damper. Shasi's specialities are eel, mullet and carp, caught from the pier at the bottom of its yard. They also offer simple accommodation (doubles from €30).

mix of Latin and Montenegrin as 'I came, I saw, Sit! Eat!'

Ćićkova Čarda   SEAFOOD, ITALIAN **€€**
(Bojana River; mains €5.50-13) Seemingly constructed Robinson Crusoe–style from flotsam and jetsam, this very atmospheric restaurant on the Ada Bojana side of the river serves lots of traditional seafood dishes as well as the usual selection of pasta, risotto, steaks and grills. It's a wonderful spot to watch the sunset from. Add your name to the hundreds scrawled all over its wooden walls.

❶ Getting There & Away

➼ There's a day rate to visit Ada Bojana (€6/1/2 per car/passenger/pedestrian).

➼ You'll need your own car to get here, as public transport options are few and far between.

Central Montenegro

Best Places to Eat

➡ Stari Most (p98)

➡ Konoba Badanj (p100)

➡ Pod Volat (p105)

➡ Pekara (p109)

Best Places to Sleep

➡ Apartments Athos (p103)

➡ Hotel Hemera (p104)

➡ Hotel Trebjesa (p108)

➡ La Vecchia Casa (p97)

Why Go?

Ogle the splendid cap of northern mountains and impeccable drape of glittering coastline by all means, but to truly get to know Montenegro, a visit to the country's core is a must.

Its beating heart is Mt Lovćen, a 1749m-high symbol of national identity and the very black mountain that gives Crna Gora its name. To the south, Lake Skadar is the country's lungs, a clean, green oasis of lily-strewn waterways and rare bird havens. Swoop north to Ostrog to discover the very soul of the nation in a gravity-defying cliff-face monastery that literally brings pilgrims to their knees. And you'll find character galore in Montenegro's two capitals; the modern-day seat of Podgorica is home to hip bars and a happening arts scene, while the royal city of Cetinje proudly preserves its gallant past in a collection of richly endowed museums and galleries.

When to Go

➡ May is late spring and the perfect time to visit the capital, before the sizzling summer.

➡ August offers great weather for exploring Lake Skadar; Danilovgrad hosts the River Zeta Festival.

➡ September is not as scorching but still warm enough, and an ideal time to drive the panoramic Circuit Around Korita.

Central Montenegro Highlights

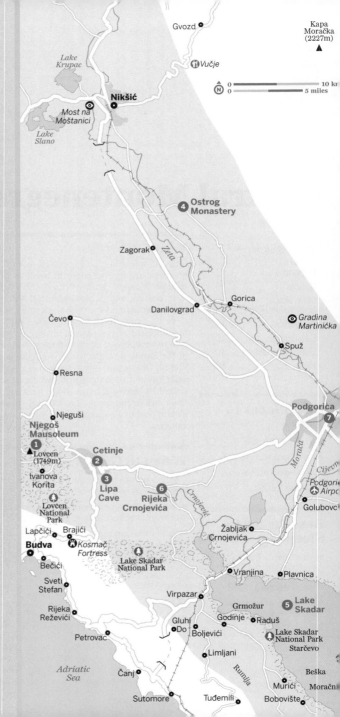

1 Njegoš Mausoleum (p93)
Marvelling at the majesty of both the mountains and the monument at the top.

2 Museums (p000) Delving into history, art and culture in the former royal capital Cetinje.

3 Lipa Cave (p96) Diving even deeper into the past on a tour of one of the country's largest caves.

4 Ostrog Monastery (p107) Gazing in wonder at the improbable cliff-face construction of this holy site.

5 Lake Skadar (p97) Cruising the sparkling waters to the island monasteries and bird sanctuaries.

6 Rijeka Crnojevića (p98) Feasting on the sublime seafood and serene setting.

7 Nova Varoš (p106) Soaking up the nocturnal buzz of Podgorica's party precinct.

Climate

Extremes are more noticeable in this region than on the coast. Podgorica is scorching in summer and can reach above 40°C. In the mountains the climate is considerably cooler. Temperatures can drop below freezing any time from October to March.

❶ Getting There & Away

Podgorica has an international airport and is the country's main bus and train hub. The main highway from the coast starts near Sutomore and takes a 4km-long tunnel (toll charge €3.50) through the mountains to Virpazar and on to Podgorica .

❶ Getting Around

Regular bus services head from Podgorica to Cetinje, Nikšić and Virpazar. Trains connect Podgorica to Virpazar, Danilovgrad and Nikšić.

Lovćen National Park

Directly behind Kotor is **Mt Lovćen** (Ловћен; 1749m), the black mountain that gave Crna Gora (Montenegro) its name; *crna/negro* means 'black', and *gora/monte* means 'mountain' in Montenegrin and Italian respectively. This locale occupies a special place in the hearts of all Montenegrins. For most of its history it represented the entire nation – a rocky island of Slavic resistance in an Ottoman sea. A striking shrine to Montenegro's most famous son, Petar II Petrović Njegoš, peers down from its heights, with views stretching as far as Albania and Croatia.

The park's main hub is **Ivanova Korita**, near its centre, where there are a few eateries and accommodation providers and, in winter, a beginners' ski slope. **Njeguši**, on the park's northern edge, is famous for being the home village of the Petrović dynasty and for making the country's best *pršut* (smoke-dried ham) and *sir* (cheese). Roadside stalls sell both, along with honey.

◎ Sights

★**Njegoš Mausoleum**   MAUSOLEUM
(Njegošev mauzolej; adult/child €3/1.50; ☺9am-6pm) Lovćen's star attraction, this magnificent mausoleum (built 1970 to 1974) sits at the top of its second-highest peak, Jezerski Vrh (1657m). Take the 461 steps up to the entry where two granite giantesses guard the tomb of Montenegro's greatest hero. Inside,

under a golden mosaic canopy, a 28-tonne Petar II Petrović Njegoš rests in the wings of an eagle, carved from a single block of black granite.

The actual tomb lies below, and a path at the rear leads to a dramatic circular viewing platform providing the same utterly spectacular views that caused George Bernard Shaw to exclaim, 'Am I in paradise or on the moon?'

A photographer stationed near the entrance has a stash of folk costumes and a computer set up to print out quirky souvenirs (€10).

Njegoš Birth House   HOUSE
(Njegoševa rodna kuća; www.mnmuseum.org; Erakovići bb; adult/child €2/1; ☺9am-5pm May-Oct) The humble house where Petar II Petrović Njegoš was born has been turned into a small museum. There's not much inside, but it's an interesting insight into how 19th-century Montenegrins lived.

✶ Activities

The mountains are criss-crossed with hiking paths and mountain-biking trails, which can be accessed from Kotor, Budva or Cetinje. If you're planning on hiking, come prepared; the temperature is, on average, 10°C cooler than on the coast and the weather is prone to sudden changes. Water supplies are limited.

Quad Biking   ADVENTURE
(☑033-451 020; www.globtourmontenegro.com; adult/child €87/77) These exhilarating day-long bush-bashing tours leave from Ivanova Korita, bumping up Mt Lovćen to take in some of Montenegro's best mountain and sea views. Prices include pick-ups from coastal towns.

🍽 Sleeping & Eating

The **National Park Visitor Centre** (☑067-344 678; www.nparkovi.me; Ivanova Korita bb; ☺9am-5pm) offers accommodation in four-bed bungalows (€30). Informal camping is possible within the park (small/large tent €3/5), with additional charges for using established campgrounds (€10) or lighting fires in designated places (€5, including wood).

Konoba kod Radonjića   MONTENEGRIN €€
(☑041-239 820; Njeguši bb; mains €6-13; ☺8am-7pm; 🐾) With stone walls, and meat hanging from the ceiling, this atmospheric

family-run tavern serves up delicious roast lamb as well as the local specialities, *pršut* (smoke-dried ham) and *sir* (cheese). Enjoy them along with olives on a Njeguški plate (€9.50) or in sandwiches (€2.50).

ⓘ Getting There & Away

If you're driving, the park can be approached from either Kotor (20km) or Cetinje (7km); pay the entry fee (€2) at the booths on each approach. Tour buses are the only buses that head into the park. Be aware that this is a *very* twisty-turny and narrow road; the large tour buses that hog it in summer don't make the driving experience any easier. Don't be distracted by the beyond-spectacular views.

Cetinje

☑ 041 / POP 13,900

Rising from a green vale surrounded by rough grey mountains, Cetinje (Цетиње) is an odd mix of erstwhile capital and over-grown village, where single-storey cottages and stately mansions share the same street. Several of those mansions – dating from the days when European ambassadors rubbed shoulders with Montenegrin princesses – have become museums or schools for art and music.

The city was founded in 1482 by Ivan Crnojević, the ruler of the Zeta state, after abandoning his previous capital near Lake Skadar, Žabljak Crnojevića, to the Ottomans. A large statue of him stands near the main square. Cetinje was the capital of Montenegro until the country was subsumed into the first Yugoslavia in 1918. After WWII, when Montenegro became a republic within federal Yugoslavia, it passed the baton – somewhat reluctantly – to Titograd (now Podgorica). Today it's billed as the 'royal capital', and is home to the country's most impressive collection of museums.

◉ Sights

The **National Museum of Montenegro** is actually a collection of four museums and two galleries. Two museums housed within the imposing former Parliament building (1910). On the ground floor, the fascinating **History Museum** (Istorijski muzej; Map p95; ☑ 041-230 310; www.mnmuseum.org; Novice Cerovića 7; adult/child €3/1.50; ⊙ 9am-5pm Apr-Oct, to 4pm Mon-Sat Nov-Mar) follows a timeline from the Stone Age to 1955. There are few English signs but the enthusiastic staff will

give you an overview. Bullet holes are a theme of some of the most interesting relics: there are three in the back of the tunic that Prince Danilo was wearing when assassinated; Prince Nikola's standard from the battle of Vučji Do has 396; while, in the communist section, there's a big gaping one in the skull of a fallen comrade.

Upstairs you'll find the excellent **Montenegrin Art Gallery** (Crnogorska galerija umjetnosti; Map p95; www.mnmuseum.org; Novice Cerovića 7; adult/child €4/2; ⊙ 9am-5pm Apr-Oct, to 4pm Mon-Sat Nov-Mar), with a small but important collection of icons. The most precious of them all is the bejewelled 9th-century *Our Lady of Philermos*, traditionally believed to be painted by St Luke himself. It's spectacularly presented in its own blue-lit 'chapel'.

For something more edgy, head to the **Miodrag Dado Đurić Gallery** (Galerija; Map p95; Balšića Pazar; ⊙ 10am-2pm & 5-9pm Tue-Sun) FREE. Housed in a striking five-storey concrete and glass building, it promotes and displays 20th-century and contemporary Montenegrin art. One ticket covers both this and the national gallery.

Opposite the History Museum, the wonderfully castle-like **Biljarda** (Njegoš muzej biljarda; Map p95; www.mnmuseum.org; Dvorski Trg; adult/child €3/1.50; ⊙ 9am-5pm May-Oct, to 4pm Mon-Sat Nov-Apr) was the residence of Montenegro's favourite son, prince-bishop and poet Petar II Petrović Njegoš. It was built and financed by the Russians in 1838 and housed the nation's first billiard table (hence the name). The bottom floor is devoted to military costumes, photos of soldiers with outlandish moustaches and exquisitely decorated weapons. Upstairs are Njegoš' personal effects, including his bishop's cross and garments, documents, fabulous furniture and, of course, the famous billiard table.

When you leave Biljarda, turn right and follow the walls to the glass pavilion housing an astonishing large-scale **Relief Map of Montenegro** (Reljef Crne Gore; Map p95; €1), created by the Austrians in 1917. Peek through the windows if it's closed. A **lapidarium** in the courtyard beside it is dotted with ancient inscribed tombstones collected from across Montenegro.

Entry to the **King Nikola Museum** (Muzej kralja Nikole; Map p95; www.mnmuseum.org; Dvorski Trg; adult/child €5/2.50; ⊙ 9am-5pm Apr-Oct, to 4pm Mon-Sat Nov-Mar) – a stunning 1871

Cetinje

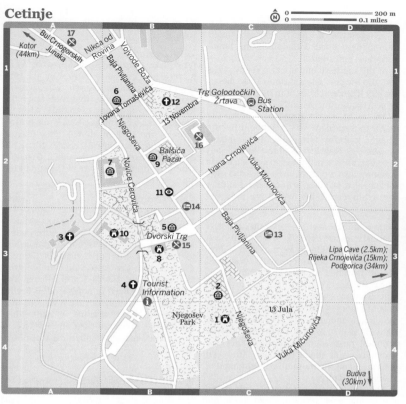

Cetinje

⊙ Sights
1 Blue Palace	C4
2 British Embassy	C3
3 Cetinje Monastery	A3
4 Court Church	B3
5 Ethnographic Museum	B3
6 French Embassy	B1
7 History Museum	B2
8 King Nikola Museum	B3
9 Miodrag Dado Đurić Gallery	B2
Montenegrin Art Gallery	(see 7)
10 Njegoš Museum Biljarda	B3
Relief Map of Montenegro	(see 10)
11 Ulica Njegoševa	B2
12 Vlach Church	B1

🛏 Sleeping
13 La Vecchia Casa	C3
14 Royal Square Apartment	B2

🍴 Eating
15 Gradska Kafana	B3
16 Green Market	B2
17 Kole	A1

maroon-and-white palace that was home to the last sovereign of Montenegro – is by guided tour (you may need to wait for a group to form). Although looted during WWII, it retains enough plush furnishings, stern portraits and taxidermied animals to capture the spirit of the court.

If you haven't worn yourself out yet, pop into the **Ethnographic Museum** (Etnografski muzej; Map p95; Dvorski Trg; adult/child €2/1; ⊘9am-5pm Mon-Sat), where you'll find a well-presented collection of costumes and tools explained by English notations.

Ulica Njegoševa
STREET

(Map p95) Cetinje's main street is pretty Njegoševa, a partly pedestrianised thoroughfare lined with interesting buildings, cafes and shops.

At the southern end are two shady parks and the elegant **Blue Palace** (Plavi dvorac; Map p95; Njegoševa bb), built in 1895 for Crown Prince Danilo but recently commandeered by the Montenegrin president – hence the manicured gardens. Its neighbour is the equally graceful former **British Embassy** (Map p95; Njegoševa bb), built in 1912 but Georgian in its sensibilities; it's now a music academy. Just north of the pedestrian-only section is a striking art-nouveau building covered in glazed tiles, which was once the **French Embassy** (Map p95; Njegoševa bb).

Cetinje Monastery
CHRISTIAN MONASTERY

(Cetinjski manastir; Map p95; ⊘8am-6pm) It's a case of four times lucky for the Cetinje Monastery, having been repeatedly destroyed during Ottoman attacks and rebuilt. This sturdy incarnation dates from 1786, with its only exterior ornamentation being the capitals of columns recycled from the original building, founded in 1484. The chapel to the right of the courtyard holds the monastery's proudest possessions: a shard of the True Cross (a claim made by many European churches) and the mummified right hand of St John the Baptist.

The monastery treasury (admission €2) is only open to groups, but if you are persuasive enough and prepared to wait around, you may be able to get in (mornings are the best time to try). It holds a wealth of fascinating objects including the jewel-encrusted crown of 14th-century Serbian king – and later saint – Stefan Uroš III Dečanski, icons and a copy of the 1494 *Oktoih* (Book of the Eight Voices), the first book printed in Serbian.

ℹ A ROYAL ROUND TRIP

From Cetinje, a 53km, day-long, circular mountain-biking route follows roads through Lovćen National Park. You'll ascend 890m in your first 20km to the entrance of the Njegoš Mausoleum, where you can stop for the views and a bite to eat. It's mainly downhill from here, heading in the direction of Kotor before looping through Njeguši and back to Cetinje.

Dress modestly or you'll either be denied entry or given an unflattering smock to wear.

Vlach Church
CHURCH

(Vlaška crkva; Map p95; Baja Pivljanina bb) While its present appearance dates from the 19th century, this stone church was actually founded around 1450, thus predating the Montenegrin founding of Cetinje. A sumptuous gilded iconostasis (1878) is the centrepiece of the current church. Take a close look at the churchyard's fence: it's made from 1544 barrels of guns taken from the Ottomans during the wars at the end of the 19th century.

Court Church
CHURCH

(Dvorska crkva; Map p95; Novice Cerovića bb) Built in 1886 on the ruins of the original Cetinje Monastery, this little church has a lovely gilded iconostasis, but its main claim to fame is as the burial place of Cetinje's founder, Ivan Crnojević, and Montenegro's last sovereigns, Nikola I and Milena. The pair may have been unpopular after fleeing the country for Italy during WWI, but they received a hero's welcome in 1989, when their bodies were returned and interred in these white-marble tombs in a three-hour service.

Lipa Cave
CAVE

(Lipska pećina; ☑067-003 040; www.lipa-cave. me; adult/child €11/7; ⊘tours 10am, 11.30am, 1pm, 2.30pm & 4pm May-Oct) Cetinje may indeed be littered with old-time reminders of its days as Montenegro's capital city, but just 4km away lies an attraction that makes the town look positively modern. Millions of years old, Lipa Cave is one of the country's largest caves – and the only one open for organised visits – with 2.5km of illuminated passages and halls filled with stalactites, stalagmites and freaky natural pillars. Tours take 60 minutes, including a road-train ride and short walk to the entrance.

🎉 Festivals & Events

Summer in the Old Capital
PERFORMING ARTS

(Ljeto u Prijestonici; ⊘Jul-Sep) Summer-long festival, with live music, art exhibitions, folkloric dancing, classic car displays, literary events, food stalls...if it's cultural, edible or just plain fun, this whopping festival has it going on.

KOSMAČ FORTRESS

High up in the hills midway between Budva and Cetinje, this artfully abandoned 19th-century fortress looms over some spectacular high-altitude scenery. Once the southernmost fortress in the Austro-Hungarian Empire, the large, formerly three-storey limestone complex was the scene of two bloody rebellions in the late 1800s, and was garrisoned by Italian troops in WWII. Now roofless and ruined, **Kosmač** (Tvrdjava Kosmač) is nevertheless a fascinating and haunting place to explore, though curious adventurers do so at their own risk; the fortress is not staffed or maintained, and large chunks of stone have a habit of toppling without notice.

Kosmač is near the village of Brajići on the Budva–Cetinje road. Park near the signpost, then walk just over a kilometre through the village to get to the fortress itself. It's also reachable via a three-hour hike from Kamenovo, near Pržno on the coast.

🛏 Sleeping

⭐ **La Vecchia Casa**   GUESTHOUSE **€**
(Map p95; 📞 067-629 660; www.lavecchiacasa. com; Vojvode Batrica 6; s/d/apt €20/34/38; 🅿 ❄ 🛜) With its gorgeous rear garden and pervading sense of tranquillity, this period house captures the essence of old Cetinje. The clean, antique-strewn rooms retain a sense of the home's history, and there's a guest kitchen (stocked with do-it-yourself breakfast supplies) and a laundry.

Royal Square Apartment   APARTMENT **€**
(Map p95; 📞 067-678 206; petrai22@hotmail.com; Njegoševa 52; apt from €39; ❄ 🛜) Get in quick if you want to snag yourself these cheap, central and colourful digs right in the heart of Cetinje's historic pedestrian zone. It's a popular place, and so it should be: the town's main attractions are but a stumble from the door, the apartments – while they don't look any great shakes from outside – are comfortable and well equipped, and the host couldn't be more helpful.

🍴 Eating

Head to the local **market** (Zelena pijaca; Map p95; Baja Pivljanina 24) for fresh produce and local specialities.

Kole   MONTENEGRIN **€€**
(Map p95; 📞 069-606 660; www.restaurant kole.me; Bul Crnogorskih junaka 12; mains €4-16; ⏱ 7am-midnight) They serve omelettes and pasta at this popular restaurant, but it's worth delving into artery-clogging local specialities such as *Njeguški ražanj* (smoky spit-roasted meat stuffed with prosciutto and cheese) or *popeci na cetinjski način* ('Cetinje-style' veal schnitzel, similarly stuffed, rolled into logs, breaded and deep-fried). Serves are massive; try one between two, with a side salad.

Gradska Kafana   INTERNATIONAL **€€**
(Map p95; Dvorski Trg; mains €4-14; ⏱ 9am-midnight) Situated within the endearingly run-down old Bulgarian Embassy, this local favourite is a top spot for a good-sized meal (Cetinje may not be by the sea, but Gradska Kafana still whips up excellent fish and chips), a relaxing tipple and watching the world go by.

ℹ Information

Accident & Emergency Clinic (Hitna pomoć; Map p95; 📞 041-233 002; Vuka Mićunovića 2)

Tourist Information (Map p95; 📞 041-230 250; www.cetinje.travel; Novice Cerovića bb; ⏱ 8am-6pm Mar-Oct, to 4pm Nov-Feb) Helpful office that also rents bikes (€2/3 per half-/full day). Short sightseeing tours start from here, taking to Cetinje's streets in golf buggies (€2/3 per 30/45 minutes).

ℹ Getting There & Away

➡ Cetinje is just off the main Budva–Podgorica highway and can also be reached by a glorious back road from Kotor via Lovćen National Park.

➡ The **bus station** (Map p95; 📞 041-241 744; Trg Golootočkih Žrtava; ⏱ 6am-10pm) has regular services from Herceg Novi (€8, 2½ hours), Tivat (€5, 1¼ hours), Budva (€4, 40 minutes), Kotor (€5, 1½ hours) and Podgorica (€3, 30 minutes).

Lake Skadar National Park

Dolphin-shaped Lake Skadar (Скадарско Језеро), the Balkans' largest, has its tail and two-thirds of its body in Montenegro and its nose in Albania. On the Montenegrin side, an area of 400 sq km has been protected by a national park since 1983; today, Skadar is renowned as one of Europe's top bird habitats. It's a blissfully pretty area encompassing steep mountains, island monasteries, clear waters, and floating meadows of water lilies. The main – albeit tiny – towns here are Virpazar and Vranjina, though if you've got wheels, you can easily explore the timeless villages sprinkled along the shore.

Lake Skadar is a popular escape for nature lovers, outdoor-activity aficionados and locals fleeing the heat of Podgorica. Legend has it that the lake was created by the tears of a pixie; that may be fanciful, but after one look at magical Skadar, you may find yourself believing in fairy tales, too.

🛏 Sleeping

Plavnica Eco Resort   RESORT €€€
(📞020-443 700; www.plavnica.me; Donja Plavnica bb; ste from €110; 🅿✳🛜🏊) Day trippers from Podgorica escape the summer heat at this unusual resort, where there's an impressive pool set within an amphitheatre and a cavernous restaurant with all the ambience of a reception hall. Upstairs are four lavishly furnished suites. The resort has a boat that's used for lake tours, and you can hire catamarans, canoes, kayaks and pedal boats.

Rijeka Crnojevića
📱 041 / POP 215
The northwestern end of Lake Skadar thins into the serpentine loops of the Rijeka Crnojevića (Ријека Црнојевића; Crnojević River) and terminates near the pretty village of the same name. It's a charming, tucked-away kind of place.

When Montenegro was ruled from Cetinje, this is where the royals came to escape the Black Mountain's winter. The relatively modest house of Vladika Petar I Petrović (St Peter of Cetinje) still stands; you'll recognise it by its ground-floor arches and upper rooms jutting out over the road.

👁 Sights & Activities

During the tourist season there are usually small boats lined up on the river, offering cruises for around €25 per hour.

Danilo's Bridge   BRIDGE
(Danilov Most) This arched limestone bridge is the telegenic trademark of Rijeka Crnojevića. It was built in 1853 by Prince Danilo.

Obod Walking Track   WALKING
Rijeka Crnojevića is the starting point of a two-hour, 7.6km circular walking track that passes a pretty swimming hole with icy-cold water, through the ruins of Obod, the site of the region's first printing press, and on to Obod Cave (Obodska pećina) at the source of the river. This large cavern is home to over a dozen species of bats, which you'll smell before you see.

🍴 Eating

Stari Most   SEAFOOD €€
(📞067-339 429; Rijeka Crnojevića bb; mains €8-20; ⊙noon-10pm) Perhaps surprisingly – given its sleepy village location – Stari Most is one of Montenegro's finest restaurants. It's well located on the marble riverside promenade, looking to the old bridge from which it derives its name. Fish (particularly eel, trout and carp) is the speciality here and the fish soup alone is enough to justify a drive from Podgorica.

ℹ Getting There & Away
A car is a must if you want to visit. The two closest towns of note are Cetinje (16km) and Podgorica (26km); the village is accessed by side roads that lead off the highway.

Virpazar
📱 020 / POP 300
This tiny town, gathered around a square and a river blanketed with water lilies, serves as the main gateway to Lake Skadar National Park.

Virpazar (Вирпазар) may be a small speck on the map now, but it was once considered so strategically important that the occupying Turks built a large fortress on the hill looming above the village. After their downfall, Virpazar became an important trading town (pazar means marketplace) with a lively port; in the early 1900s, it was connected to Bar by Montenegro's first narrow-gauge railway. It was also the site of one of the country's first significant uprisings against Axis invaders in WWII. Two reminders of its bloody past still stand in – and over – the town.

If you're interested in sampling local wines, you'll find family-run vineyards and tasting cellars in and around Virpazar.

◉ Sights

Besac Fortress FORTRESS

(Tvrđava Besac; €1) Looking out over Virpazar, this recently reconstructed fortress was built by the Turks in 1478, and was the scene of many a bloody battle; it was also used as a prison by the occupying Italians in WWII. These days, it's an easy uphill stroll from Virpazar and offers splendid views of the village and its surrounds.

The path leading to Besac is signposted from the road to Murići about 400m after the post office.

🏃 Activities & Tours

You'll find plenty of boats (and their operators will definitely find you) doing one- to two-hour lake cruises from Virpazar's small marina. Trips generally cost about €25 to €35 per hour. Many of the operators can also organise fishing and birdwatching tours.

★ Undiscovered Montenegro ADVENTURE

(☑069-402 364; www.undiscoveredmontenegro.com; Boljevići bb; week incl accommodation €645-745; ☉Apr-Oct) This excellent agency specialises in week-long, lake-based itineraries including accommodation in its lovely stone cottage near Virpazar (three-day stays are possible outside of peak season). Guided hikes, kayaking and wine/gastronomy tours are included in the price, and boat trips, canyoning, horse riding, wilderness canoeing, white-water kayaking and specialist birdwatching can be arranged. Afterwards, relax around the barbecue and pool.

Zabes Holidays BOATING

(☑069-998 737; www.zabesholidays.me) Run by experienced, multilingual locals, Zabes runs a range of boat tours (from €10 per person) that take in tons of different sights along Skadar. They also organise birdwatching, kayaking, fishing and gastronomic tours; contact them for details. Those after the full Skadar experience can rent out their beautifully furnished holiday home (from €50 per night) or pitch a tent at their campground (from €3) in the village of Zabes, 2.5km from Virpazar.

Mountain Riders HORSE RIDING

(☑067-343 411; www.mountainriders.me; €60; ☉Apr-Oct) Day-long trail rides (and horse-and-rider swims) through Lake Skadar's fairy-tale-like Orahovštica Valley.

🛏 Sleeping

Locals with budget-friendly rooms to rent often linger around the main square in the afternoons. Check out www.lake-skadar.com/accommodation for a good list of hotels, rooms and apartments.

Virski Pub PUB €

(☑068-630 036; r per person from €10; ☎) Sink a few then spend the night at this welcoming watering hole. Rooms aren't posh, but they're comfortable enough. There's a shared kitchen for guests' use, or you can stagger next door to the bakery *(pekara)* to load up on cheap, fattening treats.

Jovičević Apartments APARTMENT €€

(☑069-091 185; office@outdoorandmore.me; apt from €40; ❊) The Jovičević family rents a couple of atmospheric apartments right in the centre of town. The Cave Apartment (sleeping four) is built into a natural rock

CENTRAL MONTENEGRO LAKE SKADAR NATIONAL PARK

FEATHERS, FINS & FUR: THE WILDLIFE OF LAKE SKADAR

Covering between 370 and 540 sq km (depending on the time of year), Lake Skadar is one of the most important reserves for wetland birds in Europe. The endangered Dalmatian pelican nests here along with around 280 other species, including a quarter of the global population of pygmy cormorants. You might spot whiskered terns making their nests on the water lilies.

The average depth of the lake is 5m, with some spots plunging below sea level; these underwater spring holes are called 'eyes', attracting fish by the hundreds. The deepest eye, Radus, sinks down at least 60m. At least 48 species of fish lurk beneath Skadar's smooth surface, the most common of which are carp, bleak and eel. The park offices sell fishing permits; if you join a tour, these will be provided.

Mammals within the park's confines include otters, foxes, weasels, moles, groundhogs and the occasional wolf.

wall and has its own ornamental well. A hammock is strung up between the oaks outside, and bikes are available to rent (€10 per day). Better still is the light-filled apartment in an old building right by the monument (sleeping three).

✕ Eating

Konoba Badanj   MONTENEGRIN €€
(☑069-508 019; www.facebook.com/badanjoffi cial; Virpazar bb; mains €5-14; ☺10am-midnight; ☜) A cool stone-walled interior with solid wooden beams, views of the river and interesting art make this an atmospheric eating option. The fish soup comes with big chunks of fish and delicious sconelike homemade bread, or try the eel straight out of Lake Skadar. It also stocks a good range of wine by small, local producers.

❶ Information

Virpazar Tourist Office (☑069-091 183; www. visitbar.org; ☺8am-8pm Mon-Sat, to 2pm Sun May-Sep, 9am-5pm Mon-Fri Oct-Apr; ☜) This big office on the main square can assist you with arranging anything on the lake, including boat trips, wine tastings and private accommodation. The office operates as a storefront for the region's small wine producers. The National Parks office is upstairs, selling park entry tickets (€4) and fishing permits (per day €5).

You'll find an ATM out the front of Hotel Pelikan, but apparently it often runs out of money; bring cash just in case.

❶ Getting There & Away

Virpazar doesn't have a bus station but buses on the Bar–Podgorica route stop on the highway (near Hotel Pelikan). A bus from Podgorica takes 30 minutes (€2.50); you'll have to tell the driver that you want to get off at Virpazar.

The train station is off the main road, 800m south of town. There are several trains to/from Bar (€2, 23 minutes) and Podgorica (€2.20, 30 minutes) every day.

Murići

☑085 / POP 110

The southern edge of Lake Skadar is the most dramatic, with the Rumija Mountains rising precipitously from the water. Murići (Мурићи), a cluster of traditional buildings set around a mosque, is home to one of the lake's best swimming spots. The water's clear, if a little weedy, and swarms of little fish follow your feet as you kick up the nutrients beneath.

🛏 Sleeping

Murići Vacation Resort   CAMPGROUND €
(☑069-688 288; www.nacionalnipark-izletiste murici.com; cabin per person from €20, campsite per person/car/campervan €5/5/10; ☺May-Sep) This shady, pleasant place has simple log cabins sharing a decent ablutions block, nestled within an olive grove on the lakeshore. There's also a good outdoor restaurant (mains €4 to €11) but if you're nervous about dogs, this might not be for you.

❶ Getting There & Away

From Virpazar, there's a wonderful 40-minute drive (or 56km mountain-biking route) following the contours of the lake through the mountains and an enchanting (possibly even enchanted) chestnut forest. The road heads towards the Albanian border before crossing the range and turning back towards Ulcinj. About halfway along the lake, take the steep side road that descends to Murići.

Islands

An archipelago of islands traces the southern edge of Lake Skadar and, in true Montenegrin fashion, many of them shelter monasteries.

Moračnik island's monastery dates from at least the early 15th century. Its small domed stone church dedicated to the Holy Virgin is watched over by a tower-like accommodation block occupied by a friendly monk.

In the early years of the new millennium, an exceedingly welcoming community of nuns revived **Beška Monastery** after 300 years of abandonment. Fourteenth-century St George's Church is still undergoing slow reconstruction work, but the smaller Church of the Annunciation is in active use. It was built in 1440 and contains traces of once extensive frescoes.

Beška and its neighbour on **Starčevo** were once famous for producing religious scripts. Starčevo was named somewhat unflatteringly after the hermit who founded the monastery in 1377; it translates as 'Old Man's Monastery'. Revived in the last three decades, Starčevo again has an old man – a monk who would prefer not to be disturbed (entertaining tourists isn't part of the hermit job description).

Grmožur, the closest island to Virpazar, is topped by a Turkish-built fortress (1843). It served as a prison until the early 20th century and was nicknamed 'the Montenegrin Alcatraz'.

In the swampy northwestern reaches of Lake Skadar near Žabljak Crnojevića, the Church of the Dormition (1415) of **Kom Monastery** (☑067- 887 711; www.manastirkom. org) has the best-preserved frescoes of the lake's many churches.

❶ Getting There & Away

Moračnik, Beška and Starčevo are best reached from Murići. Boats are easy to find in summer, but you might need to ask around at other times. Expect to pay about €25 per hour.

Grmožur is a regular stop on boat trips from Virpazar and Vranjina (the boats are considerably cheaper from Virpazar).

Kom is most easily reached by boat from Vranjina. In the height of summer, it can be approached by a path leading through the marshes from near Žabljak Crnojevića.

Vranjina

☑020 / POP 220

The twin hills on Vranjina (Врањина) island are nicknamed 'Sofia Loren' by the locals for wink-wink-nudge-nudge reasons that become apparent when they're viewed from afar. The village itself has the slightly improbable nickname 'the Montenegrin Venice'. In centuries past, the island was used as a hideaway for those embroiled in blood feuds.

Some boat tours leave from Vranjina, though they're generally more expensive than those departing from Virpazar.

❂ Sights & Activities

Lesendro Fortress   FORTRESS
(Lesendro Tvrđava) The remains of the 19th-century fortress Lesendro lie just along the causeway. The busy highway and railway tracks prevent land access to the site, but you'll get great views on a boat tour.

Vranjina Walking Trail   HIKING
This 4km hiking trail begins at the visitor centre and winds its way up towards the 13th-century **St Nicholas' Monastery** (Manastir Sv Nikole). The trail gets steep and rough in parts, but the views from the top are jaw-dropping. Bring plenty of water and

wear suitable boots. The visitor centre has maps and information on hand.

✖ Eating

Jezero   SEAFOOD €€
(☑020-879 106; www.plantaze.com; mains €6-18) This restaurant serves up wonderful, fresh *krap* and bleak (easy now; they're freshwater fish); savour it on the lovely lakeside terrace while enjoying a glass of local vino.

❶ Information

National Park Visitor Centre (☑020-879 103; www.nparkovi.me; €2, free with national park entry ticket; ⊙8am-7pm May-Sep, to 4pm Oct-Apr) The main visitor centre rests on the opposite side of the causeway leading to Podgorica from Virpazar. It has excellent displays about all of Montenegro's national parks, including lots of taxidermal critters and an ethnographic section with folk costumes and tools. You can buy national park entry tickets (€4) and fishing permits (per day €5) from a kiosk outside.

❶ Getting There & Away

There are frequent trains between Vranjina and Podgorica (€1.20, 25 minutes).

Vranjina is 20km from Podgorica.

Žabljak Crnojevića

For a brief time in the 15th century, between the fall of Skadar (now Shkodra in Albania) and the founding of Cetinje, this was the capital of Zetan ruler Ivan Crnojević. Now the enigmatic ruins stand forlornly on a lonely hillside surrounded by lush green plains with only some rather large snakes and spiders as occupants.

As you walk up from the small village at its base, the 14m-high, 2m-thick walls look intimidating, yet even these couldn't withstand the hammering the Ottoman invaders gave them in 1478 when the town was finally abandoned.

The site's a little hard to find but worth the effort. Heading towards Podgorica, turn left at the only traffic lights in Golubovci. After the railway bridge and the one-way bridge, turn left. Continue for about 4.5km until you see a bridge to your left. Cross it and continue to the car park near the village. Take the stone stairs heading up from the path near the river and follow your nose past the village church and along the overgrown path.

CENTRAL MONTENEGRO LAKE SKADAR NATIONAL PARK

Podgorica

📋 020 / POP 151,000

Given it's undergone five name changes, passed through the hands of everyone from the Romans to the Turks to the Austro-Hungarians, and twice been wiped off the map entirely, it's little wonder that Podgorica (Подгорица) seems permanently gripped by an identity crisis. Its streets are a hotchpotch of Ottoman oddments, Austrian shopfronts, brutalist blocks and shiny new malls, and it has a fraction of the big-smoke buzz other European capitals can claim. But with some excellent galleries, plenty of parks and a vibrant cafe culture, pint-sized Podgorica is worth a look.

The city sits at the confluence of two rivers. West of the Morača is the business district, while the Ribnica divides the eastern side in two. The south side is Stara Varoš, the old Ottoman town, while north is Nova Varoš, home to a lively mixture of shops and bars.

⊙ Sights

For a city formerly known as Titograd (literally 'Tito City'), there is an inordinate number of royal sculptures dotted around its many parks. The most imposing is the huge bronze **statue of Petar I Petrović Njegoš** (Map p104; Bul Džordža Vašingtona bb), standing on a black marble plinth on the Cetinje edge of town. A large **equestrian statue of Nikola I** (Map p104; Park Ivana Milutinovića) struts grandly at the head of a lovely park with manicured hedges and mature trees. There's also a spectacularly cheesy sculpture of Russian singer-songwriter **Vladimir Visotsky** (Map p104) near the **Millennium Bridge** (Map p104), pictured shirtless with a guitar and a skull at his feet. In late 2018 Tito himself made a comeback by way of a bronze statue, re-erected in a city park.

Stara Varoš   AREA
(Map p104) Podgorica's oldest neighbourhood retains traces of the 400 years in which it was the centre of a bustling Ottoman Turkish town. The blocky **clock tower** (Sahat Kula; Map p104; Trg Bećir-Bega Osmanagića) overlooking the square was useful for signalling Muslim prayer times. In the maze of streets behind it, two mosques remain. You wouldn't know to look at it, but the **Starodoganjska Mosque** (Map p104; Nemaljića bb) has its origins in the 15th century. More

impressive is the 18th-century **Osmanagić Mosque** (Osmanagića džamija; Map p104; Spasa Nikolića bb), which Turkish donations have helped to restore.

At the confluence of the two rivers is the ruin of the **Ribnica Fortress** (Tvrđava na Ribnici; Map p104), built by the Ottomans after their conquest in 1474. The best-preserved element is a little arched bridge crossing the Ribnica.

The rocky Morača riverbank serves as Podgorica's main **beach** (Map p104). It's a far cry from the sea beaches Montenegro's famous for – and locals have a bad habit of littering here – but in the middle of a Podgorica heatwave, it's heavenly.

**Museums & Galleries
of Podgorica**   MUSEUM
(Muzeji i Galerije Podgorice; Map p104; 📋 020-242 543; www.pgmuzeji.me; Marka Miljanova 4; ⊙9am-8pm Tue-Sun) 𝗙𝗥𝗘𝗘 Despite Cetinje nabbing most of the national endowment, Podgorica is well served by this collection of art, artefacts and folk costumes. There's an interesting section on Podgorica's history that includes antiquities exhumed from Doclea, its Roman incarnation, the remains of which are in the northern fringes of the modern city. Look out for Petar Lubarda's large canvas *Titograd* (1956) in the foyer.

Petrović Palace   PALACE
(Dvorac Petrovića; Map p104; 📋 020-243 914; www.csucg.me; Park Petrovića; ⊙8am-8pm Mon-Fri, 10am-2pm Sat) 𝗙𝗥𝗘𝗘 The Montenegro Contemporary Art Centre stages high-profile exhibitions in this pale-pink 19th-century palace. The surrounding park is peppered with interesting sculptures and a tiny church.

Temporary exhibitions are also displayed in the small **Galerija Centar** (Map p104; 📋 020-665 409; Njegoševa 2; ⊙hours vary) 𝗙𝗥𝗘𝗘 in the heart of the city.

**Cathedral of Christ's
Resurrection**   CATHEDRAL
(Saborni hram Hristovog vaskrsenja; Map p104; www.hramvaskrsenja.me; Bul Džordža Vašingtona bb) Finally consecrated in 2013 after 20 years of construction, the large dome, white stone towers and gold crosses of this immense Serbian Orthodox cathedral are a striking addition to Podgorica's skyline. The exterior features an unusual contrast between roughly hewn stone at the bottom and intricately carved details above. Inside, huge

THE CIRCUIT AROUND KORITA

If you've got wheels and a desire to get off the beaten track, rev up and head out along Montenegro's first fully signposted panoramic road. Starting off in Podgorica and skirting the Albanian border before looping back down again, the new Circuit Around Korita (Krug oko Korita) offers 65km of winding, wonderful roads that take in stunning vistas up to 1400m, pit stops in out-of-the-way museums, scenic villages and easy-going hikes – the best of which is a two-hour walk to the Grlo Sokolovo (Falcon's Throat) lookout, where you'll be rewarded with jaw-dropping views of the Cijevna Canyon and Prokletije Mountains.

The circuit is fully paved and well marked (keep an eye out for the brown signs), though the roads – in typical Montenegrin fashion – are narrow; the drive isn't recommended for caravans and is best driven between May and October. Fill up before you go; there are no petrol stations along the circuit. The Montenegrin National Tourist Organisation (p174) and Tourist Organisation of Podgorica (p106) offices can help with maps and information.

chandeliers blaze against an overwhelming expanse of gilded frescoes. One controversial image, in the apse above the front door, depicts Tito, Karl Marx and Friedrich Engels burning in hell.

Niagara Falls WATERFALL
(Nijagarini vodopadi; Rakića Kuće) They may not be the thundering cascades so beloved by honeymooners in North America, but these waterfalls make for a fantastic day trip from Podgorica. The falls are at their dramatic best after the spring thaws, but you'll find plenty of locals taking a dip in their somewhat depleted depths in early summer; by August they're often completely dried up. There's a good traditional restaurant, also called Niagara, beside the falls.

Niagara is a 10-minute drive from Podgorica; you'll need a car as there's no public transport. Take the signposted road to Tuzi, then turn right before passing the bridge over the Cijevna River and follow the signs to Rakića Kuće until you reach the restaurant's car park.

🏃 Activities & Tours

Montenegro Eco Adventures ADVENTURE
(Map p104; ☏069-123 078; www.montenegro-eco.com; Njegoševa 9; ☺9am-5pm Mon-Fri) 🍃 Promoting sustainable 'soft adventure' tours ranging from day trips to countrywide tailored, multiday expeditions.

Montenegro Adventures ADVENTURE
(Map p104; ☏020-208 000; www.montenegro-adventures.com; Jovana Tomaševića 35; ☺8am-6pm Mon-Fri, 9am-3pm Sat) This well-respected and long-standing agency creates

tailor-made adventure tours, countrywide. It can organise mountain guides, cycling logistics, kitesurfing, hiking, cultural activities, accommodation, flights...you name it.

🎭 Festivals & Events

December Arts Scene (DEUS) CULTURAL
(Decembarska umjetnička scena; ☺Dec) Monthlong celebration of art, music, literature and theatre.

🛏 Sleeping

Montenegro Hostel HOSTEL €
(Map p104; ☏069-255 501; www.montenegrohostel.com; Spasa Nikolića 52; dm €14-15, r without bathroom €40; [P][❄][@][📶][❄]) Tucked behind an old stone gate in Stara Varoš, this welcoming place feels more like a home than a hostel, with an enticing common room (and flop-worthy purple couches), a kitchen and cosy private rooms. Dorms are sparse but sparkling, with privacy curtains on the lower bunks. Note, taxi drivers may be more familiar with the street's old name, Radoja Jovanovića.

Athos APARTMENT €€
(Map p104; ☏067-227 595; www.apartments athos.com; Bul Ivana Crnojevića 58/2; apt €66-115; [P][❄][📶]) Enormous, easy on the eye and close to everything, these exceptional apartments are the best of Podgorica's private pads. All are supremely well equipped (think laundries and dishwashers), come with large terraces (some overlooking the lively cafe below) and have big, comfortable beds. Staff speak English and go out of their way to help guests. There's even a lift.

Podgorica

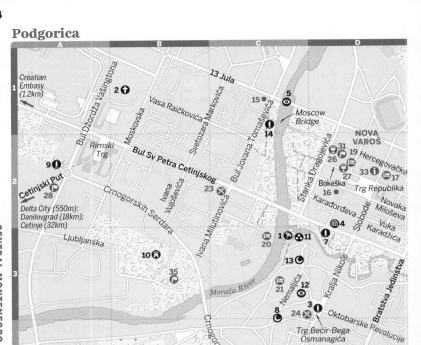

Hotel Hemera
BOUTIQUE HOTEL €€

(Map p104; ☑020-221 650; www.hotelhemera. com; Njegoševa 17; s/d from €61/81) Exceedingly atmospheric and gorgeously designed, Hemera is a top choice for those who like a bit of chic in their shelter. Rooms and suites have eclectic art covering the walls, and handmade walnut furniture used to fantastic effect. There's a superb restaurant attached, and a common-use library that gives every impression of having apparated straight from Hogwarts.

7 Hills Bed & Bike
B&B €€

(Map p104; ☑068-322 808; www.sevenhills. me; L1 Slobode 64; s/d/ste €30/45/50; [P][❄][🛜]) Geared towards cyclists – but welcoming everyone – this B&B is professionally run, spotless and very central. Self-caterers will appreciate the well-equipped communal kitchen. As you'd expect, they rent bikes, organise cycling tours and have plenty of bike storage for those travelling by pedal

power. In keeping with their athletic ethos, smoking is banned here.

Aria
HOTEL €€

(☑020-872 572; www.hotelaria.me; Mahala bb; d/ste from €83/153; [P][❄][🛜][🏊]) An oasis of green lawns in the scorched field surrounding the airport, this stylish hotel offers better value than its city equivalents and is a great option if you've got a badly timed flight. There's an excellent pool lined with loungers, and a huge kids' playground. Airport transfers are included.

Hotel Podgorica
HOTEL €€

(Map p104; ☑020-402 500; www.hotelpodgori ca.co.me; Svetlane Kane Radević 1; s/d €90/100; [P][❄][🛜]) A wonderful showcase of 1960s Yugoslav architecture, the Podgorica has been modernised yet retains its period charm – right down to the unsmiling staff. The river-stone cladding blends into stone the same shade as Montenegro's moun-

CENTRAL MONTENEGRO PODGORICA

tains; the best rooms have terraces facing the river.

✕ Eating

Podgorica offers a variety of cuisines you'll be hard-pressed to find elsewhere in the country. Head to the **green market** (Zelena pijaca; Map p104; Bratstva Jedinstva bb; ⊘6am-6pm Mon-Sat, to 3pm Sun May-Oct, 6am-4pm Nov-Apr) for fresh fruit and vegetables, or to one of the many large supermarkets.

Pod Volat BALKAN €€
(Map p104; ☏069-618 633; Trg Bećira-Bega Osmanagića; mains €3-11; ⊘7am-midnight) The food on offer here may be kind to the hip pocket, but not so much to the hips themselves; this is gloriously fattening Balkan cuisine at its best. The mixed grill is massive, but it's so good you won't mind loosening your belt a notch. It's a popular locals haunt, and its Stara Varoš location is awesomely atmospheric.

Mantra INDIAN €€
(Map p104; ☏020-242 888; www.mantrapodgorica.com; Ivana Milutinovića 21; mains €6.60-12; ⊘8am-midnight; ✓) In a country where any cuisine from further away than Italy is considered exotic, this opulently decorated Indian restaurant comes as a pleasant surprise – and a relief for vegetarian travellers bored of pizza and pasta, and vegans sick of salad. Their curry omelettes are a treat for

WORTH A TRIP

ŠIPČANIK WINE CELLAR

Wine tasting doesn't get more curious than at **Šipčanik Wine Cellar** (☑020-444 125; www.plantaze.com; tours & tastings €12-32; ⊘9am-5pm Mon-Fri), 8km southeast of Podgorica, operated by Plantaže, Montenegro's largest wine company. The cellar occupies a 356m-long tunnel that was once a secret underground Yugoslav-era aircraft hangar. Partially destroyed by NATO bombing in 1999 and abandoned immediately afterwards, the revamped hangar now houses millions of litres of wine, ageing gently in oak barrels and bottles. Call ahead to book a tour. Four options are available, starting with an hourlong tour and tastings of three standard wines accompanied by cheese and olives. The most expensive option includes five premium wines paired with food.

early risers. Ask for 'spicy' if you want any hint of a kick.

Ziya   MIDDLE EASTERN €€€
(Map p104; ☑020-230 690; www.hotelziya.me; Beogradska 10; mains €10-22; ⊘7am-11pm; 🖋) Attached to the boutique hotel of the same name – but welcoming all comers – Ziya serves delectable mains and meze in equally tasty surrounds. It's a bit more upmarket than your hometown kebabery, so be sure to scrub up.

🍷 Drinking & Nightlife

Podgorica's nightlife is centred on Nova Varoš, particularly in the blocks west of Ulica Slobode. The hippest strip right now is Ulica Bokeška. Keep an eye out for posters listing live music events and other happenings.

⭐**Culture Club Tarantino**   BAR
(Map p104; ☑067-055 333; www.cultureclub.me; Bokeška 6; ⊘7am-midnight; 🖈) Exemplifying the offbeat flavour of the Bokeška strip, this quirky spot promotes local music, art and other alternative happenings. It's a good place for a coffee and local-watching by day; at night it throngs with drinking, dancing students, creative types and other hip folk.

Buda Bar   BAR
(Map p104; www.facebook.com/Budabarpg; Stanka Dragojevića 26; ⊘8am-3am Mon-Sat) A golden Buddha smiles serenely as you meditate over your morning coffee or search for the eternal truth at the bottom of a cocktail glass. This is one slick watering hole; the tentlike, semi-enclosed terrace is the place to be on balmy summer nights, especially when there's a local starlet performing.

Shopping

The pedestrian-only sections of Hercegovačka and Ulica Slobode are Podgorica's best window-shopping strips. There are various large malls on Podgorica's outskirts, home to luxury boutiques and international brands.

ⓘ Information

Accident & Emergency Clinic (JZU zavod za hitnu medicinsku pomoć; Map p104; ☑020-226 081; www.zhmp.org; Vaka Đurovića bb; ⊘24hr)

Tourist Organisation of Podgorica (Map p104; ☑020-667 535; www.podgorica.travel; Slobode 47; ⊘8am-8pm Mon-Fri) Operates out of two offices on the same street; the second is at Slobode 30.

ⓘ Getting There & Away

AIR

Podgorica Airport (TGD; ☑020-444 244; www.montenegroairports.com) welcomes flights from across Europe.

BUS

Podgorica's **bus station** (Map p104; ☑020-620 430; Trg Golootočkih Žrtava 1; ⊘24hr) has a left-luggage service, an ATM, a restaurant and regular services to all major towns, including Herceg Novi (€10, three hours), Kotor (€7.50, 2¼ hours), Budva (€6, 1½ hours), Ulcinj (€7, two hours) and Cetinje (€3, 30 minutes). International destinations include Dubrovnik, Sarajevo, Pristina, Belgrade and Tirana.

CAR

The Sozina tunnel and toll road (one way €3.50) connects Podgorica to the Adriatic coast.

Car-hire agencies with counters at Podgorica Airport include Avis, Budget, Europcar and Sixt. Local agency **Meridian** (Map p104; ☑020-234 944; www.meridian-rentacar.com; Bul Džordža Vašingtona 85) also has a city office.

TRAIN

From Podgorica's **train station** (📞 020-441 209; www.zpcg.me; Trg Goolootočkih Žrtava 13) there are services to Bar (€2.40, one hour, 12 daily), Virpazar (€1.40, 30 minutes, 10 daily) and Belgrade (€21, 11¾ hours, two daily).

ℹ Getting Around

BUS

It's not difficult to explore Podgorica on foot, but if you fancy trying a local bus, they cost 80c for a short journey.

TAXI

Taxis in Podgorica are cheap and reliable, although they can be in short supply late at night.
City Taxi (📞 19711; www.citytaxi.com)
Halo Taxi (📞 19700; www.facebook.com/HaloTaxi19700)

Danilovgrad

📞 020 / POP 5200

Little Danilovgrad (Данилоград) could've been a contender. Originally conceived by Petar II Petrović Njegoš as a new capital (to replace then-capital Cetinje), all the sophisticated plans for its supremacy were swept away by the 1878 Congress of Berlin, which gave Montenegro possession of the far-grander cities of Nikšić, Podgorica and Bar.

Despite being dumped, Danilovgrad – 18km northwest of Podgorica – is a cheery place, and worth a short stop en route to Ostrog or Nikšić. The town's main street, Ulica Baja Sekulića, runs between two attractive squares. The one nearest the Zeta River is dominated by an impressive socialist realist **monument** featuring two likely lads and a staunch woman topped by a red star.

If you're around town on a Saturday, take a trip out to the wonderful nearby **Donkey Farm** (Farma Magaraca Martinici; 📞 067-245 006; Gradina Martinića; ⊙ 10am-1pm Sun) FREE, a welcoming sanctuary for abused and neglected donkeys.

☆☆ Festivals & Events

River Zeta Festival   CULTURAL
(⊙ late Aug) Three days of fun on the Zeta, featuring wooden raft and kayak races, diving, fishing and beauty contests plus an organic-food festival.

ℹ Information

Tourist Organisation of Danilovgrad (📞 020-816 015; www.tod.co.me; Sava Burića 2)

ℹ Getting There & Away

There are frequent buses running along the Podgorica–Nikšić route that call in at Danilovgrad. It's half an hour and €2 to either city.

There are seven trains per day between Podgorica (€1.20) and Nikšić (€1.60).

Ostrog Monastery

Resting improbably – miraculously? – in a cliff face 900m above the Zeta valley, the gleaming white **Ostrog Monastery** (Manastir Ostrog; www.manastirostrog.com) FREE is the most important site in Montenegro for Orthodox Christians, attracting up to a million visitors annually. Even with its numerous pilgrims, tourists and souvenir stands, it's a strangely affecting place.

The **Lower Monastery** (Donji manastir) is 2km below the main shrine. Stop here to admire the vivid frescoes in the **Holy Trinity Church** (Crkva Sv Trojice; 1824). Behind it is a natural spring where you can fill your bottles with deliciously cold, sweet water (and potentially benefit from an internal blessing as you sip it).

From here the faithful, some of them barefoot, plod up the steep road to the top. Halfway up, the beautiful stone walls of the little domed **Church of St Stanko the Martyr** (Crkva Sv Mučenika Stanka) gleam golden in the sunset. Non-pilgrims and the pure of heart may drive directly to the main car park and limit their penitence to just the final 200m.

The **Upper Monastery** (Gornji manastir; the really impressive one) is dubbed 'Sv Vasilije's miracle', because no one seems to understand how it was built. Constructed in 1665 within two large caves, it gives the impression that it has grown out of the very rock. Sv Vasilije (St Basil), a bishop from Hercegovina, brought his monks here after the Ottomans destroyed Tvrdoš Monastery near Trebinje.

Pilgrims queue to enter the atmospheric shrine where the saint's fabric-wrapped bones are kept. To enter you'll need to be wearing a long skirt or trousers (jeans are fine) and cover your shoulders. Most women also cover their heads with a scarf. It's customary to back out of the doorways and devout visitors might kiss lintels and make signs of the cross. At the very top of the monastery is another cave-like chapel with faded frescoes dating from 1667.

The monastery is so firmly entrenched in the country's psyche that many Montenegrins – even non-believers – commonly 'swear to Ostrog' (*'Ostroga mi...'*) when promising to do something.

🛏 Sleeping

In summer, sleeping mats are provided for free to pilgrims in front of the Upper Monastery.

ℹ Getting There & Away

There's no direct public transport to Ostrog, but numerous tour buses (€20 to €30 for a day trip) head here from all of the tourist hotspots. Trains from Podgorica go to Ostrog train station (€1.80, 45 minutes, seven daily) way down at the bottom of the hill; it's about an hour's hike from there to the Lower Monastery.

If you're driving, we strongly recommend that you take the excellent road from Danilovgrad to the monastery. The old road leaves the main Podgorica–Nikšić highway 19km past Danilovgrad. It's extremely narrow, twisting and steep, and in a very poor state of repair; in short, it's terrifying.

Nikšić

☑ 040 / POP 57,000

With no show-stopping sights, Montenegro's second-biggest city isn't high on most travellers' must-see lists. But if you fancy a blow-out in a lively student town, Nikšić (Никшић; pronounced '*nik*-shich') has an array of establishments that offer a more genuine (not to mention cheaper) Montenegrin experience than the tourist-populated bars of Budva. What else would you expect in the town that produces Nikšićko Pivo, the nation's favourite beer? Nikšić is also in the grip of a cultural revival; it's one of the best places in Montenegro to check out alternative, avant-garde art.

It's not all parties and paintings here: Nikšić is one of Montenegro's main industrial centres, supporting a large steel mill and bauxite mine.

👁 Sights

Nikšić Heritage Museum   MUSEUM, PALACE
(Zavičajni muzej Nikšić; Trg Šaka Petrovića, King Nikola's Palace; adult/child €1/50c; ⊙ 9am-1pm & 5-8pm Tue-Sat, 9am-noon Sun) King Nikola must have kept the country's builders busy as there's yet another of his palaces here (adding to those in Cetinje, Podgorica and

Bar). Now used as a museum, it's badly in need of renovating.

Start upstairs in the prehistoric section (where there are various flints dating to the 3rd millennium BC) and progress to the lovingly decorated guns, jewel-encrusted armour and embroidered clothes in the ethnographic section. WWII is covered by photographs and memorabilia (no English explanations); the graves of many of the fallen Partisans pictured are in the nearby cemetery.

Bedem Fortress   FORTRESS
The original Nikšić was built within sturdy walls on a rocky hill to the west of the current town. This was the site of a 4th-century Roman military base that was taken over by the Goths and fortified. Today, the partially restored fortress hosts an annual **music festival** (www.bedemfest.me; ⊙ late Aug-early Sep).

From Ulica Njegoševa, take Ulica Narodnih Heroja to the end, where you'll see the fortress ahead of you. It's near the train station.

St Basil of Ostrog's Cathedral   CATHEDRAL
(Saborna crkva Svetog Vasilija Ostroškog; Trg Šaka Petrovića) Sitting grandly on top of a pine-covered hill, Nikšić's hefty Serbian Orthodox cathedral was built between 1895 and 1900. A central dome floods the interior with light and massive chandeliers hang from the ceiling. The exquisite iconostasis is painted in the realistic style popular in the early 20th century, as opposed to the Byzantine look of the more recent icons. Look for local saints Peter of Cetinje and Basil of Ostrog on either side of the sanctuary doors.

🏃 Activities & Tours

Anitra Travel Agency   ADVENTURE
(☑ 040-200 598; www.tara-grab.com; Njegoševa 12) Owned by the same company as Camp Grab (p118), this local agency can arrange all kinds of active expeditions, including rafting, canyoning, hiking, fishing, mountain biking and jeep safaris.

🛏 Sleeping & Eating

Hotel Trebjesa   HOTEL €€
(☑ 077-200 060; www.hoteltrebjesa.me; Trebjesa bb; d €55-70, apt €95) Overlooking Nikšić from its forested perch in Trebjesa park, this sparkling hotel offers a literal breath of fresh air. All rooms are clean, comfortable and have beautiful mountain and city views; some have Jacuzzis. It's an easy five-minute drive

PUNKT ROCKS: HOW NIKŠIĆ GOT ITS GROOVE BACK

Think of Nikšić – if you think at all of Nikšić – and 'bohemia' is probably the last thing that springs to mind. But behind the city's industrial landscape lies a vibrant history of art and culture, a heritage that – after centuries in bloom – wilted in sync with the collapse of Yugoslavia in the 1990s. But creativity is once again flowering in Montenegro's second city, all thanks to a visionary collective called PUNKT.

Set up in 2015 by a group of young creatives, PUNKT is putting Nikšić back on the boho map by bombarding the city with the artistic and musical works of hitherto voiceless up-and-coming locals. Their first exhibition – for which they commandeered a dilapidated Yugoslav Army building – featured a wooden orchestra created by chainsaw, a room painted with eyeballs, avant-garde films and punk performances. Since then, they've held well-received exhibitions and concerts at bars, cafes and galleries across town, and have been revitalising – or, in the words of the crew, 'PUNKTing' – the cityscape with public murals. Keep up with them on www.facebook.com/KCPUNKT; if there's a happening when you're in town, it's well worth checking out.

up the hill from the centre of town, or you can toodle about on the hotel's free bikes.

Pekara INTERNATIONAL €€
(☑067-267 943; Marka Miljanova bb; mains €3-10; ☺7am-11pm) Its name means 'bakery', but there's more to this wildly popular hang-out than bread rolls. While their baked offerings – waffles, cakes and outrageously stacked pancakes – are indeed divine, it's also worth a visit to sample their burgers, grills and local stews served in hearty, edible bowls.

Forest INTERNATIONAL €€
(cnr Ivana Milutinovića & Manastirska; mains €4-15; ☺8am-midnight) The sidewalk seating at this buzzy corner cafe-restaurant makes for an excellent people-watching spot. Goggle at passers-by over a bowl of pasta (reputed to be the best in town) and a glass of wine from their long list. They also make tasty coffees and cakes.

 Drinking & Nightlife

Propaganda Bar BAR, CAFE
(Trg Slobode; ☺8am-midnight) This vibrant cafe-bar is populated by friendly, arty locals nattering over superb coffees by day and even better cocktails by night.

Blues Brothers Bar BAR
(Njegoševa 9) Fantastic bar that often hosts various cultural events, from music (orchestra, blues, rock, you name it) to alternative art and cinema exhibitions.

❶ Information

The helpful **Tourist Organisation of Nikšić** (☑040-213 262; www.niksic.travel; Ivana Milutinovića 10) is a short stroll south of Trg Slobode.

General Hospital (Opšta bolnica; ☑040-231 111; www.bolnica-nk.com; Radoja Dakića bb)

❶ Getting There & Away

BUS
The **bus station** (☑040-213 018; Gojka Garčevića bb) is next to the main roundabout and has toilets, restaurants and a left-luggage counter (€1). Domestic destinations include Kotor (€8, three hours, seven daily), Budva (€8.70, two hours, 10 daily), Podgorica (€3.50, one hour, frequent), Plužine (€5.50, one hour, six daily) and Žabljak (€6, 2½ hours, six daily). International services include Trebinje (€6.50, two hours, four daily), Sarajevo (€15, five hours, five daily) and Belgrade (€26, 10¾ hours, one daily).

CAR
A good road leads south from Nikšić directly down to Risan on the Bay of Kotor; heading north, it will take you to Žabljak.

TRAIN
Train Station (☑040-211 912; www.zpcg. me; Gojka Garčevića bb) Seven trains a day head to/from Podgorica (€2.80, one hour) via Danilovgrad and Ostrog.

Around Nikšić

As you travel west on the road to Trebinje in Hercegovina, a large sign on the left (3.5km after the small roundabout on the edge of town) points to **Most na Moštanici**, a 3rd-century Roman bridge. It's a bit hard to find as there are no other signs once you leave the main road. Coming off the road, turn sharp left and then right. Veer left after about 300m and head alongside the village. After a kilometre you'll see the bridge near a sturdy little church. The bridge's five graceful arches once spanned a flowing river that is today a dry ditch.

Heading in the same direction, a few kilometres past the turn-off to the bridge, you'll see **Lake Slano** (Slansko jezero) on your left. Although it's an artificial structure (there's a dam at one edge), Slano's sparkling blue waters, low-lying islands and green borders make for a beautiful vista. There are a few tiny villages on the shore but there's no straightforward route down to the water; take whatever turn-off you can find and wind your way down. You'll be unlikely to find more than a few people fishing or sunbathing.

More popular is **Lake Krupac** (Krupačko jezero), another dammed lake to the northwest of town that's been given the local nickname 'Nikšić's sea'. It has a small sandy beach, a couple of beach bars, picnic spots and pedal boats, jet skis and kayaks for hire. The **Lake Fest** (www.lakefest.me; ⊘ mid-Aug) music festival is held on its shores.

There are four ski slopes at **Vučje** (☑ 067-319 719; www.vucje.me; day pass adult/child €10/5), 21km northeast of Nikšić on the road to Šavnik.

Northern Mountains

Best Places to Eat

➡ Sočica (p125)

➡ Lupo D'argento (p120)

➡ Vodenica (p115)

➡ Savardak (p114)

➡ Krojet (p124)

Best Places to Sleep

➡ Eko-Oaza Suza Evrope (p119)

➡ Bianca Resort & Spa (p114)

➡ Etno Selo Šljeme (p120)

➡ Zvono (p125)

Why Go?

The mountainous north is the beefy brawn to the coast's polished pulchritude. Peaking at 2534m, this is the roof of Montenegro, where profound massifs, otherworldly vistas and a picturesque smattering of old-school villages offer a literal and metaphorical breath of fresh air.

The region's main drawcards are its three national parks. Durmitor is a dizzying combination of soaring peaks and the plunging depths of the Tara River Canyon, making for spectacular skiing in winter and rip-roaring rafting in summer. The remote treks and trails of Prokletije's Accursed Mountains are more heaven than hell for serious alpinists, while the less hardcore can catch their breath in Biogradska Gora's gentle lakes and timeless forests.

There's not much in the way of infrastructure outside of Kolašin and Žabljak, but don't let that stop you. Hire a car, steady your nerves, and let the twisty, turny, white-knuckle roads take you where they will.

When to Go

➡ In January and February, spend your days skiing and your nights feasting in front of an open fire.

➡ July and August have the best hiking weather, with average Durmitor temperatures in the low 20s.

➡ Watch the forest explode in colour in September and October as autumn hits Biogradska Gora.

NORTHERN MOUNTAINS

Northern Mountains Highlights

1 Tara Canyon (p117) Rafting between the kilometre-plus canyon walls in Durmitor National Park.

2 Prokletije National Park (p126) Tackling the trails and treks of the Accursed Mountains.

3 Biogradska Gora National Park (p115)

Searching for wood nymphs in the primordial forest.

4 Morača Monastery (p113) Time-warping to the 13th century as you step through the gates.

5 Rožaje (p122) People-watching as the evening promenade descends on the main street.

6 Gusinje (p124) Soaking up the peaceful Eastern vibe between the mosques and mountains.

7 Piva Canyon (p125) Taking a white-knuckle ride between the sheer cliffs and green depths.

Climate

It shouldn't surprise anyone that this mountainous region is cooler than the rest of the country. Average high temperatures range from just above freezing in January to the low 20s in August.

ℹ️ Getting There & Away

The main highway between Podgorica and Belgrade cuts through Mojkovac and Bijelo Polje and is well served by buses. A major road connects Nikšić to Durmitor National Park; this same road leads south to Risan on the Bay of Kotor. You can travel to Kolašin, Mojkovac and Bijelo Polje by train from Serbia in the north or Podgorica and Bar in the south. There are also road connections with Bosnia, Serbia and Kosovo.

ℹ️ Getting Around

South of Bijelo Polje, the Podgorica–Belgrade highway joins another highway leading through Berane and Rožaje. Buses take both of these routes. The road from Mojkovac to Žabljak is in excellent condition but gets twistier as it leaves the Tara Canyon and climbs into the mountains; this isn't a regular bus route. Plav is the most isolated town but it's reached by a scenic road used by frequent buses to Berane. It's possible to circle the Bjelasica Mountains completely in a 136km loop. The most spectacular section is from Kolašin to Andrijevica, but it is prone to landslides in bad weather and avoided by buses.

It's possible to travel between Kolašin, Mojkovac and Bijelo Polje by train.

Morača Canyon

Heading north from Podgorica, it doesn't take long before the scenery becomes breathtaking. The highway – a thrilling, spectacular stretch of road – gets progressively more precarious as it follows the Morača River into a nearly perpendicular canyon, 300m to 400m deep. If you're driving, pull over into one of the viewing areas to enjoy it properly: this is an extremely busy and unforgiving stretch of road.

The river continues after the canyon recedes; you'll find the **Morača Monastery** (Manastir Morača) near its banks. Founded in 1252, this is one of the most important Orthodox monasteries in Montenegro, with some of its most accomplished religious art.

As you enter the walled compound into a garden courtyard where the bees from the monks' hives dance between the hydrangeas and roses, it's like stepping back into the 13th century. To the right, the small **St Nicholas' Church** (Crkva Sv Nikole) has faded frescoes on its facade that were once as vivid as those inside.

The larger **Church of the Dormition** (Crkva Uspenja Bogorodice) has external frescoes by the celebrated master Djordje Mitrofanović, plus beautiful doors inlaid with geometric patterns. The church's treasures include Mitrofanović's *The Virgin Enthroned with Child, Prophets and Hymnographers* (1617). The other master at work here was Kozma, whose icon of *Saints Sava and Simeon* (1645), on the right-hand wall,

includes a border showing the construction of the monastery (the latter saint was the founder's grandfather).

This is an active monastery (albeit with only four monks); dress appropriately.

Kolašin

📓 020 / POP 3000

Sitting 960m above sea level, Kolašin (Колашин; pronounced 'ko-*la*-shin') is Montenegro's main mountain resort. Although the skiing's not as reliable as in Durmitor, Kolašin's much easier to get to (it's just off the main highway, 71km north of Podgorica) and has ritzier accommodation offerings. Like most ski towns, it looks far prettier under a blanket of snow, but even in summer it's a handy base for exploring Biogradska Gora National Park or other parts of the Bjelasica Mountains.

Most things of interest, including banks and a post office, are set around the two central squares (Trg Borca and Trg Vukmana Kruščića) and the short street that connects them (Ulica IV Proleterske).

👁 Sights

Botanic Garden GARDENS
(Botanička bašta; botanybasta@t-com.me; Put Braće Vujisić) With a huge, unique collection of indigenous mountain flora and medicinal herbs, this fascinating, privately owned garden has attracted botanists from around the world. The founder and keeper of the garden, Daniel Vincek, may be getting along in years, but his knowledge – and the infectious way he shares his passion for plants in excellent English – is timeless.

Hours are at Daniel's whim; if you're keen to visit, ask the tourist office to give him a call, or drop him an email yourself.

Heritage Museum MUSEUM
(Zavičajni muzej; Trg Borca 1; ☉ 8am-3pm) **FREE**
Trg Borca contains a stirring statue of a young man and woman marching forward, guns and communist flag aloft. They look like they're about to liberate the museum building, which served as a prison during WWII. Inside, the collection consists mainly of photos and there aren't any English explanations, but the idealistic faces of the town's young comrades, many of whom lost their lives fighting the Nazis, are captivating. There's also an ethnographic section and an art gallery.

🏃 Activities

Three marked **hiking paths** start from Trg Borca and head into the Bjelasica Mountains. From the ski centre there's a 16km, five-hour loop route through forest to **Mt Ključ** (1973m) and on to Eco Katun Vranjak before heading back. If you're staying at the *katun* (traditional shepherd's mountain hut) you can take another scenic trail that knocks off **Zekova Glava** (2117m) and passes **Lake Pešić** (Pešićko jezero), skirting beneath Bjelasica's highest peak. On the loop back it visits the spring that is the source of the Biogradska River before heading up **Troglava** (2072m). The 16km path is easy and well marked and should take less than five hours. For detailed descriptions and maps of both trails, pick up a copy of the *Mountains of Bjelasica* booklet available at either of the tourist offices.

A 93km **mountain-biking route** runs through remote countryside from Podgorica to Kolašin. There are plenty of places in Kolašin to hire bikes, so you could pick one up here, catch the train to Podgorica and cycle back over a few days.

Kolašin 1450 Ski Resort SKIING
(📞068-041 450; www.kolasin1450.com; day/week ski pass €15/98) Located 10km east of Kolašin, at an elevation of 1450m, this ski centre offers 30km of runs (graded green, blue, red and black) reached by various ski lifts, as well as a cafe and restaurant in attractive wooden chalets. You can hire a full ski or snowboard kit from €13 per day. The ski season lasts roughly from December to mid-April.

In winter, there are shuttle buses from the Bianca and Lipka hotels; they're free if you're a guest or if you purchase your ski pass from the hotels.

Explorer Tourist Agency ADVENTURE
(📞020-864 200; www.explorer.co.me; Mojkovačka bb) Located near the bus station, this agency specialises in action-packed holidays. It can arrange hiking, skiing, rafting, mountain biking, canyoning, caving, mountain climbing, jeep safaris, horse riding, paragliding and fishing expeditions. It also hires out mountain bikes.

🛏 Sleeping

Premium prices are charged during the ski season, with the absolute peak being around New Year. In summer it's possible to stay high in the mountains in a traveller-friendly version of a traditional *katun* (wooden shepherd's hut); enquire at the tourist office or book through one of the adventure travel agencies.

Apartments Life APARTMENT €€
(📞068-003 056; www.apartments-life.com; Toška i Jovana bb; apt from €45; 🅿🛜) Centrally located and very welcoming, this cosy place offers the choice of a one-bedroom apartment, a private cottage or an entire house; all are cosy, clean and great value. During winter, it rents out ski equipment; in the warmer months, guests can socialise around the communal barbecue. It's a top spot for self-caterers; all accommodations have kitchens, and it's just a quick stroll to Kolašin's produce market.

Brile HOTEL €€
(📞020-865 021; www.brile.co; Buda Tomovića 2; s/d €35/74; 🛜) On the edge of the main square, this attractive family-run hotel has comfy rooms with polished wooden floors. There's a sauna for an après-ski defrost and a restaurant downstairs serving warming comfort food such as roasts, grilled meat, pizza and pasta. It also rents out bikes and skis.

Bianca Resort & Spa RESORT €€€
(📞020-863 000; www.biancaresort.com; Mirka Vešovića bb; d/ste from €120/200; 🅿🛜🏊) Take one large angular hotel with quirky hexagonal windows, completely gut it, add a heap of rakish, rustic touches, and voila! You get this atmospheric, idiosyncratic first-rate ski resort. After a hard day on the slopes, you can soothe out any bumps and bruises in the luxury spa, which includes a large indoor pool, sauna, Turkish bath and gym.

🍴 Eating

Konoba MONTENEGRIN €€
(📞069-609 144; Trg Vukmana Kruščića; mains €6-8; ⏲8am-midnight) Sitting on the square that was the heart of the old Turkish town, this rustic eatery is a standard-bearer for Montenegrin mountain cuisine, such as *kačamak* (polenta porridge with mashed potato), *cicvara* (creamy polenta), *popara* (bread-based porridge) and tender roast lamb that falls off the bone.

Savardak MONTENEGRIN €€
(📞069-051 264; savardak@t-com.me; mains €8-9) Located 2.8km from Kolašin on the road to the ski centre, Savardak serves traditional food in what appears to be a big haystack with a chimney attached. Eat in the atmos-

pheric interior or sit at outdoor tables by the stream. Four-person apartments (€40) are available in a thatch-roofed wooden chalet next door.

Vodenica MONTENEGRIN €€
(☑069-241 507; Dunje Dokić bb; mains €6-9; ⊙9am-11pm) Set in a traditional watermill, Vodenica offers a taste of traditional stodgy mountain food designed to warm your belly on cold nights. Ease back and let your arteries clog over a bowl of *cicvara* (creamy polenta) or *kačamak* (polenta porridge with mashed potato).

ℹ️ Information

Bjelasica & Komovi Regional Tourism Organisation (☑020-860 670; www.bjelasica-komovi.me; Trg Borca 2; ⊙9am-8pm Mon-Fri, 9am-noon & 4-8pm Sat & Sun) When it's open (hours can be hit or miss), this impressive wooden information centre should be your first port of call for information on hiking and mountain-biking routes. It can help arrange all manner of mountain activities and tours, including visits to local honey and cheese producers. It also rents out mountain bikes (per half-day/day €7/10). You'll find it prominently located near the main square. The organisation is also involved in the Northern Exposure project (www.northernexposure.me), an EU-backed project promoting year-round activities in the mountainous regions of Montenegro and Bosnia. See the website for tons of information on year-round activities in the Bjelasica, Komovi and Prokletije regions.

Kolašin Tourist Office (☑020-864 254; www.to-kolasin.me; Mirka Vešovića bb; ⊙8am-8pm Mon-Fri, 9am-3pm Sat) The town's tourist office is very useful for arranging private accommodation (including *katun* – wooden mountain hut – stays) and for information on local activities.

ℹ️ Getting There & Away

The **bus station** (☑020-864 033; Mojkovačka bb) is a wooden shed by a scrappy parking lot on the road leading into town, about 200m north of the centre. Destinations include Pljevlja (€7, 2½ hours, five daily), Podgorica (€5, 1½ hours, frequent), Bar (€6.50, 2½ hours, five daily), Budva (€10, three hours, seven daily) and Kotor (€10.50, 3¾ hours, five daily).

Kolašin's **train station** (☑020-441 492; www.zpcg.me) is 1.5km east from the centre, with services to Bijelo Polje (€2.20, 30 minutes, six daily), Podgorica (€3.20, 90 minutes, six daily), Bar (€5.40, 2½ hours, five daily) and Belgrade (€16, 6½ hours, two daily). Buy your tickets on the train.

Biogradska Gora National Park

Nestled within the Bjelasica mountain range, pretty Biogradska Gora (Биоградска Гора) has as its heart 1600 hectares of virgin woodland – one of Europe's last three remaining primeval forests. King Nikola is to thank for its survival; on a visit in 1878 he was so taken by the beauty of **Lake Biogradska** (Biogradsko jezero) that the locals gifted him the land and he ordered it to be preserved.

Many of the trees in the forest are more than half a millennium old, with some soaring to dizzying heights of 60m. The park is also home to five high-altitude (1820m) glacial lakes.

There are many signposted **hiking trails** within the park, ranging in difficulty from chilled (a 3.4km amble around Lake Biograd) to challenging (35km trek up to Crna Glava and beyond). The **park office** (☑020-865 625; www.nparkovi.me; ⊙9am-5pm Sep-May, to 7pm Jun-Aug) has information on hikes and trails; if you're not keen to go it alone, ask about their expert mountain guides (four/eight hours €60/80). The office also rents rowing boats (€8 per hour) and kayaks (from €3 per hour).

🍽 Eating

Bring your own picnic or try the lakeside **Restoran Biogradsko Jezero** (mains €8-9; ⊙9am-6pm), much beloved by tour groups and hungry hikers.

ℹ️ Getting There & Away

The main entrance to the park is between Kolašin and Mojkovac on the Podgorica–Belgrade highway. After paying an entry fee (€3/1.50 adult/child), you can drive the further 4km to Lake Biograd.

Getting here via public transport (plus a bit of hoofing it) is also possible. Buses to/from Kolašin and Mojkovac stop (on request) at Kraljevo Kolo, the entrance to the park. From there it's about an hour's walk to the lake. The nearest train station (Štitarička Rijeka, on the Podgorica–Belgrade route) is a 90-minute walk away.

Mojkovac

☑050 / POP 4000

Despite being on the doorstep of two national parks, Mojkovac (Мојковац; pronounced '*moy*-ko-vats') hasn't cashed in on

THE BJELASICA MASSIF

The Bjelasica massif dominates northeastern Montenegro with 10 grand peaks higher than 2000m. The unfortunately named Crna Glava (Black Head) is the highest at 2139m.

Any preconception you may have of Montenegro's mountains as grey and barren will be shattered as the snows recede and reveal virgin forest (within the protected environs of Biogradska Gora National Park) and meadows teeming with wildflowers. In the higher pastures you'll find *katuns*, round thatched structures that have been used for centuries by semi-nomadic shepherds when they bring their flocks here in summer. It's a much more forgiving environment than the Orjen, Lovćen or Durmitor ranges, and therefore easier to explore.

Trails are accessed from the towns that encircle the mountain: Kolašin, Mojkovac, Bijelo Polje, Berane and Andrijevica. The best times for hiking are at the end of summer and in autumn when the forests are a mash of colours. Be prepared for sudden drops in temperature and storms. Local tourist offices should be able to provide you with maps, information, advice and contacts for guides. Otherwise, talk to one of the agencies specialising in adventure holidays. The excellent website www.northernexposure.me has loads of useful information on year-round activities in and around the Bjelasica region.

its potential – at least not yet. Over recent years there's been a concerted effort to clean up the toxic legacy of centuries of silver, lead and zinc mining. Now that the task has been largely completed, the United Nations Development Programme has turned its attention to encouraging adventure tourism and organic farming – watch this space. In the meantime, don't drink the water.

The centre of town is triangular Trg Ljubomira Bakoča, encompassing a pretty little park and a large pompous statue of Janko Vukotić, who led Montenegrin forces to a bloody, underdog victory against Austria-Hungary in the WWI Battle of Mojkovac.

A steep hiking path leads from the centre to a 17km (six-hour) loop through the surrounding mountains; take trail 310 and return on 319 and then 301. Mojkovac's railway station is the starting point of a 309km, six- to seven-day mountain-biking loop (Top Biking Trail 3: Eastern Enchantment), which takes in Biogradska Gora National Park, Gusinje, Plav and Rožaje. The **Mojkovac Tourism Organisation** (www.mojkovac. travel; Serdara Janka Vukotića bb) can help with trail and trek information.

🛏 Sleeping & Eating

Hotel & Resort Gacka B&B €€€
(☏ 050-474 720; www.imanjerakocevic.me; tw/d €95/110, 1-/2-bedroom chalets from €120/200; 🛜 🐾) Less than 5km from Mojkovac's centre but a million miles from its (relative) bustle, this lovely spot is dotted with pristine wooden cabins enjoying picture-perfect mountain views. The 'luxury' cottages have saunas, though all guests can use the spa's indoor pool. There's an excellent on-site restaurant dishing up fattening local fare, which goes a long way towards soaking up their home-made wines and *rakija* (fruit brandy).

ℹ Getting There & Away

Mojkovac's large **bus station** (☏ 050-472 247; Podgorica-Belgrade Hwy) is a major stop on the Podgorica–Belgrade route. Destinations include Podgorica (€6, two hours, frequent), Kolašin (€2.50, 35 minutes, frequent), Pljevlja (€6, two hours, two daily) and Belgrade (€17, 9½ hours, six daily). The station is 200m north of the main square.

The train station is on the southern outskirts of town. Trains head from here to Bar (€6.20, 2¾ hours, five daily), Podgorica (€4.40, two hours, six daily) and Bijelo Polje (€1.20, 20 minutes, six daily).

Durmitor National Park

The impossibly rugged and dramatic Durmitor (Дурмитор) is one of Montenegro's – and Mother Nature's – showpieces. Carved out by glaciers and underground streams, Durmitor stuns with dizzying canyons, glittering glacial lakes and nearly 50 limestone peaks soaring to over 2000m; the highest, **Bobotov Kuk**, hits 2523m. From December to March, Durmitor is a major ski resort, while in summer it's popular for hiking, rafting and other active pursuits.

The national park covers the Durmitor mountain range and a narrow branch heading east along the Tara River towards Mojkovac. West of the park, the mighty Tara marks the border with Bosnia and joins the Piva River near Šćepan Polje.

Durmitor is home to 163 bird species, about 50 types of mammals and purportedly the greatest variety of butterflies in Europe. It's very unlikely you'll spot bears and wolves, which is either a good or bad thing depending on your perspective.

All roads (and ski runs and bumpy trails) lead to **Žabljak**, regional capital and – at 1450m – one of the highest towns in the Balkans. Quaintly ramshackle – though slowly smartening up – it's the gateway to Durmitor's mountain adventures. You'll find restaurants, hotels and a supermarket gathered around the car park that masquerades as Žabljak's main square.

◎ Sights

★ Tara Canyon   CANYON

Slicing through the mountains at the northern edge of the national park, the Tara River forms a canyon that is 1300m deep at its peak (the Grand Canyon plummets a mere 200m deeper). The best views are from the water, and rafting (p118) along the river is one of the country's most popular tourist activities. If you'd rather admire the canyon from afar, head to the top of **Mt Ćurevac** (1625m) – although even this view is restricted by the canyon walls.

The viewpoint isn't well signposted and can be difficult to find. From central Žabljak, take the road north and follow the signs marked 'Panoramic Road 2'. Leave this route at the fork to the right marked 'Tepca'. Eventually there are some small wooden signs pointing to Ćurevac or *vidikovac* (viewpoint). Stop at the grassy parking spot opposite the drink stall and clamber up the small track behind.

Tara Bridge   BRIDGE

(Đurđevića Tara) The elegant spans of the 150m-high Tara Bridge were completed just as WWII was starting. At the time it was the largest concrete arched vehicular bridge in Europe. Its 365m length is carried on five sweeping arches, the largest of which is 116m wide.

In May 1942, with large numbers of Italian and German troops stationed in Žabljak, the Partisan command gave the order to blow up the bridge. The honour went to one of its engineers, Lazar Jauković, who planted the bomb that destroyed his beautiful creation.

Jauković was captured by the Italians and executed on the remains of his bridge. When it was rebuilt in 1946, Jauković's bravery was acknowledged by a plaque that still stands by the bridge today.

★ Black Lake   LAKE

(Crno jezero) Eighteen glittering glacial lakes known as *gorske oči* (mountain eyes) dot the Durmitor range. The spectacular Black Lake, a pleasant 3km walk from Žabljak, is the largest of them and the most visited part of the national park. The rounded mass of **Međed** (the Bear; 2287m) rears up behind it, casting an inky shadow into the pine-walled waters. An easy 3.6km walking track circles the lake.

Stećci Sites   CEMETERY

These mysterious carved stone tomb monuments – dating from between the 12th and 16th centuries – can be found across northern Montenegro and neighbouring Bosnia. There are two extremely significant *stećci* sites in Durmitor National Park (both were added to Unesco's World Heritage list in 2016): the Bare Žugića necropolis, with 300 *stećci*, and Grčko groblje (Greek graveyard), with 49. Many of the stones at both sites are intricately decorated.

Though neither site is signposted or staffed, they're easy to visit if you've got wheels. Around 5km south from Žabljak, turn left towards Devil's Lake (Vražje Jezero) – a gorgeous swimmable lake with a deep green centre and a lighter ring of green surrounding it. Continue on and, when you see the sign to Novakovići village, Grčko groblje can be spotted on the hill to your left; Fish Lake (Riblije Jezero) is on the right.

Continue along the road to the left and the Bare Žugića necropolis is to the left of

NORTHERN MOUNTAINS DURMITOR NATIONAL PARK

ⓘ PARK FEES

The road to Black Lake is blocked off just past the National Park Visitors Centre and an entry fee is charged (per person per day €3, free for children under seven). If you're planning on staying in the area, it's worth purchasing a three-day (€6) or weekly (€12) ticket. Drivers will need to park outside the gates (€2) and walk the remaining 500m to the lake. Keep hold of your ticket, in case you bump into a ranger.

the road, shortly after a monument topped by an Orthodox cross.

Dobrilovina Monastery CHRISTIAN MONASTERY
Near the eastern boundary of the national park, 28km from Mojkovac, this monastery has an idyllic setting in lush fields hemmed in by the mountains and the Tara River. If you knock at the accommodation wing, a black-robed nun will unlock the church, but only if she's satisfied that you're appropriately attired. The frescoes that remain inside the church, dedicated to St George (Sv Ðorđe), are faded but very beautiful.

🏃 Activities

Rafting
A rafting expedition along the Tara is the best way to revel in glorious river scenery that's impossible to catch from land. Trips are suitable for everyone from the white-water novice to experienced foam-hounds. Though it's not the world's most white-knuckled ride, there are a few rapids; if you're after speed, visit in April and May, when the last of the melting snow revs up the flow. Various operators run trips between April and October.

The 82km section that is raftable starts from Splavište, south of the Tara Bridge, and ends at Šćepan Polje on the Bosnian border. The classic two-day trip heads through the deepest part of the canyon on the first day, stopping overnight at Radovan Luka. Summit Travel Agency offers a range of rafting trips on this route, with transfers from Žabljak.

Most of the day tours from the coast traverse only the last 18km from Brstanovica – this is outside the national park and hence avoids hefty fees. You'll miss out on the canyon's depths, but it's still a beautiful stretch, including most of the rapids. The buses follow a spectacular road along the Piva River, giving you a double dose of canyon action.

It's important to use a reputable operator; in 2010 two people died in one day on a trip with inexperienced guides. At a minimum make sure you're given a helmet and life jacket – wear them and do them up. Some noteworthy operators are **Camp Grab** (✆069-101 002; www.tara-grab.com; half-day incl lunch €44, 3-day all-inclusive rafting trips from €200), **Tara Tour** (✆069-086 106; www.tara-tour.com; Šćepan Polje bb) and **Waterfall Rafting Centre** (✆069-310 848; www.

raftingmontenegro.com). Many of the rafting groups also offer other activities, including horse riding, canyoning and jeep safaris. If you've got your own wheels you can save a few bucks and avoid a lengthy coach tour by heading directly to Šćepan Polje and hooking up with the rafting tours there.

Hiking
Durmitor is one of the best-marked mountain ranges in Europe, with 25 marked trails making up a total of 150km. Some suggest it's a little *too* well labelled, encouraging novices to wander around seriously high-altitude paths that are prone to fog and summer thunderstorms. Ask the staff at the National Park Visitors Centre (p120) about tracks that suit your level of experience and fitness.

One rewarding route is the hike to the two **Škrčka Lakes** (Škrčka jezera), in the centre of a tectonic valley, where you can enjoy magnificent scenery and stay overnight in a mountain hut (June to September only). Another popular hike is from the Black Lake to the **ice cave** *(ledina pećina)* – home in cooler months to stalactite- and stalagmite-like shapes made of ice – on Obla Glava. It's a six- to seven-hour return hike.

If you're considering an assault on Bobotov Kuk or a serious winter expedition, it's best to arrange a local guide.

In any case, check the weather forecast before you set out, stick to the tracks, and prepare for rain and sudden drops in temperature. A compass could be a lifesaver. *Durmitor and the Tara Canyon* by Branislav Cerović (€12 from the visitors centre) is a great resource for mountaineers and serious hikers. The **Mountaineering Association of Montenegro** (www.pscg.me) has contacts and info on the peaks and paths of Durmitor.

Via Dinarica Hiking Trail HIKING
(www.viadinarica.com) The Montenegrin part of this 1930km 'megatrail' – which traverses Slovenia, Croatia, Bosnia, Montenegro and Albania – connects Durmitor with Bosnia's Sutjeska National Park. See the website for details, or contact Black Mountain (p40) to organise hiking tours.

Skiing
With 120 days of snow cover, Durmitor offers the most reliable – and cheapest – skiing in Montenegro.

Javorovača Ski Centar (☑067-800 971; www.javorovaca.me; adult/child day passes €8/5, week passes €48/30) rents out equipment and offers lessons. See www.skiresortmontene gro.com (in Montenegrin) for more information on all of Montenegro's ski centres.

Free-riding snowboarders and skiers should check out www.riders.me for off-piste adventure ideas.

Canyoning

Nevidio Canyon CANYONING
Just south of the national park, near Šavnik, is the remarkable 2.7km-long Nevidio Canyon. Cut by the Komarnica River, at points it is only metres wide, hence the name (*nevidio* means 'invisible'). It's extremely beautiful but equally dangerous. Canyoning expeditions generally take about three to four hours and participants should be able to swim and have a high level of fitness.

July and August are the safest months to explore, and then only in the company of professional guides. **Montenegro Canyoning** (☑069-565 311; www.montenegro-canyoning. com; trips without/with lunch per person €90/100) is a highly recommended group that focuses solely on expeditions to Nevidio. Otherwise, **Anitra/Grab** (www.tara-grab.com) organises expeditions out of Nikšić (price on application), and Summit Travel Agency and Durmitor Adventure do so out of Žabljak (€100 per person including lunch, minimum two people).

Ziplining

Get a bird's-eye view of Durmitor's delights with a zoom on a zipline. Three competing outfits are set up near the Tara Bridge; **Red Rock Zipline** (☑069-440 290; www. redrockzipline.com; Đurđevića Tara; adult €10; ☉10am-8pm Apr-Oct), on the Pljevlja side of the bridge, is the longest established of them. **Crno Jezero Avanturistički Park** (☑069-214 110; www.avanturistickipark.me; Black Lake; adult/child €9/8; ☉10am-7pm Jul & Aug, 10am-6pm Sat & Sun Jun & Sep) has a zipline over the Black Lake.

Rock Climbing

Two rock walls have been prepared on the side of the mountain at **Pirlitor**, but you'll need your own ropes. To get to Pirlitor from Žabljak, head towards the Tara Bridge, turn left at Vrela and follow the signs. The access road is very rough and

is best attempted with a four-wheel drive. The easier eastern wall has six lines graded 3+ to 4+ on the French scale, reaching to about 10m. There are 14 routes on the 30m-high western wall, graded from 5b to 7b+.

Jeep Safaris

Simply driving in Durmitor is a delight. If you haven't got your own wheels – or are rightfully nervous about braving the precipitous, twisty-turny roads – a jeep safari is an excellent and easy way to take in the region's magnificent scenery. Safaris generally include village visits, traditional lunches and off-road bushwhacks.

☞ Tours

Durmitor Adventure ADVENTURE
(☑069-629 516; www.durmitoradventure.com)
This well-regarded group offers tandem paragliding (€90), canyoning expeditions to Nevidio (€100), climbing at Pirlitor (€50) and a range of guided mountain hikes, including treks to Bobotov Kuk and the ice cave (€70 for a group).

Summit Travel Agency ADVENTURE
(☑068-535 535; www.summit.co.me; Njegoševa 12, Žabljak; half-/1-/2-day rafting trips €45/110/200) As well as all-inclusive rafting trips departing from Žabljak, this long-standing agency can arrange jeep tours and canyoning expeditions. It also has accommodation in the form of rental apartments in Žabljak.

🛏 Sleeping

Campgrounds and Žabljak's lone hostel are generally open from April to October.

★**Eko-Oaza Tear of Europe** CAMPGROUND €
(Eko-Oaza suza Evrope; ☑069-444 590; www. eko-oaza.me; Gornja Dobrilovina; campsites per 1/2/3 people €7.50/11/15, campervans €13-15, cabins €50, without bathroom €20; ☉Apr-Oct; 🛜) Consisting of a handful of comfortable wooden cottages with bathrooms (each sleeping five people), small cabins without bathrooms, well-equipped apartments and a fine stretch of lawn above the river, this magical, family-run 'eco oasis' offers a genuine experience of Montenegrin hospitality. Home-cooked meals are provided on request, and rafting, kayaking, canyoning and jeep safaris can be arranged. Truly memorable.

ⓘ PEDAL OFF THE METAL

The gloriously swooping, zigzaggy roads around the Durmitor area seem to inspire reckless racing-car driver fantasies in many locals, but whatever you do, don't follow their lead. Not only are these roads incredibly dangerous, they're heavily patrolled by the traffic police. We've had reports of people being pulled over for even the most minor infractions, so play it straight and watch your speed.

Autokamp Mlinski Potok CAMPGROUND €
(☏069-821 730; www.facebook.com/camp.dur mitor.mlinskipotok; Pitomine bb; campsites per person/car €4/2, r €10; ☺May-Oct; Ⓟ) With a fabulously hospitable host (there's no escaping the *rakija* shots), this private campsite above the visitors centre is a sociable option. It's a fairly basic set-up but there are hot-water showers and clean sit-down toilets. Private rooms are also available.

Etno Selo Šljeme CABIN €€
(☏063-229 294; www.etnoselosljeme.com; Smrčevo brdo bb; cabins €90; Ⓟ☎) Šljeme's two-bedroom A-frame cabins are more swish than some of the other *'etno'* (rustic and vaguely traditional) offerings in the vicinity, and much better than the rooms above the on-site restaurant. There's also a playground, and bikes for hire. It's located 6km south of Žabljak.

Polar Star HOTEL €€
(☏067-609 444; www.polarstar.me; Borje; d/apt €80/110; Ⓟ☎) A quick 4km drive from Žabljak, this recently renovated hotel is a clean, comfy and comradely option for those who want to be near town but not in it. Apartments have full kitchens and dishwashers; all guests have access to the free sauna. The hotel can organise various excursions (including quad-bike tours through the national park); during winter, guests can rent snowmobiles (€70, with guide).

✖ Eating

Zlatni Papagaj PIZZA €
(Vuka Karadžića 5, Žabljak; mains €3.50-12; ☎) The 'Golden Parrot' has the feel of a pirate lair, with wine-barrel tables, a wooden ceiling hung with chandeliers and a thick fug of cigarette smoke (though there is a non-smoking section, a rarity round these parts). The menu offers a crowd-pleasing selection of pizza, creamy pastas and steaks.

Lupo D'argento ITALIAN, STEAK €€
(☏069-111 555; Vuka Karadžića bb, Žabljak; mains €4-15; ☺8am-1am) This shiny, modern place is undoubtedly Žabljak's hippest restaurant; so hip, in fact, that you may wonder why it's here at all. Don't question, just enjoy. The menu covers all the Italian classics, and they do wonderful things with steak. Portions are big, the espressos are strong, and if you just can't tear yourself away, the place morphs into a trendy nightclub after 9pm.

ⓘ Information

Durmitor National Park Visitors Centre
(☏052-360 228; www.nparkovi.me; Njegoševa bb, Žabljak; ☺7am-5pm Mon-Fri, 10am-5pm Sat & Sun Jan & Jun–mid-Sep, 7am-3pm Mon-Fri mid-Sep–Dec & Feb-May)

Žabljak Tourist Office (☏052-361 802; www. tozabljak.com; Trg Durmitorskih ratnika, Žabljak; ☺7am-10pm mid-Jun–Sep, 8am-8pm Oct–mid-Jun)

ⓘ Getting There & Away

All of the approaches to Durmitor are spectacular. The most reliable road to Žabljak follows the Tara River west from Mojkovac. In summer this 70km drive takes about 90 minutes. If you're coming from Podgorica, the quickest way is through Nikšić and Šavnik. The main highway north from Nikšić follows the dramatic Piva Canyon to Šćepan Polje. There's a wonderful back road through the mountains leaving the highway near Plužine, but it's impassable as soon as the snows fall.

The bus station is at the southern edge of Žabljak, on the Šavnik road. Buses head to Podgorica (€8, 2½ hours, eight daily), Belgrade (€21, nine hours, daily) and, in summer, to the Bay of Kotor.

Pljevlja

☏052 / POP 19,500

The road over the vertigo-inducing Tara Bridge, 23km east of Žabljak, heads north to Montenegro's third-largest city. Although it has a long and fascinating history – excavations have revealed life in the town dating back 20,000 years, and the Romans also had a long stint here – Pljevlja (Пљевља) today doesn't quite live up to its previous glories. It's an industrial town, with a large coalmine and thermal powerplant. That said, Pljevlja is not without its charms: Montenegro's most impressive mosque is found here, there's a pleasant park to idle in, and much of the surrounding countryside is extremely pretty.

Despite its prominent mosques, Pljevlja is predominantly an Orthodox town (73%) and nearly half of the population identifies their ethnicity as Serbian, no surprise given the Serbian border is less than 10km away.

☉ Sights

Hussein Pasha Mosque　　　　MOSQUE
(Husein Pašina Džamija; ✆052-323 509; Vuka Kneževića bb) Built in 1569 and boasting the highest minaret in the Balkans (42m), this is the most beautiful mosque in Montenegro. Its interiors are unusual as they're painted with elaborate frescoes featuring geometric patterns and floral motifs. If it's locked (as it often is), you'll get a taste from the paintings around the entrance.

Holy Trinity Monastery　CHRISTIAN MONASTERY
(Manastir Sv Trojice) Dating from 1537, this impressive monastery occupies a sublimely peaceful nook tucked into the hills, 1km north of the town. Ottoman-style buildings hung with flowerboxes form a backdrop to a solid church with a sumptuously painted interior and gilded iconostasis. Behind the church, a small waterfall tumbles into a pond.

Pljevlja Heritage Museum　　　MUSEUM
(Zavičajni muzej; ✆052-322 002; www.muzejpljevlja.com; Trg 13 Jula bb; ◷8am-4pm Mon-Fri) FREE Though crammed into a small space in a dreary building, this little museum is home to some truly exceptional collections including ancient jewellery, rare costumes and prehistoric art discovered nearby. Its star attraction is an exquisite glass 'cage cup' from the 4th century BC. The cup is available for viewing if you make an appointment beforehand.

🛏 Sleeping & Eating

Hotel Pljevlja　　　　HOTEL €€
(✆052-323 140; hotelpljevlja@gmail.com; Kralja Petra bb; r/ste €30/60; P🅿❄🛜) This old state-run hotel may not be posh, but it's smack bang in the middle of town, and you won't find cheaper. All rooms have balconies, and

there's a decent restaurant on-site. You'll find it above a Maxi supermarket.

Tri Šešira　　　　MONTENEGRIN €
(✆052-352 005; Njegoševa 26; mains €4-9) Locals love this little place. The meals are huge, simple and hearty, and if you're looking to have a few drinks and meet the natives, this is a top place to do it.

ⓘ Information

Tourist Office (✆052-300 148; www.pljevlja.travel; Kralja Petra 43; ◷8am-4pm Mon-Fri)

ⓘ Getting There & Away

From the **bus station** (cnr Miloša Tošica & III Sandžačke; 🕿) buses head to Žabljak (€3.50, 1¼ hours, three daily), Mojkovac (€6, two hours, five daily), Kolašin (€7, 2½ hours, five daily), Podgorica (€7.50, four hours, eight daily) and Budva (€14, 5½ hours, two daily). International destinations include Belgrade (€19, seven hours, three daily) and Sarajevo (€10, five hours, daily).

Bijelo Polje

✆050 / POP 15,900

Montenegro's fourth-largest city, Bijelo Polje (Бијело Поље; pronounced 'bi-*ye*-lo po-lye') was once part of the evocatively named Sandžak of Novi Pazar, the Ottoman-controlled region that separated Montenegro from Serbia until 1912. Today almost 54% of the town's population identify as Orthodox and 45% as Muslim, with mosque minarets and church bell towers sprouting in nearly equal profusion. It's one of the most diverse cities of Montenegro.

'Bijelo Polje' means 'white field', a reference to centuries past when the area was supposedly covered in white flowers. Alas, it's not quite as picturesque today, but still, it's far from being derelict. The broad Lim River skirts the town centre, where you'll find lots of cafe-bars, pizzerias, banks and the post office.

🛏 Sleeping & Eating

Hotel Franca　　　　HOTEL €€
(✆050-433-442; www.francahotels.me/bijelopolje.html; Munib Kučevića bb; s/d/apt €40/60/100; P🅿❄🛜) This clean, modern hotel is right in the middle of town. Rooms are spacious, staff are helpful and there's a very good restaurant attached. It's the best option in Bijelo Polje.

ⓘ Information

Bijelo Polje Tourist Office (☑ 050-484 795; www.tobijelopolje.me; Nedeljka Merdovića bb)

ⓘ Getting There & Away

The bus station is on the highway, near the town centre. Services head in both directions on the Podgorica–Belgrade highway. There are frequent buses to Podgorica (€5.50, 2¼ hours), Mojkovac (€2, 40 minutes) and Belgrade (€15, seven hours).

There's a large train station further along the highway, 2.5km north of town, with services to Bar (€7.20, 3¼ hours, five daily), Podgorica (€5.20, two hours, six daily), Kolašin (€2.20, 30 minutes, six daily), Mojkovac (€1.20, 15 minutes, six daily) and Belgrade (€15, eight hours, two daily).

Rožaje

☑ 051 / POP 9500

Rožaje (Рожаје) is Montenegro's most easterly town, nestled within the mountainous folds bordering Serbia and Kosovo. Almost 95% of its population are Muslim, and the song of muezzins can be heard echoing from its minarets at prayer times. It's fascinating to sit by the main square and watch the evening promenade. While this social ritual is common to every town in Montenegro, here you'll spot plenty of men strolling together arm in arm and some women wearing hijabs (head coverings).

With a backdrop of rocky cliffs and plenty of old wooden houses achieving a look bordering on designer decrepitude, Rožaje could be very pretty indeed. The main thing preventing that happening is the scandalous state of the Ibar River, which seems to be used as the main waste disposal. Plastic bags full of household refuse line its banks as it gurgles through town.

◎ Sights

Ganića Kula　　　　　　　　　　TOWER
(Trg IX Crnogorske Brigade bb; ☺8am-4pm Mon-Fri)
FREE Residential towers of this sort were once common throughout eastern Montenegro, Kosovo and Albania. Not just a defence against invaders, a *kula* was particularly useful for protecting the menfolk during interfamily blood feuds. There's a revamped ethnographic **museum** inside the tower, with a well-presented collection of costumes, crafts and artefacts. The tower is a two-minute walk north from the main square.

ⓘ Information

Tourist Office (☑ 051-270 158; www.to.rozaje. me; 13 Juli bb; ☺8am-4pm)

ⓘ Getting There & Away

From Rožaje, the main highway continues into Serbia, 22km to the northeast. Montenegro's only border crossing with Kosovo is on a winding road heading southeast.

The **bus station** (☑ 051-271 115) is on the highway above the town centre, with services to Herceg Novi (€18, 7¼ hours, four daily), Bar (€10.50, five hours, daily), Ulcinj (€12, 5¾ hours, daily), Podgorica (€9.50, four hours, four daily) and Berane (€2.50, 40 minutes) for onward services to Plav and Gusinje. International destinations include Peja (€6.50, 1½ to three hours, daily), Prishtina (€11.50, four hours, daily) and Belgrade (€14, six hours, four daily).

Plav

☑ 051 / POP 3800

Heading from Andrijevica, the road to Plav (Плав) follows the Lim River through lush fields, and the imposing Prokletije Mountains (Montenegro's highest) begin to reveal themselves.

As if knowing that such beauty demands a mirror, Lake Plav (Plavsko jezero) has positioned itself to provide it. Devastatingly pretty, it swarms with tiny fish swimming between the reeds and water lilies, and a chorus of birds and frogs sing their contentment to call it home. The human occupants seem rather less appreciative, judging by the amount of rubbish washing into it from the township. The lakeside road passes a crop of massive turreted houses that either take their inspiration from fairy tales or nightmares, take your pick.

Plav is a predominantly Muslim town, with 80% of locals identifying their ethnicity as Bosniak or Muslim and a further 9% as Albanian.

Plav and nearby Gusinje are the best towns to access Prokletije National Park.

Plav is one of those towns that doesn't believe in street names, so you'll have to either ask for directions or wander through the twisting laneways of its hilly *čaršija* (old market area). The post office has an ATM attached and is near the main roundabout leading down to the *čaršija*. The area around the bus station is called Racina.

PEAKS OF THE BALKANS HIKING TRAIL

Winding 192km through the Accursed Mountains range, the border-hopping **Peaks of the Balkans** (PoB; www.peaksofthebalkans.com) hiking trail is the epitome of epic. The waymarked circuit, which runs through eastern Montenegro, northern Albania and western Kosovo, follows shepherds' paths and alpine trails along verdant valleys, remote villages and up (literally) breathtaking mountains; the highest point of the trail is 2300m. While there are other transnational hiking paths in Europe, this one is extra impressive, not only for its otherwise inaccessible, utterly astonishing scenery, but also the fact that it exists at all, given the centuries of bad blood between the countries and previously rigorously guarded borders.

Being a circular route, the trail has multiple entry points. Though the full hike takes between 10 and 13 days to complete, you can tailor your own trek; there are almost limitless shorter or alternative hikes to choose from, and it's possible to hop on and off to visit nearby historical sites, clamber up off-trail peaks or simply take a breather in relative civilisation.

Apart from wild camping, the only accommodation options along the trail are village guesthouses and homestays; the cultural immersion and traditional hospitality you'll receive are as magical as the mountains themselves. It's best to arrange your digs ahead of time; if you're not on an organised trek, local tourist offices can help.

Don't be lulled by its marketable name, the flash website and the fact that it's (mostly) signposted; the Peaks of the Balkans is not a journey to be undertaken lightly. Hikers should be fit and come equipped with proper equipment, including sturdy hiking boots, torches, GPS, phone (though don't count on reception), first-aid kit, sleeping bag, tent and waterproof clothing. June to October is the best time to make the trek, though inclement weather can strike at any time.

The trail meanders through some incredibly isolated areas: tackling it on your own is not recommended. Cross-border permits are required from each country you plan to cross in and out of, but these can be hard to arrange, especially from the Montenegrin side. We highly recommend engaging the services of a local adventure-travel agency to plan your trip. At present, Albania seems to have the best infrastructure for this, and there's also a good agency operating out of Kosovo.

If you don't want to join an agency-organised group trek, at the very least go with two or more friends. Better yet, hire a local guide; those listed on the PoB website have been trained by the DAV (Deutscher Alpen Verein; German Alpine Club).

◉ Sights & Activities

Redžepagića Kula TOWER
(Redžepagića tower) This defensive tower, slightly up the hill from the Redžepagić Mosque, officially dates to 1671, although it's possibly 16th century. The bottom two floors have stone walls over a metre thick, capped by a wooden storey with lovely jutting balconies.

Brezojevica Monastery CHRISTIAN MONASTERY
Three kilometres north of Plav, Brezojevica Monastery is a study in rural tranquillity. Meadows of yellow and purple flowers line the riverbank broken by the occasional abandoned stone building.

A stone gate, topped by a shiny golden Orthodox cross, leads from the highway. Inside the **Holy Trinity Church** (Crkva Sv Trojice) are the faded remains of original frescoes, although the only subject that's easy to discern is the Dormition of the Mother of God over the door.

The present structure of Holy Trinity Church was built in the 16th century on 13th-century foundations, but was damaged during WWII and left to decay, used only by the local Orthodox community for funerals. It's a testimony to the religious revival of recent years that the monastery is (very slowly) being restored.

Ask at the Plav Tourist Office if someone can let you in, or try your luck at the monastery; there's often someone about.

Lake Plav SWIMMING
(Plavsko jezero) The pier extending over the lake is a good spot to swim from, or you can hire paddle boats (€2 per hour) or kayaks (€1.50 per hour) nearby.

🛏 Sleeping & Eating

Aqua
BUNGALOW €

(📞069-889 759; visitaqua@gmail.com; Brezojevica bb; r/cabin €35; 🅿🛜) Hugging Lake Plav's western shore near the beginning of the road to Gusinje, this complex has simple free-standing bungalows (sleeping up to four people) and a handful of rooms with three single beds. It's a simple set-up but reasonably comfortable. Upstairs, the restaurant (mains €4 to €12) offers lake views to accompany pizza, pasta, salad, fish and gigantic meat dishes.

Komnenovo Etno-Selo
HOTEL €€

(📞067-638 311; www.kuladamjanova.com; Vojno Selo bb; s/d/ste from €40/55/70; 🅿🛜) Located on the south shore of the lake (reached by the back road from Plav), this large complex conjures up an 'ethno' ambience with its wood and stone construction. The theme continues with the traditional specialities served in the restaurant (breakfast is included in the room rates). Activities on offer include fishing, horse riding and guided mountain expeditions.

Restoran Abas
MONTENEGRIN €€

(📞069-611 503; www.facebook.com/restaurant. abas; mains €5-17; ⊙7am-11pm) Don't be put off by the alarming intergalactic-castle exterior; this is possibly the best restaurant in Montenegro's north. Inside, its elegant decor sets the tone for a superb dining experience, with excellent fresh lake fish, mouth-watering grills and a handful of vegetarian offers all crafted with flair and local, organic ingredients. The owners have extensive overseas restaurant experience, and it shows.

Abas is a three-minute drive from Plav's centre, just before the Lake Views campground. They also have some rooms (€20) available upstairs if you want to stick around for breakfast the next morning.

ℹ Information

Plav Tourist Office (📞051-250 151; www. toplav.me; Racina bb; ⊙8am-4pm Mon-Fri, 9am-3pm Sat) They don't speak much English but the staff here are friendly and surprisingly helpful, considering. They stock the *Prokletije Hiking & Biking* map (€5, scale 1:50,000), which outlines 10 bike paths and 15 hiking tracks.

Police Station (Jezerska bb) In theory at least, the Plav police should be able to help with organising cross-border permits for those taking on the Peaks of the Balkans trans-national hiking trail.

Gusinje

📞051 / POP 1700

Along with its big sister Plav, 10km away, Gusinje (Гусиње; pronounced '*gu*-si-nye') is the main gateway to the Prokletije National Park. It's a tidy, laid-back place with an idyllic setting, surrounded by verdant farmland and hemmed in by the rugged majesty of the Prokletije Mountains. You could easily lose a day exploring the back roads and villages by bicycle or car.

While the 1700-strong community is overwhelmingly Muslim, the town's two mosques coexist comfortably with both an Orthodox and a Catholic church. The most architecturally impressive is the 1626 **Vizier's Mosque** (Vezirova Džamija), a stone structure with a wooden porch and minaret similar to – but better preserved than – the mosques in Plav.

In the centre of Gusinje you'll find a post office, an ATM, cafes and plenty of options for pizza or *burek* (meat or cheese pastry).

⊙ Sights

Ali Paša Springs
SPRING

(Ali Pašini izvori) In a beautiful, bucolic setting at the foothills of the Prokletije Mountains, these karst springs are an ideal spot for a picnic. Locals extol the health benefits of drinking the springs' water, purportedly rich in therapeutic minerals. The springs are a five-minute drive – or an easy 25-minute hike – south of Gusinje.

🛏 Sleeping & Eating

Hotel Rosi
HOTEL €

(📞069-610 999; Gusinje bb; d/tr €35/50; 🅿🛜) On top of a supermarket and right by the bus stop, the family-run Rosi isn't big on glamour, but it is convenient, clean and comfortable. Its good restaurant will fatten you up nicely.

The family also offers village accommodation (from €25) in Vusanje, 5km south of Gusinje on the border with Albania.

Krojet
MONTENEGRIN €

(📞068-432 587; mains €4-9.50) At the Ali Paša Springs, this excellent restaurant and attached campground (sites €5) enjoy a beautiful, bucolic location. The atmospheric restaurant was once a watermill, and its rustic charm – not to mention the heaped dishes of local specialities – makes a meal here a memorable one.

ℹ️ Information

The **Prokletije National Park Visitors Centre**
(☑ 051-250 130; www.nparkovi.me; Alipašina
bb; ⊙ 9am-5pm Jun-Aug, 8am-4pm Mon-Fri
Sep-May) is at the southern end of town, en
route to Ali Paša Springs. They can help with
organising and recommending park activities, mountain guides and accommodation;
the attached shop sells books, guides and all
manner of locally made souvenirs. It also rents
snowshoes (€4 per day) and hiking sticks (€3
per day).

ℹ️ Getting There & Away

Buses to and from Plav (€2, four daily) stop
here. Four buses a day go to Podgorica (€11.50).
To access other bus routes, you'll need to go to
Berane (€4.50, 1½ hours).

Piva Canyon

The highway north from Nikšić meets the
Piva River after passing through 40km of
verdant farmland. It then tangos with the
river until they both reach the border at
Šćepan Polje. The river was blocked in 1975
by the building of the 220m-high hydroelec-
tric Mratinje Dam (Brana Mratinje), flooding part of the Piva Canyon (Кањон Пива) to
create the tremendously turquoise Lake Piva
(Pivsko Jezero), which plummets to depths
of more than 180m.

The road alongside the river is a feat of engineering in itself, clinging to the cliffs and
passing through 56 small tunnels carved out
of the stone. The narrow but equally spectacular route through the mountains from
Žabljak joins this road near Plužine, the Piva
region's unofficial capital. Heading north
from here the route gets even more dramatic, with the steep walls of the canyon reflecting in the toothpaste-blue waters below.

◉ Sights & Activities

Piva Monastery   CHRISTIAN MONASTERY
(Manastir Piva) Small Piva Monastery has an
intriguing history: originally constructed
between 1573 and 1586, it was the only Serbian Orthodox monastery to be built during
the Ottoman occupation (the Grand Vizier
was a relative of Piva's founder; connections
have always been everything in Montenegro). It hulked by the Piva River until the
late 1960s when plans for the Mratinje Dam
forced it to be moved – brick by brick, fresco
fragment by fresco fragment – over 12 years
to its current location near Gorankso village.

Piva Lake Cruises   BOATING
During summer, boats ply Lake Piva offering
cruises and expeditions to secret swimming
spots. The **tourist centre** (☑ 040-270 068;
www.pluzine.travel; Baja Pivljanina bb, Plužine) in
Plužine can give you the heads up on the
season's offerings, or you could go direct to
Zvono, where the English-speaking owner
runs excellent trips around the lake's coves
and caves, with breaks for hikes, beers and
swims. It also has a four-seater canoe available for lake jaunts.

🛏️ Sleeping & Eating

In addition to private rooms and apartments
in town, accommodation is available at the
rafting camps around Šćepan Polje and in
various *etno sela* ('ethno villages' offering
traditional digs) scattered around Plužine
and the back road to Žabljak.

The Plužine tourist centre website lists
loads of hotels and village accommodation
in the Piva region.

Zvono   GUESTHOUSE €
(☑ 069-471 893; www.zvono.me; ul Baja Pivljanina
bb, Plužine; s/d from €20/35; ℗ 🛜) Plužine's
surprisingly cosmopolitan Zvono ('Bell') offers characterful cottage accommodation,
fresh trout lunches and homemade *medovi-
na* (honey wine), best sipped in the cosy,
cluttered restaurant with Zvono's jazz-cat
owner. It also runs some of Plužine's best
boat cruises and offers canoe hire.

Sočica   MONTENEGRIN
(Baja Pivljanina bb, Plužine) This gorgeous old
cottage is worth a stop even if you're not
staying in Plužine. The traditionally dressed
waiters may take their time getting the delectable local specialities (think lamb, just-
caught trout and *cicvara*, akin to a creamy
polenta dish) to your table, but if you've got
a glass of their homemade *kruška rakija*
(pear brandy), you won't care one bit.

ℹ️ Information

Opening hours are seemingly decided on a daily
whim, but if they're open, drop into the Plužine
tourist centre for maps and information on activities, accommodation and more in and around
Plužine.

ℹ️ Getting There & Away

Plužine's tatty bus stop is on the highway at
the entrance to town. There are four buses a
day to Nikšić (€5.30, two hours). If you want to

get to Šćepan Polje (€2, 30 minutes), hop on a bus bound for Sarajevo (€9.50, four hours). A hideously timed 1am bus leaves nightly for Herceg Novi (€15, five hours).

There is no public transportation in Piva. If they don't have a car (usually an old VW Golf), locals travel by thumb.

Prokletije National Park

The Prokletije Mountains (Проклетије) are a huge, hulking expanse of wilderness forming the border with Albania and Kosovo. They're the southernmost – and highest – part of the Dinaric Alps. Surreally scenic and eerily remote, this magnificent area may well be one of Europe's least explored corners.

In 2009 a 160 sq km chunk of the Montenegrin side of the range was declared the country's fifth national park. Ambitious plans are afoot for the entire range to be declared a cross-border Balkans Peace Park (see www.balkanspeacepark.org). The epic Peaks of the Balkans (p123) hiking trail is a 192km circuit that crosses through all three countries.

Both the Montenegrin and the Albanian names for the range (Prokletije and Bjeshkët e Namuna, respectively) translate to the rather ominous-sounding 'Accursed Mountains'. Leave your hoodoo at home; this is a reference to the harsh environment of these sky-punching, jagged peaks rather than any high-altitude jinx.

🛏 Sleeping & Eating

Plav and Gusinje are good bases if you need access to facilities. Otherwise, the gorgeous Grbaja Valley, 8km from Gusinje and in the shadows of the range, has mountain huts and other basic accommodation. Wild camping is possible in the mountains, as are home stays in shepherds' huts; Gusinje's Prokletije National Park Visitors Centre can help with arrangements. Book ahead for all accommodation.

If you're heading up the mountains, you'll need to take all of your own supplies, including water.

Eko Katun Grebaje CABIN €
(☎069-044 572; ekokatungrebaje@live.com; Grebajska bb; per bed €10; ☺Apr-Oct) This collection of rustic, charming cabins is as flash as it gets out here. It's comfortable and quaint, the owner is a font of local knowledge, and its setting at the foot of the mountains can't be beaten. There's a restaurant attached, serving hearty regional dishes.

❶ Getting There & Away

From both Gusinje and Plav – the gateways to the park – yellow signs point to various walking tracks and give both the distance and estimated time required for each. Within a few hours, you can reach glacial lakes and mountain springs. Many trails run to and from the Grbaja Valley (*Dolina Grbaje*), 8km from Gusinje and 20km from Plav. There is no public transport out here, but you can catch a taxi to Grbaja from Plav or Gusinje.

Dubrovnik (Croatia)

POP 28,500

Best Places to Eat

➡ Pantarul (p138)

➡ Restaurant 360° (p138)

➡ Nishta (p138)

➡ Shizuku (p138)

➡ Amfora (p138)

Best Places to Sleep

➡ Karmen Apartments (p136)

➡ Villa Klaić (p136)

➡ Hotel Kompas (p137)

➡ Villa Dubrovnik (p136)

➡ Hostel Angelina (p136)

Why Go?

Why have we included a Croatian city in a book on Montenegro? The first reason is practical: many travellers to Montenegro fly into Dubrovnik Airport, which is, after all, only 17km from the border. More importantly, it seems inconceivable that you'd come this close and not visit one of the most beautiful cities in the entire Mediterranean, if not the world. Its proximity to the Bay of Kotor makes at least a day trip practically obligatory.

Dubrovnik is simply unique; its beauty is bewitching, its setting sublime. Regardless of whether you are visiting Dubrovnik for the first time or the hundredth, the sense of awe when you set eyes on the remarkable old town, ringed by its mighty defensive walls, never fades. Indeed it's hard to imagine anyone becoming jaded by the city's marble streets, baroque buildings and the endless shimmer of the Adriatic.

When to Go

➡ May and June offer warm sunny days, without the scorching heat or crowds of midsummer.

➡ Sate your cultural appetite during Dubrovnik's prestigious Summer Festival in July and August.

➡ September and October are still warm enough for swimming and the beaches aren't as crowded.

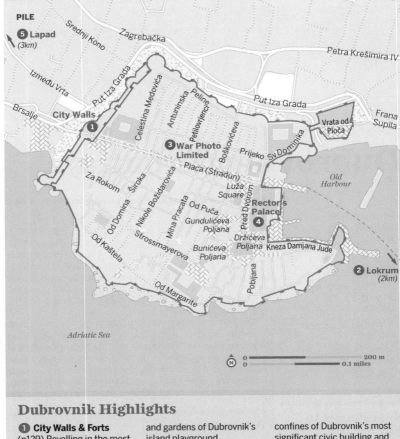

Dubrovnik Highlights

1 City Walls & Forts
(p129) Revelling in the most fascinating and touristy of activities: seeing Dubrovnik from the vantage point of its venerable walls.

2 Lokrum (p134) Taking the short ferry ride out to the beaches, forest, monastery

and gardens of Dubrovnik's island playground.

3 War Photo Limited
(p131) Visiting this affecting gallery and putting recent Balkan history in perspective.

4 Rector's Palace (p132) Wandering the rarefied

confines of Dubrovnik's most significant civic building and learning about the unique republic it once served.

5 Lapad (p135) Swimming in the crystal-clear waters of the bays scattered around the peninsula.

History

After the Slavs wiped out the Roman city of Epidaurum (site of present-day Cavtat) in the 7th century, survivors fled to the safest place they could find – a rocky islet separated from the mainland by a narrow channel. By the end of the 12th century the city they founded, Ragusa (later called Dubrovnik), had become an important trading centre on

the coast. It came under Venetian authority in 1205, finally breaking away from its control in 1358. Through canny diplomacy, the Republic of Ragusa maintained good relations with everyone – even the Ottoman Empire, to which it began paying tribute in the 16th century.

Centuries of peace and prosperity allowed art, science and literature to flourish, but most of the Renaissance art and architecture in Dubrovnik was destroyed in the earthquake of 1667, which killed 5000 people and left the city in ruins. The earthquake also marked the beginning of the economic decline of the republic. The final *coup de grâce* was dealt by Napoleon in 1808.

Caught in the cross-hairs of the war that ravaged former Yugoslavia, Dubrovnik was pummelled with some 2000 shells in 1991 and 1992.

◉ Sights

◉ Old Town

★ City Walls & Forts FORT
(Gradske zidine; Map p132; ☑ 020-638 800; www.wallsofdubrovnik.com; adult/child 200/50KN; ⊗8am-6.30pm Apr-Oct, 9am-3pm Nov-Mar) No visit to Dubrovnik would be complete without a walk around the spectacular city walls, the finest in the world and the city's main claim to fame. From the top, the view over the old town and the shimmering Adriatic is sublime. You can get a good handle on the extent of the shelling damage in the 1990s by gazing over the rooftops: those sporting bright new terracotta suffered damage and had to be replaced.

The first set of walls to enclose the city was built in the 9th century. In the middle of the 14th century the 1.5m-thick defences were fortified with 15 square forts. The threat of attacks from the Turks in the 15th century prompted the city to strengthen the existing forts and add new ones, so that the entire old town was contained within a stone barrier 2km long and up to 25m high. The walls are thicker on the land side – up to 6m – and range from 1.5m to 3m on the sea side.

Round **Fort Minčeta** (Tvrđava Minčeta; Map p132) protects the landward edge of the city from attack; **Fort Bokar** (Tvrđava Bokar; Map p132) and **Fort Lawrence** (Tvrđava Lovrjenac; Map p132; www.citywallsdubrovnik.hr; Pile; 50KN, free with city walls ticket; ⊗8am-6.30pm Apr-Oct, 9am-3pm Nov-Mar) look west and out to sea; while **Fort Revelin** (Map p132; Trg Oružja) and **Fort St John** (Tvrđava sv Ivana; Map p132) guard the eastern approach and the Old Harbour.

There are entrances to the walls from near the Pile Gate, the Ploče Gate and the **Maritime Museum** (Pomorski muzej; ☑ 020-323 904; www.dumus.hr; Tvrđava Sv Ivana; multi-

museum pass adult/child 120/25KN; ⊗9am-6pm Tue-Sun Apr-Oct, to 4pm Nov-Mar). The Pile Gate entrance tends to be the busiest, so entering from the Ploče side has the added advantage of getting the steepest climbs out of the way first (you're required to walk in an anticlockwise direction). Don't underestimate how strenuous the wall walk can be, especially on a hot day. There's very little shelter and the few vendors selling water on the route tend to overcharge.

Pile Gate GATE
(Gradska vrata Pile; Map p132) The natural starting point to any visit to Dubrovnik is this imposing city gate, built in 1537. While crossing the drawbridge, imagine that this was once lifted every evening, the gate closed and the key handed to the rector. Notice the statue of St Blaise, the city's patron saint, set in a niche over the Renaissance arch.

Large Onofrio Fountain FOUNTAIN
(Velika Onofrijeva fontana; Map p132; Poljana Paska Miličevića) One of Dubrovnik's most famous landmarks, this circular fountain was built in 1438 as part of a water-supply system that involved bringing water from a spring 12km away. Originally the fountain was adorned with sculptures, but it was heavily damaged in the 1667 earthquake and only 16 carved masks remain, with their mouths dribbling drinkable water into a drainage pool. Its

---

ℹ️ MUSEUMS OF DUBROVNIK PASS

Perhaps a cunning plan to get you through the doors of some of the town's smaller museums, nine of Dubrovnik's institutions can only be visited by buying a multimuseum pass (adult/child 120/25KN); individual tickets aren't available. Cleverly, the Rector's Palace is one of them – one of the city's higher-profile sights.

If you've bought the ticket mainly to visit the Rector's Palace and want to get your money's worth in a limited amount of time, we suggest you prioritise the rest in the following order: Museum of Modern & Contemporary Art, Maritime Museum, Archaeological Museum, Dulčić Masle Pulitika Gallery, Natural History Museum, Ethnographic Museum, Marin Držić House, Pulitika Studio.

Dubrovnik

DUBROVNIK (CROATIA)

0 0.5 miles

0 1 km

N

Adriatic Sea

Lapad Bay

BABIN KUK

LAPAD

GRUŽ

Gruž Harbour

Dubrovnik Bus Station

Dubrovnik Bus Station

Gruž Tourist Office

Jadrolinija

Obala Stjepana Radića

Ferry Terminal

SRĐ

PLOČE

PILE

Danče Beach

Gradac Park

Airport (25km)

Villa Dubrovnik (650m)

Old Harbour

See Dubrovnik Old Town Map (p132)

Jadranska Cesta

Jadranska Cesta

Vladimira Nazora

Petra Bakića

Gornji Kono

Od Gaja

Andrije Hebranga

Ante Starčevića

Pera Čingrije

Branitelja Dubrovnika

Ante Boškoviće

Zagrebačka

Gornji

Petra Krešimira IV

Frana Supila

Iva Vojnovića

Josipa Kosora

Liechtensteinov Put

Dr Roka Mišetića

Iva Dulči

Ivana Zajca

Vatroslava Lisinskog

Riječka

Kneza Domagoja

Primorska

Šetalište Kralja Zvonimira

Kardinala Stepinca

Šetalište Nika i Meda Pucića

Masarykov Put

Kralja Tomislava

Nikole Tesle

Dalmatinska

Od Batale

Sv Mihajla

Ispod Petke

Lapadska Obala

Lapad Peninsula

Obala Pape Ivana Pavla II

Don Frana Bulića

Srd

Srđ

Tourist Office

Tourist Office

Lapad

1
6

2
3
19

14
11

12
4

15

17

16

10
9
13
8

18

5

7

Dubrovnik

sibling, the ornate **Little Onofrio Fountain**, is in Luža Sq at the other end of Stradun.

Franciscan Monastery & Museum
CHRISTIAN MONASTERY

(Franjevački samostan i muzej; Map p132; ☑020-321 410; Placa 2; 30KN; ☺9am-6pm Apr-Oct, to 2pm Nov-Mar) Within this monastery's solid stone walls are a gorgeous mid-14th-century **cloister**, a historic **pharmacy** and a small **museum** with a collection of relics and liturgical objects, including chalices, paintings and gold jewellery, and pharmacy items such as laboratory gear and medical books.

★ War Photo Limited
GALLERY

(Map p132; ☑020-322 166; www.warphotoltd.com; Antuninska 6; adult/child 50/40KN; ☺10am-10pm May-Sep, to 4pm Wed-Mon Apr & Oct) An immensely powerful experience, this gallery features compelling exhibitions curated by New Zealand photojournalist Wade Goddard, who worked in the Balkans in the 1990s. Its intention is to expose the everyday, horrific and unjust realities of war. There's a permanent exhibition on the up-

per floor devoted to the wars in Yugoslavia; the changing exhibitions cover a multitude of conflicts.

Synagogue & Jewish Museum
SYNAGOGUE

(Sinagoga i Židovski muzej; Map p132; Žudioska 5; 50KN; ☺10am-5pm) With a religious practice that can be traced back to the 14th century, this is said to be the second-oldest still-functioning synagogue in Europe and the oldest Sephardic one. Sitting on a street that was once the Jewish ghetto, the synagogue also houses a small museum exhibiting religious relics and documentation on the local Jewish population, including records relating to their persecution during WWII.

Dominican Monastery & Museum
CHRISTIAN MONASTERY

(Dominikanski samostan i muzej; Map p132; ☑020-321 423; www.dominicanmuseum.hr; Sv Dominika 4; adult/child 30/20KN; ☺9am-5pm) This imposing structure is an architectural highlight, built in a transitional Gothic-Renaissance style and containing an impressive art collection. Constructed around the same time as the city walls in the 14th century, the stark exterior resembles a fortress more than a religious complex. The interior contains a graceful 15th-century **cloister** constructed by local artisans after the designs of the Florentine architect Maso di Bartolomeo.

Sponza Palace
PALACE

(Palača Sponza; Map p132; ☑020-321 031; Placa bb; May-Oct free, Nov-Apr 25KN; ☺archives display & cloister 10am-10pm May-Oct, cloister 10am-3pm Nov-Apr) One of the few buildings in the old town to survive the 1667 earthquake, the Sponza Palace was built from 1516 to 1522 as a customs house, and it has subsequently been used as a mint, treasury, armoury and bank. Architecturally it's a mixture of styles beginning with an exquisite Renaissance portico resting on six Corinthian columns. The 1st floor has late-Gothic windows and the 2nd-floor windows are in a Renaissance style, with an alcove containing a statue of St Blaise.

St Blaise's Church
CHURCH

(Crkva Sv Vlahe; Map p132; Luža Sq; ☺8am-noon & 4-5pm Mon-Sat, 7am-1pm Sun) Dedicated to the city's patron saint, this exceptionally beautiful church was built in 1715 in the ornate baroque style. The interior is notable

DUBROVNIK (CROATIA) SIGHTS

Dubrovnik Old Town

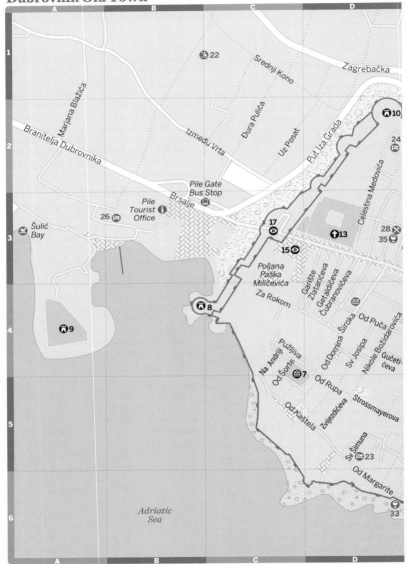

for its marble altars and a 15th-century silver gilt statue of St Blaise (within the high altar), who is holding a scale model of pre-earthquake Dubrovnik. Note also the stained-glass windows designed by local artist Ivo Dulčić in 1971.

⭐ **Rector's Palace** PALACE

(Knežev dvor; Map p132; ☑020-321 497; www.dumus.hr; Pred Dvorom 3; adult/child 80/25KN, incl in multimuseum pass adult/child 120/25KN; ⊘9am-6pm Apr-Oct, to 4pm Nov-Mar) Built in the late 15th century for the elected rec-

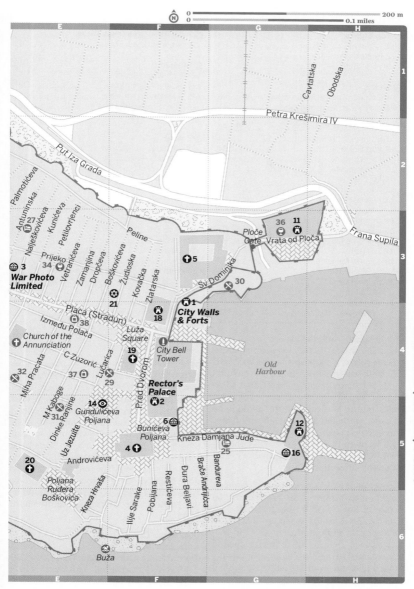

tor who governed Dubrovnik, this Gothic-Renaissance palace contains the rector's office and private chambers, public halls, administrative offices and a dungeon. During his one-month term the rector was unable to leave the building without the permission of the senate. Today the palace has been turned into the **Cultural History Museum**, with artfully restored rooms, portraits, coats of arms and coins, evoking the glorious history of Ragusa.

Dubrovnik Old Town

Dulčić Masle Pulitika Gallery   GALLERY
(Map p132; ☎020-612 645; www.ugdubrovnik.hr; Držićeva poljana 1; multimuseum pass adult/child 120/25KN; ☺9am-8pm Tue-Sun) This small off-shoot of the city's main gallery unites three friends beyond the grave: local artists Ivo Dulčić, Antun Masle and Đuro Pulitika, who all came to the fore in the 1950s and 1960s. There's a permanent collection featuring the trio's work on the lower floor, while the upper gallery is given over to temporary exhibitions by current artists.

Cathedral of the Assumption   CATHEDRAL
(Katedrala Marijina Uznesenja; Map p132; Držićeva poljana; treasury 20KN; ☺8am-5pm Mon-Sat, 11am-5pm Sun Easter-Oct, 9am-noon & 4-5pm Mon-Sat Nov-Easter) Built on the site of a 7th-century basilica, Dubrovnik's original cathedral was enlarged in the 12th century, supposedly funded by a gift from England's King Richard I, the Lionheart, who was saved from a shipwreck on the nearby island of Lokrum. Soon after the first cathedral was destroyed in the 1667 earthquake, work began on this, its baroque replacement, which was finished in 1713.

◎ Surrounds

★ Lokrum   ISLAND
(☎020-311 738; www.lokrum.hr; adult/child incl boat 150/25KN; ☺Apr-Nov) Lush Lokrum is a beautiful, forested island full of holm oaks, black ash, pines and olive trees, only a 10-minute ferry ride from Dubrovnik's Old Harbour. It's a popular swimming spot, although the beaches are rocky. Boats leave roughly hourly in summer (half-hourly in July and August). The public boat ticket price includes the entrance fee, but if you arrive with another boat, you're required to pay 120KN at the information centre on the island.

Dubrovnik During the Homeland War   MUSEUM
(Dubrovnik u Domovinskom ratu; Map p130; ☎020-324 856; Fort Imperial, Srđ; adult/child 30/15KN; ☺8am-10pm; Ⓟ) Set inside the crumbling Napoleonic Fort Imperial (completed in 1812) near the cable-car terminus, this permanent exhibition is dedicated to the siege of Dubrovnik during the 'Homeland War', as the 1990s war is dubbed in Croatia. By re-

taining control of the fort, the local defenders ensured that the city wasn't captured. If the displays are understandably one-sided and overly wordy, they still provide in-depth coverage of the events, including video footage.

Museum of Modern Art   GALLERY
(Umjetnička galerija; Map p130; ☑020-426 590; www.ugdubrovnik.hr; Frana Supila 23, Ploče; with multimuseum pass adult/child 120/25KN; ☺9am-8pm Tue-Sun) Spread over three floors of a significant modernist building east of the old town, this excellent gallery showcases Croatian artists, particularly painter Vlaho Bukovac from nearby Cavtat. Head up to the sculpture terrace for excellent views.

🏃 Activities

Swimming

Banje Beach   SWIMMING
(Map p130; www.banjebeach.com; Frana Supila 10, Ploče) Banje Beach is the closest beach to the old town, just beyond the 17th-century Lazareti (a former quarantine station) outside Ploče Gate. Although many people rent lounge chairs and parasols from the beach club, there's no problem with just flinging a towel on the beach if you can find a space.

Bellevue Beach   SWIMMING
(Map p130; Montovjerna) The nicest beach within an easy walk of the old town is below the Hotel Bellevue. This pebbly cove is sheltered by high cliffs, which provide a platform for daredevil cliff divers but also cast a shadow over the beach by late afternoon – a boon on a scorching day. Public access is via a steep staircase off Kotorska.

Lapad Bay   SWIMMING
(Uvala Lapad; Map p130; Lapad) Bounded by the forested Petka hills on one side and the crest of Babin Kuk on the other, Lapad Bay is a busy string of pebble beaches, beachfront hotels and pedestrianised promenades. There are plenty of diversions here, both in and out of the water, including a kids' playground and lots of cafes and bars.

Copacabana Beach   SWIMMING
(Map p130; www.thebeachdubrovnik.com; Ivana Zajca bb, Babin Kuk) Facing the bridge on the northern coast of Babin Kuk, this pebbly strip has lots of facilities including showers, loungers, an inflatable floating playground, a vine-covered restaurant, masseurs, and kayaks and jet skis for hire.

Kayaking

Adriatic Kayak Tours   KAYAKING, CYCLING
(Map p132; ☑020-312 770; www.adriatickayak tours.com; Zrinsko Frankopanska 6, Pile; half-day from 280KN; ☺Apr-Oct) Offers sea-kayak excursions (from a half-day paddle to a weeklong trip), hiking and cycling tours, and Montenegro getaways (including rafting).

Outdoor Croatia   KAYAKING
(Map p130; ☑020-418 282; www.outdoorcroatia. com; day trip 440KN) Rents kayaks and offers day trips around the Elafiti Islands, along with multiday excursions and kayaking-cycling combos.

Other Activities

Blue Planet Diving   DIVING
(Map p130; ☑091 89 90 973; www.blueplanet-diving.com; Dubrovnik Palace Hotel, Masarykov put 20, Lapad; half-day introductory/shore/boat dive €73/50/61) There's some great diving around Dubrovnik, including at the wreck of the *Taranto*, an 1899 Italian merchant ship that hit a mine during WWII. Blue Planet's experienced crew offers recreational dives and PADI courses.

Buggy Safari Dubrovnik   ADVENTURE
(Map p130; ☑098 16 69 730; www.buggy dubrovnik.com; cable-car terminus, Srđ; 1-/2-people trip 400/600KN; ☺Mar-Nov) Take a trip in a souped-up quad bike through the mountainous nether regions of Srđ, visiting forts and a farm. Expect to come back caked in mud and dust.

ℹ DUBROVNIK CARD

If you want to get through all the essential sights of Dubrovnik in one day, it's well worth buying the Dubrovnik Card (250KN). If you were already planning on walking the city walls (200KN) and buying a museum pass (120KN), the 250KN card makes a lot of sense. Plus it scores you free rides on buses and discounts at various restaurants and shops. The card is available from tourist offices, hotels and museums.

✨ Festivals & Events

Feast of St Blaise
CULTURAL

(⊘3 Feb) A city-wide bash in honour of the town's patron saint, marked by pageants and a procession listed by Unesco as an 'Intangible Cultural Heritage' for remaining largely unchanged for almost a thousand years.

Carnival
CARNIVAL

(⊘Feb) Venetian-style masked high jinks, held in the lead-up to Lent (usually February).

Dubrovnik Summer Festival
CULTURAL

(Dubrovačke ljetne igre; ☑020-326 100; www. dubrovnik-festival.hr; ⊘Jul-Aug) The most prestigious summer festival in Croatia presents a program of theatre, opera, concerts and dance on open-air stages throughout the city from 10 July to 25 August. Tickets are available online, from the festival office just off Placa, and at various venues (up to one hour before the performance).

🛏 Sleeping

Dubrovnik is the most expensive city in Croatia. You should book well in advance, especially in summer. There's limited accommodation in the compact old town itself. If you want to combine a beach holiday with your city stay, consider the leafy Lapad Peninsula, 4km west of the centre.

🛏 Old Town

Hostel Angelina
HOSTEL €

(Map p132; ☑091 89 39 089; www.hostelange linaoldtowndubrovnik.com; Plovani skalini 17a; dm from €49; ❉🛜) Hidden away in a quiet nook of the old town, this cute little hostel offers bunk rooms, a small guest kitchen and a bougainvillea-shaded terrace with memorable views over the rooftops. Plus you'll get a great glute workout every time you walk up the lane. It also has private rooms in three old-town annexes (from €110).

★Karmen Apartments
APARTMENT €€

(Map p132; ☑020-323 433; www.karmendu.com; Bandureva 1; apt from €95; ❉🛜) These four inviting apartments enjoy a great location a stone's throw from Ploče harbour. All have plenty of character with art, splashes of colour, tasteful furnishings and books to browse. Apartment 2 has a little balcony, while apartment 1 enjoys sublime port views. Book well ahead.

City Walls Hostel
HOSTEL €€

(Map p132; ☑091 79 92 086; www.citywallshostel. com; Sv Šimuna 15; dm/r from €46/104; ❉@🛜) Tucked away by the city walls, this classic backpackers is warm and welcoming with a lively character. Downstairs there's a small kitchen and a space for socialising. Upstairs you'll find clean and simple dorms and a cosy double with a sea view.

Rooms Vicelić
GUESTHOUSE €€

(Map p132; ☑095 52 78 933; www.rooms-vicelic. com; Antuninska 10; r €80-120; ❉🛜) Situated on one of the steeply stepped old-town streets, this friendly, family-run place has four atmospheric stone-walled rooms with private bathrooms. Guests have use of a shared kitchenette with a microwave and a kettle. There's also a studio apartment for rent two streets down.

🛏 Viktorija

★Villa Dubrovnik
BOUTIQUE HOTEL €€€

(☑020-500 300; www.villa-dubrovnik.hr; Vlaha Bukovca 6; r/ste from €720/1260; 🅿❉🛜🏊) Gazing endlessly at the old town and Lokrum from its prime waterfront position, this elegant, low-slung, boutique hotel gleams white against a backdrop of honey-coloured stone. The windows retract completely to bring the indoor pool into the outdoors, but sun seekers can laze on a lounger by the sea or commandeer a day bed in the rooftop prosciutto-and-wine bar.

🛏 Pile

Guest House Biličić
GUESTHOUSE €€

(Map p130; ☑098 802 111; Privežna 2; r from 740KN; ❉🛜) The main attraction of this long-standing guesthouse is its gorgeous subtropical garden, with a guest kitchen on the terrace. Bedrooms are simple and clean, although you have to cross the corridor to reach your private bathroom. It doesn't have its own website but you can find it on major booking sites.

★Villa Klaić
B&B €€

(Map p130; ☑091 73 84 673; www.villaklaic dubrovnik.com; Šumetska 9; r from €120; 🅿❉🛜🏊) Just off the main coastal highway, high above the old town, this outstanding guesthouse offers comfortable modern rooms and wonderful hospitality courtesy of the owner, Milo Klaić. Extras include a small swimming pool, continental breakfast, free pick-ups (for longer stays) and free beer!

ENTER THE GAME OF THRONES

Dubrovnik is like a fantasy world for most people, but fans of *Game of Thrones* have more reason to indulge in flights of fancy than most, as a large chunk of the immensely popular TV series was filmed here. While Split and Šibenik were also used as locations, Dubrovnik has featured the most prominently, standing in for the cities of King's Landing and Qarth. If you fancy taking your own Walk of Shame through the streets of Westeros, here are some key spots:

Fort Lawrence (p129) King's Landing's famous Red Keep. Cersei farewelled her daughter Myrcella from the little harbour beneath it.

City Walls (p129) Tyrion Lannister commanded the defence of King's Landing from the seaward-facing walls during the Battle of the Blackwater.

Minčeta Tower (p129) The exterior of Qarth's House of Undying.

Rector's Palace (p132) The atrium featured as the palace of the Spice King of Qarth – they didn't even bother moving the statue!

Sv Dominika street The street and staircase outside the Dominican Monastery (p131) were used for various King's Landing market scenes.

Uz Jezuite The stairs connecting the **St Ignatius of Loyola Church** (Crkva Sv Ignacija Lojolskoga; Map p132; ☑ 020-323 500; Poljana Ruđera Boškovića 6; ⊙ 7am-7pm) to **Gundulić Square** (Gundulićeva Sq; Map p132) were the starting point for Cersei Lannister's memorable naked penitential walk. The walk continued down Stradun.

Gradac Park The site of the Purple Wedding feast, where King Joffrey finally got his comeuppance.

Ethnographic Museum (Etnografski muzej; Map p132; ☑ 020-323 056; www.dumus.hr; Od Rupa 3; multimuseum pass adult/child 120/25KN; ⊙ 9am-4pm Wed-Mon) Littlefinger's brothel.

Lokrum (p134) The reception for Daenerys in Qarth was held in the monastery cloister.

MirÓ Studio Apartments　　APARTMENT €€€
(Map p132; ☑ 099 42 42 442; www.mirostudio apartmentsdubrovnik.com; Sv Đurđa 16; apt €145-200; ❄🛜) Located in a quiet residential nook only metres from the sea, hidden between the old-town walls and Fort Lawrence, this schmick complex is an absolute gem. The decor marries ancient stone walls and whitewashed ceiling beams with design features such as uplighting, contemporary bathrooms and sliding glass partitions.

🛏 Lapad

Apartments Silva　　GUESTHOUSE €€
(Map p130; ☑ 098 244 639; Kardinala Stepinca 62, Babin Kuk; r from 660KN; 🅿❄🛜) Lush Mediterranean foliage lines the terraces of this lovely hillside complex, a short hop up from the beach at Lapad. The rooms are comfortable and well priced, but best of all is the spacious top-floor apartment (sleeping five). It doesn't have a website, but you'll find it on major booking sites.

Begović Boarding House　　GUESTHOUSE €€
(Map p130; ☑ 020-435 191; www.begovic-boarding-house.com; Primorska 17, Babin Kuk; r/ste/apt €90/140/160; 🅿❄🛜) At the time of writing, major renovations were under way at this long-standing family-run place. Plans for the two new floors include large two-bedroom apartments with amazing sea views. Below, the six private rooms all have bathrooms and fridges.

★**Hotel Kompas**　　HOTEL €€€
(Map p130; ☑ 020-299 000; www.adriaticluxury hotels.com; Kardinala Stepinca 21, Babin Kuk; r/ ste from €261/632; 🅿❄🛜🏊) Right by the beach at Lapad, this big hotel has more personality that you'd expect for its size, due in large part to interesting art, slick design and charming staff. The breakfast buffet is excellent and the outdoor pool is pleasantly cool on a scorching day (the indoor one's warmer).

Hotel Bellevue HOTEL **€€€**

(Map p130; ☑020-330 000; www.adriaticluxury hotels.com; Pera Čingrije 7, Montovjerna; r from €383; P✳@🛜🌊) Positioned on a cliff near the very beginning of the Lapad Peninsula (a 20-minute walk west of Pile Gate), this classy hotel has modern decor (despite its dated smoky-glass facade), excellent facilities and a top-notch restaurant. Best of all is the direct lift access to the gem of a cove below.

🍴 Eating

Oliva Pizzeria PIZZA **€€**

(Map p132; ☑020-324 594; www.pizza-oliva.com; Lučarica 5; mains 74-105KN; ⊘10am-11pm; 🛜🍴) There are a few token pasta dishes on the menu, but this attractive little restaurant is really all about pizza. And the pizza is worthy of the attention. Grab a seat on the street and tuck in.

★**Pantarul** MEDITERRANEAN **€€€**

(Map p130; ☑020-333 486; www.pantarul.com; Kralja Tomislava 1, Lapad; mains 108-180KN; 5-course tasting menus 390-410KN; ⊘noon-4pm & 6pm-midnight Tue-Sun; P🛜) This breezy bistro aligns its menu with the seasons and has a reputation for exceptional homemade bread, pasta and risotto, alongside the likes of steaks, ox cheeks, burgers and various fish dishes. There's a fresh, modern touch to most dishes.

★**Shizuku** JAPANESE **€€**

(Map p130; ☑020-311 493; www.facebook.com/ ShizukuDubrovnik; Kneza Domagoja 1f, Batala; mains 70-85KN; ⊘5pm-midnight Tue-Sun; 🛜) Attentive local wait staff usher you to your table in the clean-lined, modern dining room of this popular restaurant, tucked away in a residential area between Gruž Harbour and Lapad Bay. The Japanese owners will be in the kitchen, preparing authentic sushi, sashimi, udon, crispy *karaage* chicken and gyoza dumplings. Wash it all down with Japanese beer or sake.

★**Nishta** VEGAN **€€**

(Map p132; ☑020-322 088; www.nishtarestaurant. com; Prijeko bb; mains 98-108KN; ⊘11.30am-11.30pm Mon-Sat; 🍴) The popularity of this tiny old-town restaurant is testament not just to the paucity of options for vegetarians and vegans in Croatia, but also to the imaginative and beautifully presented food produced within. Each day of the week has its own menu with a separate set of cooked and raw options.

Taj Mahal BOSNIAN **€€€**

(Map p132; ☑020-323 221; www.tajmahal-dubrovnik.com; Nikole Gučetića 2; mains 75-210KN; ⊘10am-midnight; 🛜🍴) This tiny restaurant is like an Aladdin's cave and oozes a distinct Ottoman vibe. Order the *džingis kan* (dried beef, sausage, peppers and spring onions with curdled milk) and get a taste of everything Bosnian, or feast on spicy *sudžukice* (beef sausage).

★**Restaurant 360°** INTERNATIONAL **€€€**

(Map p132; ☑020-322 222; www.360dubrovnik. com; Sv Dominika bb; 2/3/5 courses 520/620/860KN; ⊘6.30-10.30pm Tue-Sun Apr-Sep; 🛜) Dubrovnik's glitziest restaurant offers fine dining at its best, with flavoursome, beautifully presented, creative cuisine, an impressive wine list and slick, professional service. The setting is unrivalled – on top of the city walls with tables positioned so you can peer through the battlements over the harbour.

★**Amfora** INTERNATIONAL **€€€**

(Map p130; ☑020-419 419; www.amforadubrovnik. com; Obala Stjepana Radića 26, Gruž; mains 95-165KN; ⊘noon-4pm & 7-11pm) From the street, Amfora looks like just another local cafe-bar, but the real magic happens at the six-table restaurant at the rear. Dalmatian favourites such as *pašticada* (stew with gnocchi) feature in a globetrotting menu alongside ramen noodles, falafels and cheeseburgers.

Restaurant Dubrovnik EUROPEAN **€€€**

(Map p132; ☑020-324 810; www.restoran dubrovnik.com; Marojice Kaboge 5; mains 110-230KN; ⊘noon-midnight; 🛜) One of Dubrovnik's most upmarket restaurants has a wonderfully unstuffy setting, occupying a covered rooftop terrace hidden among the venerable stone buildings of the old town. A strong French influence pervades a menu full of decadent and rich dishes, such as confit duck and perfectly cooked steak.

🍷 Drinking & Entertainment

Buža BAR

(Map p132; off Od Margarite; ⊘8am-2am Jun-Aug, to midnight Sep-May) Finding this ramshackle bar-on-a-cliff feels like a real discovery as you duck and dive around the city walls and finally see the entrance tunnel. However, Buža's no secret – it gets insanely busy, especially around sunset. Wait for a space on one of the concrete platforms, grab a cool drink in a plastic cup and enjoy the vibe and views.

Cave Bar More
BAR

(Map p130; www.hotel-more.hr; Šetalište Nika i Meda Pucića bb, Babin Kuk; ☺10am-midnight Jun-Aug, to 10pm Sep-May) This little beach bar serves coffee, snacks and cocktails to bathers reclining by the dazzlingly clear waters of Lapad Bay, but that's not the half of it – the main bar is set in an actual cave. Cool off beneath the stalactites in the side chamber, where a glass floor exposes a water-filled cavern.

D'vino
WINE BAR

(Map p132; ☑020-321 130; www.dvino.net; Palmotićeva 4a; ☺9am-midnight Mar-Nov; ☎) If you're interested in sampling top-notch Croatian wine, this convivial bar is the place to go. As well as a large and varied wine list, it offers tasting flights presented by cool and knowledgeable staff (three wines from 55KN) plus savoury breakfasts, snacks and platters. Sit outside for the authentic old-town-alley ambience, but check out the whimsical wall inscriptions inside.

Buzz Bar
BAR

(Map p132; ☑020-321 025; www.thebuzzbar. wixsite.com/buzz; Prijeko 21; ☺8am-2am; ☎) Appropriately named, this buzzy little bar is rocky and relaxed, with craft beer and cocktails being the main poisons – aside from those being exhaled by the recalcitrant smokers in the corner.

Revelin
CLUB

(Map p132; www.clubrevelin.com; Sv Dominika 3; ☺11pm-6am daily Jun-Sep, Sat Oct-May) Housed within the vast vaulted chambers of Fort Revelin, this is Dubrovnik's most impressive club space, with famous international DJs dropping in during summer.

Lazareti
ARTS CENTRE

(Map p130; www.arl.hr; Frana Supila 8, Ploče) Housed in a former quarantine centre, Lazareti hosts cinema nights, club nights, live music, folk dancing, art exhibitions and pretty much all the best things in town.

🛍 Shopping

Grad Market
MARKET

(Map p132; www.sanitat.hr; Gundulićeva poljana; ☺6am-2pm May-Oct, to noon Nov-Apr) Stallholders sell mainly produce, local artisanal

products and crafts at this open-air market. In summer traditional craft sellers stick around until late afternoon.

Uje
FOOD & DRINKS

(Map p132; ☑020-321 532; www.uje.hr; Placa 5; ☺11am-6pm Jan-Mar, 9am-9pm Apr, May & Oct-Dec, 9am-11pm Jun-Sep) Uje specialises in olive oils, along with a wide range of other locally produced epicurean delights, including some excellent jams, pickled capers, local herbs and spices, honey, figs in honey, chocolate, wine and *rakija* (fruit brandy). There's another **branch** (☑020-324 865; www.uje.hr; Od Puča 2; ☺9am-9pm Sep-Jun, to midnight Jul & Aug) around the corner.

ℹ Information

Dubrovnik's tourist board has offices in **Pile** (Map p132; ☑020-312 011; www.tzdubrovnik. hr; Brsalje 5; ☺8am-8pm), **Gruž** (Map p130; ☑020-417 983; www.tzdubrovnik.hr; Obala Pape Ivana Pavla II 1; ☺8am-8pm Jun-Oct, 8am-3pm Mon-Fri, to 1pm Sat Nov-Mar, 8am-8pm Mon-Fri, to 2pm Sat & Sun Apr & May) and **Lapad** (Map p130; ☑020-437 460; www. tzdubrovnik.hr; Dvori Lapad, Masarykov put 2; ☺8am-8pm Jul & Aug, 8am-noon & 5-8pm Mon-Fri, 9am-2pm Sat Apr-Jun, Sep & Oct) that dispense maps, information and advice.

Dubrovnik General Hospital (Opća bolnica Dubrovnik; Map p130; ☑020-431 777, emergency 194; www.bolnica-du.hr; Dr Roka Mišetića 2, Lapad) On the southern edge of the Lapad Peninsula.

Post Office (Hrvatska pošta; Map p132; Široka 8; ☺8am-8pm Mon-Fri, to 3pm Sat May-Oct, 8am-7pm Mon-Fri, to noon Nov-Apr)

ℹ Getting There & Away

AIR

Dubrovnik Airport (p172) is in Čilipi, 19km southeast of Dubrovnik. Both Croatia Airlines and British Airways fly to Dubrovnik all year-round. In summer they're joined by dozens of other airlines flying seasonal routes and charter flights.

DUBROVNIK (CROATIA) SHOPPING

ℹ CROATIAN PHONE CODES

To call the numbers in this chapter from within Croatia, you'll need to add the area code 020 to the number. From outside Croatia, dial your country's international access code (usually 00) and then 385-20, and then the number.

GETTING TO MONTENEGRO

Airport Transfer

There are no buses from Dubrovnik Airport to Montenegro, but you should be able to prearrange a transfer through a Herceg Novi travel agent or accommodation provider for about €40.

Bus

Up to six buses head to Kotor (124KN, 2½ hours) from Dubrovnik bus station each day, stopping in Herceg Novi on the way. The duration of the trip depends entirely on how busy the border is.

Car

The distance between the old towns of Herceg Novi and Dubrovnik is only 47km but the border crossing can cause major delays, particularly on the Croatian side; to be safe, allow an hour for the crossing during the peak season. There's a smaller, lesser-known border crossing on the tip of the Prevlaka Peninsula. We have been told that it's only supposed to be for locals, but we've never had a problem crossing there.

BOAT

The **ferry terminal** (Map p130; Obala Pape Ivana Pavla II 1, Gruž) is in Gruž, 3km northwest of the old town. Ferries for Lokrum and Cavtat depart from the Old Harbour.

Local ferries head to various Croatian islands and coastal towns. From April to October, **Jadrolinija** (Map p130; ☎ 020-418 000; www.jadrolinija.hr; Obala Stjepana Radića 40, Gruž) has two to six car ferries per week travelling between Dubrovnik and Bari, Italy (passenger/car from €44/59, 10 hours).

BUS

Buses from **Dubrovnik Bus Station** (Autobusni kolodvor; Map p130; ☎ 060 305 070; www.libertasdubrovnik.hr; Obala Pape Ivana Pavla II 44a, Gruž; ⏲ 4.30am-10pm; 📶) can be crowded, so book tickets in advance in summer. The station has toilets and a *garderoba* for storing luggage (5KN for the first hour then 1.50KN per hour).

Destinations include Split (130KN, 4½ hours, 21 daily), Zagreb (219KN, 9¼ to 11¾ hours, 10 daily), Sarajevo in Bosnia (175KN, 6½ hours, two daily), Ljubljana in Slovenia (300KN, 13 hours, two daily) and Trieste in Italy (459KN, 14¾ hours, daily).

Departure times are detailed at www.libertasdubrovnik.hr.

Getting Around

TO/FROM THE AIRPORT

Atlas runs the airport bus service (40KN, 30 minutes), timed to run around flights. Buses to Dubrovnik stop at the Pile Gate and the bus station; buses to the airport pick up from the bus station and from the bus stop near the cable car.

City buses 11, 27 and 38 also stop at the airport but are less frequent and take longer (28KN, four daily, no Sunday service).

Allow up to 280KN for a taxi to Dubrovnik.

CAR

The entire old town is a pedestrian area. Cars with Montenegrin plates are targets for vandals if they're left on the street, so you're best to park in a monitored car park. The **Ilijina Glavica Car Park** (Map p130; ☎ 020-312 720; Zagrebačka bb, Pile; per hour/day/week 40/480/2400KN; ⏲ 24hr) is a 10-minute walk above the Pile Gate.

PUBLIC TRANSPORT

Dubrovnik has a superb bus service; buses run frequently and generally on time. The key tourist routes run until after 2am in summer. The fare is 15KN if you buy from the driver, and 12KN if you buy a ticket at a *tisak* (news-stand). Timetables are available at www.libertasdubrovnik.hr.

Understand
Montenegro

History

Nothing about Balkan history is straightforward. In this part of the world, events that are centuries old factor heavily in the national consciousness and in the (occasionally heated) public discourse. State boundaries have changed continuously down the ages – since WWI alone, Montenegro has gone through seven incarnations – and each ethnic and religious group has their own tales to tell, making this a complex country with many distinct histories.

The Illyrians & the Romans

The Illyrians were the first known people to inhabit the region, arriving during the late Iron Age. By 1000 BCE a common Illyrian language and culture had spread across much of the Balkans. Interaction among groups was not always friendly – hill forts were the most common form of settlement – but distinctive Illyrian art forms such as amber and bronze jewellery evolved. In time the Illyrians established a loose federation of tribes centred in what is now North Macedonia and northern Albania.

Maritime Greeks created coastal colonies on the sites of some Illyrian settlements around 400 BCE. Thereafter Hellenic culture gradually spread out from Greek centres, particularly from Bouthoe (Budva). The Romans eventually followed, initially at the behest of the Greeks who sought protection from the Illyrian Queen Teuta. The Illyrians continued to resist the Romans until 168 BCE, when the last Illyrian king, Gentius, was defeated. The Romans fully absorbed the Balkans into their provinces and established networks of forts, roads and trade routes from the Danube to the Aegean. However, outside the towns, Illyrian culture remained dominant.

The Romans established the province of Dalmatia, which included what is now Montenegro. The most important Roman town in this region was Doclea (present-day Podgorica), founded around CE 100. Archaeological finds indicate that it was a hub in an extensive trade network.

Over the centuries, the Roman Empire gradually declined. Invaders from the north and west began encroaching on Roman territory and in 395 the empire was formally split, the western half retaining Rome

TIMELINE	300 BCE	231–228 BCE	CE 100
	Illyrian tribes achieve supremacy in the Balkans, founding city states (including one at Lake Skadar near the modern Montenegro–Albania border) and establishing themselves as maritime powers in the Adriatic.	Illyrian Queen Teuta establishes her base at Risan and pirates under her command roam the Adriatic, harrying the Romans, among others. Eventually the Romans bring her reign to an end.	Doclea (present-day Podgorica), a settlement established by the Illyrians, grows to become a significant city under Roman rule. It is home to up to 10,000 people.

as capital and the eastern half (which eventually became the Byzantine Empire) choosing Constantinople (present-day Istanbul). What is now Montenegro lay on the fault line between these two entities.

In the 6th century, the Byzantine Emperor Justinian took control of the previously Roman-ruled parts of the Balkans, pushing out the Ostrogoths who had bowled through the region. He brought Christianity with him.

The Slavs Arrive

In around the early 6th century, a new group, the Slavs, began moving south from the broad plains north of the Danube. It is thought that they moved in the wake of a nomadic Central Asian people, the Avars, who were noted for their ferocity. The Avars tangled with the Byzantines, razing Doclea while roaring through the Balkans. They had too much momentum, however, rolling on and besieging the mighty Byzantine capital at Constantinople in 626. The Byzantines duly crushed them and the Avars faded into history.

Controversy remains as to the role the Slavs played in the demise of the Avars. Some claim that Byzantium called on the Slavs to help stave off the Avar onslaught, while others think that the Slavs merely filled the void left when the Avars disappeared. Whatever the case, the Slavs spread rapidly through the Balkans, reaching the Adriatic by the early 7th century.

Two closely related Slavic groups settled along the Adriatic coast and its hinterland: the Croats and the Serbs. Byzantine culture lingered on in the towns of the interior, thus fostering the spread of Christianity among the Slavs.

The Romans took advantage of the beautiful Adriatic coastline to build lavish seaside villas complete with mosaic floors, the remains of which are displayed in both Risan and Petrovac. Other Roman ruins can be seen at the site of Doclea, on the northern edge of Podgorica.

First Slavic Kingdoms

In the 7th century, the Bulgarians created the first Slavic state in the Balkans. By the 9th century, the Bulgarian Prince Boris was advocating that the Slavonic language be used for the church liturgy. The subsequent spread of Cyrillic script allowed various other Slavic kingdoms to grow as entities separate from Byzantium.

One such polity was Raška, a group of Serbian tribes that came together near Novi Pazar (in modern Serbia) to shake off Bulgarian control. This kingdom was short-lived, being snuffed out by Bulgarian Tsar Simeon around 927, but not before Raška recognised the Byzantine emperor as sovereign, further speeding the spread of Christianity in the region.

Soon another Serbian state, Duklja, sprang up on the site of the Roman town of Doclea. Under its leader Vladimir, Duklja swiftly expanded its territory to take in Dubrovnik and what remained of Raška. By 1040 Duklja was confident enough to rebel against Byzantine control, expand

395	614	800s	869
The Roman Empire is divided into two. Present-day Croatia and Bosnia land in the western half and Serbia in the eastern Byzantine Empire, while Montenegro sits on the dividing line.	The Avars sack the Roman cities of Salona (Split) and Epidaurum (Cavtat). The Slavic tribes follow in their wake, either as invited defenders or as opportunistic vacuum-fillers.	The first Serbian entity, Raška, arises near what is now the Serbian city of Novi Pazar. It is squeezed between the Byzantine and Bulgarian empires.	At the behest of Byzantium, Macedonian monks Methodius and Cyril create the Glagolitic alphabet, precursor of the Cyrillic alphabet, to help speed the spread of Christianity among the Slavic peoples.

its territory along the Dalmatian coast and establish a capital at Skadar (modern Shkodra in Albania). Around 1080 Duklja achieved its greatest extent, absorbing present-day Bosnia. Civil wars and various intrigues led to Duklja's downfall and power shifted back to Raška during the 12th century.

The Nemanjići & the Golden Age

The legacy of the Raška state can be seen in the Church of the Dormition in Reževići Monastery, founded by Stefan Nemanja, and Morača Monastery, founded by his grandson. Raškan royals feature in church frescoes throughout the country.

Stefan Nemanja (born near present-day Podgorica) was to establish the dynasty that saw Raška (which came to be known as Serbia) reach its greatest territorial extent. By 1190 he had regained Raška's independence from Byzantium, also claiming present-day Kosovo and North Macedonia for his kingdom. Nemanja later retired as a monk to Mt Athos in Greece, while his sons conquered further territory. After his death he was canonised by the Orthodox Church and became St Simeon.

Meanwhile, the Fourth Crusade in 1204 had hobbled the Byzantines, and Venetian influence began spreading through the Adriatic. In 1219 Sava, one of Nemanja's sons, made an agreement with a weakened Byzantium that the Serbian Church should be autocephalous (self-ruling), and appointed himself its first archbishop; he too was eventually canonised.

Around 1331 Dušan was proclaimed the 'young king'. He was to prove a towering figure in Serbian history, both physically (he was around 2m tall) and historically. He swiftly confirmed he was in control by chasing the Bulgarians out of Macedonia and capturing territory from the Byzantines. In expanding so rapidly under Dušan, Serbia became an 'empire', its territory doubling as it took in Serbs, Albanians, Bulgarians and Greeks. More than just an aggressive campaigner, Dušan also codified the Serbian law (known as the *Zakonik*) and established the Serbian Patriarchate. In linking the Orthodox Church with the Serbian royal line, Dušan also created a sense of cohesion among previously fractious Serbian tribes.

It seems that the Byzantines' first impressions of the Slavs weren't entirely positive. The Byzantine historian John of Ephesus remarked that they were 'rude savages'.

Nonetheless, throughout this period Zeta (as Duklja was now called) remained distinct from Serbia. Zetan nobles displayed a reluctance to submit to the Raškan rulers of Serbia, while the Raškan rulers generally appointed their sons to oversee Zeta, further indicating the separation of the two entities. As Raška became Serbia, so Duklja/Zeta is seen as the antecedent of Montenegro.

Enter the Venetians & Turks

During the reign of Dušan's son, Uroš, various factions tussled for power and the Balšić family rose to prominence in Zeta. The Balšići established a base near Skadar and began claiming territory along the Adriatic coast. In the north the Venetians reappeared, taking control of Kotor by 1420.

1015	1054	1166	1208
With the decline of the Bulgarian Empire, following the death of Tsar Samuil, Duklja arises as a Serb-controlled principality in the place of the recently departed Raška.	The Great Schism irrevocably splits Christianity into (eastern) Orthodox and (western) Catholic strands. Modern-day Montenegro lies on the fault line between the two.	Stefan Nemanja establishes the Nemanjić dynasty, a Serbian line that is to reign for more than 200 years. He is later recognised as an Orthodox saint.	Sava returns to the Balkans from the Orthodox monasteries at Mt Athos and begins to organise the Serbian Orthodox Church as a distinct ecclesiastical entity.

By the time Uroš died, Serbian barons were busy squabbling among themselves, oblivious to a greater threat that was steadily advancing through the Balkans: the Ottoman Turks.

By 1441 the Ottomans had rolled through Serbia and in the late 1470s they lunged at the previously unbowed region of Zeta. Ivan Crnojević led a beleaguered group of Zetan survivors to the easily defensible and inaccessible heights near Mt Lovćen, and in 1482 established a court and a monastery at what was to become Cetinje. Venetian sailors began calling Mt Lovćen the 'Monte Negro' (meaning 'black mountain'). Meanwhile, the Ottomans continued assailing Cetinje and succeeded in overrunning it in 1514.

Ottoman Control of the Balkans

Despite taking Cetinje, the Ottomans withdrew. This remote corner was inhospitable and barren, and in any case the Turks were more intent on controlling the Adriatic. Under Süleyman the Magnificent, the Turks took Belgrade in 1521, putting beyond doubt their dominance of the Balkans. That one rocky eyrie, Mt Lovćen, and its environs became the last bastion of Serbian Orthodox culture holding out against the Ottomans.

Despite being barely known in the rest of Europe, the Montenegrins retained a degree of autonomy. Innately warlike and uncontrollable, their behaviour was such that the Ottomans opted for pragmatism and largely left them to their own devices. With the Venetians extending their control in the Adriatic, taking Kotor and Budva, the Montenegrins found themselves caught between the Turkish and Venetian empires.

Through the 17th century a series of wars in Europe exposed weaknesses in the previously invincible Ottoman war machine. At one stage,

One of the more bizarre characters in Montenegrin history is Šćepan Mali, who emerged in 1767 claiming to be the murdered Russian Tsar Peter III. Šćepan hoodwinked the Montenegrins and succeeded in being elected to lead the *zbor* (council). His luck ran out when he was murdered in 1773.

HISTORY OTTOMAN CONTROL OF THE BALKANS

THE BATTLE OF KOSOVO POLJE

In 1386 the Ottoman Turks took the Serbian stronghold at Niš, then in 1389 at Kosovo Polje, the amassed armies of Serbian Prince Lazar and Ottoman Sultan Murat met. This proved to be one of the most pivotal events in Balkan history. Both leaders were killed and while neither side could conclusively claim victory, the Serbian empire was emphatically brought to an end and the Ottomans were free to continue their march into central Europe. Lazar's widow accepted Ottoman suzerainty and the battle entered Serbian legend, portrayed as a noble and ultimately hopeless act of Serbian bravery in the face of overwhelming odds.

The battle remains a defining part of Serbian identity to this day and partly explains Serb hostility to the notion of an independent, Albanian-dominated Kosovo. You'll see '*Kosovo je Srbija*' (Kosovo *is* Serbia) graffiti throughout Serbia and the Serb-identified parts of Montenegro, often accompanied by '1389', the date of the battle.

1331	1389	1420	1482
Allegedly the tallest man alive at the time, Dušan assumes the leadership and raises Serbia to be one of the largest kingdoms in Europe.	At the battle of Kosovo Polje, much of the Serbian nobility is killed by the invading Ottoman Turks. In time the Ottomans regroup and expand further into the Balkans.	Kotor begins 377 years under Venetian rule.	After a series of Ottoman attacks against Zeta during the late 1470s, Ivan Crnojević leads the remaining nobility to Cetinje, which will become the kernel of the Montenegrin state.

Sites related to
Ivan Crnojević
include the ruins
of his abandoned
fortress, Žabljak
Crnojevića, and
Cetinje Monas-
tery, which he
founded.

the Ottomans became determined to remove the concessions that the Montenegrins had long enjoyed and that they now considered rightfully theirs. Montenegrin resistance to the Turkish attempt to enforce a tax regime was violent and the Turkish retribution horrific. As Turkish reactions grew more violent, the bonds between previously unruly Montenegrin clans became stronger.

During the 1690s the Ottomans took Cetinje several times, but each time they were forced to retreat due to persistent harrying from Montenegrin tribesmen. At the conclusion of the Morean War in 1699, the Ottomans sued for peace for the first time ever, ceding territory at Risan and Herceg Novi to Venice. The Montenegrins' enthusiastic and effective participation in the war had brought them – and their martial virtues – to the attention of the Habsburgs and the Russians, while also furthering a sense of common purpose among the previously squabbling tribes.

It was then that the Ottomans finally realised they would not be able to control Montenegro; nonetheless they were clearly reluctant to give up their claim. To encircle it, they built a string of fort towns that attracted the Muslim population of the region. The Orthodox tribes and peasants remained in the countryside, developing a sense of solidarity and separateness from the relatively well-off town populations. For the locals, identity was tied to the notion of tribe and the Serbian Orthodox Church, rather than Serbia or Montenegro. Nonetheless, distinct Serbian and Montenegrin identities were evolving: the Serbs were directly ruled by the Ottomans, while the Montenegrins retained a degree of autonomy in their mountain fastness and had managed to avoid being entirely weighed down by the Ottoman 'yoke'.

The Vladikas

In 1696 Danilo Petrović-Njegoš was elected *vladika,* the equivalent of a bishop within the Orthodox Church hierarchy. Ambitious and warlike, he declared himself 'Vladika of Cetinje and Warlord of all the Serb lands'. In so doing, Danilo presumed a role as the leader of the Serbs, perhaps a reflection of Montenegrins dubbing themselves 'the best of the Serbs' during their years of battles against the Turks. Beyond this, Danilo succeeded in elevating the *vladika* role into that of a hereditary 'prince-bishop' – a political (and military) leader as well as a church leader – and founded the Petrović dynasty, which would rule Montenegro until WWI.

In 1766 the Ottomans established the Ecumenical Patriarchate in Constantinople, responsible for all of the Orthodox churches in the Ottoman domain. The Serbs later set up their own patriarchate in Habsburg territory, beyond the reach of Ottoman authorities. These moves effectively led to the creation of separate Montenegrin and Serbian Orthodox Churches and, while the Montenegrins retained some sense of community with the

1521	1593–1606	1667	1697
The Ottomans take Belgrade, thereby confirming their control of Serbia. The Venetians have been expanding along the Adriatic coast for more than a century and now control most of it.	During the Austrian–Ottoman wars, the pope attempts to incite the Montenegrins, as fellow Christians, to fight against the Ottomans, but with limited success. The Ottomans have control of Bar and Ulcinj.	A devastating earthquake hits the Adriatic coast, destroying much of Kotor, which is under Venetian control. The city has also recently endured an outbreak of plague.	Danilo becomes *vladika* (prince-bishop) and establishes the Petrović dynasty. He mediates disputes between tribes and clans, and within 15 years begins the fight back against the Ottomans.

Serbs, this was another factor in the divergent experience and the evolution of a separate national consciousness among the Montenegrins.

Dealing with the Great Powers

Napoleon appeared in 1797, claiming Venice's Adriatic territories, thus removing Montenegro's main rival for power in the Adriatic. The years to come saw Napoleon tangling with the Montenegrins, British and Austrians in the Adriatic. The Montenegrins operated with military support from the Russians and briefly captured Herceg Novi, a long-hoped-for Adriatic coastal town, but in the aftermath they were forced to abandon it due to diplomatic horse-trading.

In 1830 Petar II Petrović Njegoš became *vladika* upon the death of his uncle. Two metres tall, Njegoš fulfilled the requirement that the *vladika* be striking, handsome and dashing. Njegoš made further unsuccessful attempts to gain access to the sea, but in other aspects of nation-building he was more successful. He increased the role of government and developed a system of taxation for Montenegro. He also canonised his predecessor Petar I, thus bringing a saintly aspect to the role of *vladika,* in emulation of the saintly kings of medieval Serbia.

Njegoš made the now-traditional trip to St Petersburg in search of military and monetary support from the Russian tsars and set about modernising his nation, which was primitive and undeveloped. Succeeding Petrović rulers continued the process of modernisation, albeit gradually. Danilo came to power in 1851 and promptly declared himself prince, thus bringing an end to the ecclesiastical position of *vladika* as leader of the Montenegrins. In 1855 he won a great victory over the Ottomans at Grahovo and he skilfully steered a course between the interests of the Great Powers – Austria-Hungary, Russia, France and Britain – all of whom had designs on Montenegro and the broader Balkan region.

Nikola, who became prince after Danilo, pressed on with a road-building program and introduced the telegraph to Montenegro. He was also responsible for founding a school for girls in Cetinje, the first-ever such institution in Montenegro. During the 1860s Nikola established contact with Mihailo Obrenović, ruler of the Serbian principality (by then de facto independent from the Ottoman rule). The two leaders signed an agreement to liberate their peoples and create a single state. Most significantly, Nikola reorganised the Montenegrin army into a modern fighting force.

Freedom from the Ottomans

A rebellion against Ottoman control broke out in Bosnia and Hercegovina (BiH) in 1875. Both Serbs and Montenegrins joined the insurgency, Montenegrins (under Nikola) again excelling themselves and making

Elizabeth Roberts' lively and detailed history of Montenegro, *Realm of the Black Mountain,* is a must for anyone interested in the goings-on of this fascinating country.

HISTORY DEALING WITH THE GREAT POWERS

1784	1797–1815	1800s	1830
Petar I is consecrated as *vladika*, eventually becoming an enduring military and spiritual hero. In 1796 he defeats the Ottoman renegade Kara Mahmud and expands Montenegrin territory considerably.	Napoleon brings the Venetian Republic to an end; Venetian dominions are initially given to the Habsburgs, but in 1806 Napoleon gains the Adriatic coast, which he dubs the Illyrian Provinces.	Petar I courts Russia in the hope of military and financial support in the struggle against the Ottomans. Russia's interest waxes and wanes in the wake of other diplomatic priorities.	Petar II Petrović Njegoš rules as the last *vladika* and becomes one of the nation's most acclaimed leaders. His epic poem *The Mountain Wreath* is regarded as Montenegro's greatest literary work.

significant territorial gains. In the wake of the struggle for Bosnia, the Congress of Berlin in 1878 saw Montenegro and Serbia officially achieve independence from the Ottomans. Montenegro won control of upland territories in Nikšić, Podgorica and Žabljak and territory around Lake Skadar and the port of Bar, effectively tripling in size. The expansionist Austrians annexed BiH, thus stymying any further Montenegrin expansion to the north. The Montenegrins, however, managed to take control of the Ulcinj region of the Adriatic coast.

Petar I was not only a social and ecclesiastical leader; he is also credited with introducing the potato to Montenegro.

After 1878 Montenegro enjoyed a period of ongoing peace. Nikola's rule, however, became increasingly autocratic. His most popular move during these years was marrying off several of his daughters to European royalty, including two Russian monarchs. In 1910, on his 50th jubilee, Nikola raised himself from the role of prince to king.

In the early years of the 20th century, there were increasing calls for union with Serbia and rising political opposition to Nikola's rule. The Serbian King Petar Karađorđević (whose late wife was one of Nikola's daughters) was suspected of being involved in attempts to overthrow King Nikola, and Montenegrin–Serbian relations reached their historical low point.

The Balkan Wars of 1912–13 saw the Montenegrins patching things up with the Serbs to join the Greeks and Bulgarians in an effort to throw the Ottoman Turks out of Europe once and for all. During the wars, the Montenegrins gained Bijelo Polje, Berane and Plav, and in so doing bordered Serbia for the first time in more than 500 years. The idea of a Serbian–Montenegrin union gained more currency, and in the elections of 1914 many voters opted for union. King Nikola pragmatically supported the idea on the stipulation that both the Serbian and Montenegrin royal houses be retained.

WWI & the First Yugoslavia

Before the union could be realised, WWI intervened. Montenegro entered the war on the side of Serbia and the Allies. Austria-Hungary invaded shortly afterwards and swiftly captured Cetinje, sending King Nikola into exile in France. In 1918 the Serbian army entered Montenegro and the French, keen to implement the Serbian–Montenegrin union, refused to allow Nikola to leave France, formally bringing an end to the Petrović dynasty. The same year, Montenegro ceased to exist after being subsumed into the newly created Kingdom of Serbs, Croats and Slovenes – the first Yugoslavia.

Throughout the 1920s some Montenegrins, peeved at their 'little brother to Serbia' status, as well as the loss of their sovereignty and distinct identity, put up spirited resistance to the union with Serbia. This resentment increased after the abolition of the Montenegrin Church,

1851	1876–78	1910	1918
Njegoš' nephew Danilo becomes the country's first secular leader, taking the title 'prince'. He is assassinated in 1860, a victim of a blood feud with a rival Montenegrin clan.	Wars of independence see Serbia, Bulgaria and Montenegro finally win their freedom from the rapidly shrinking Ottoman Empire. Montenegro triples in size, gaining Nikšić, Podgorica, Žabljak and Bar.	Prince Nikola takes the title of 'king', raising eyebrows across Europe that such a diminutive and impoverished territory, home to only 200,000 souls, could really qualify as a kingdom.	The Kingdom of Serbs, Croats and Slovenes is created in the aftermath of WWI. Serbia's King Petar I Karađorđević assumes the monarchy. Montenegro is included within his domains.

which was subsumed into the Serbian Orthodox Patriarchate in Belgrade. Taking advantage of fears of a Serb–Croat civil war, on 6 January 1929 King Aleksandar proclaimed a royal dictatorship, abolished political parties and suspended parliamentary government, thus ending any hope of democratic change. In 1934, while on a state visit in Marseilles, King Aleksandar was assassinated by the fascist-inspired Croatian Ustaše.

Meanwhile, during the mid-1920s, the Yugoslav Communist Party arose; Josip Broz Tito was to become leader in 1937. The high level of membership of the Communist Party among Montenegrins was perhaps a reflection of their displeasure with the status of Montenegro within Yugoslavia.

WWII & the Second Yugoslavia

During WWII the Nazis invaded Yugoslavia on multiple fronts. The Italians followed on their coat-tails. After routing the Yugoslav army, Germany and Italy divided the country into a patchwork of areas of control. The Italians controlled Montenegro and parts of neighbouring Dalmatia. Some anti-union Montenegrins collaborated with the Italians in the hope that the Petrović dynasty would be reinstated. Meanwhile, Tito's Partisans and the Serbian Četniks (royalists) engaged the Italians, sometimes lapsing into fighting each other. The most effective antifascist struggle was conducted by Partisan units led by Tito. With their roots in the outlawed Yugoslav Communist Party, the Partisans attracted long-suffering intellectuals and antifascists of all kinds. They gained wide popular support with an early manifesto which, although vague, appeared to envision a postwar Yugoslavia based on a loose federation.

Although the Allies initially backed the Serbian Četniks, it became apparent that the Partisans were waging a far more focused and determined fight against the Nazis. With the diplomatic and military support of Churchill and other Allied powers, the Partisans controlled much of Yugoslavia by 1943. The Partisans established functioning local governments in the territory they seized, which later eased their transition to power. Hitler made several concerted attempts to kill Tito and wipe out the Partisans, but was unsuccessful. As the tide of the war turned, the Italians surrendered to the Allies and, with the Partisans harassing them, the Germans withdrew. On 20 October 1944 Tito entered Belgrade with the Red Army and was made prime minister.

The communist federation of Yugoslavia was established. Tito was determined to create a state in which no ethnic group dominated the political landscape. Montenegro became one of six republics – along with Macedonia, Serbia, Croatia, BiH and Slovenia – in a tightly configured union. Tito effected this delicate balance by creating a one-party state and rigorously stamping out all opposition whether nationalist, royalist

In 1904 the country was allied with Russia in the Russo-Japanese War, with Montenegrin volunteers fighting alongside their Slavic brethren in Manchuria. When peace was declared in 1905, Montenegro wasn't included in the treaty. It wasn't until 2006 – 101 years later – that a separate peace treaty was signed and the 'war' between Japan and Montenegro was formally over.

HISTORY WWII & THE SECOND YUGOSLAVIA

1941	1943	1945–48	1960s
Hitler invades Yugoslavia and divides it into areas of German and Italian control. Mussolini occupies Montenegro with plans to absorb it as an Italian protectorate.	Tito's communist Partisans achieve military victories and build a popular antifascist front. They reclaim territory from retreating Italian brigades. The Partisans eventually take control of Yugoslavia.	The Federal People's Republic of Yugoslavia is founded. In time, Tito breaks with Stalin and steers a careful course between Eastern and Western blocs, including establishing the nonaligned movement.	Tourism takes off in Yugoslavia, with a particular focus on the Adriatic coast. Hotspots such as Sveti Stefan attract the international jet set right up until the Yugoslav wars.

or religious. The border of the modern state was set: Montenegro won Kotor, but lost some areas of Kosovo in the horse-trading that Tito undertook in order to establish a balance between the various Yugoslav republics.

In 1948 Tito fell out with Stalin and broke off contacts with the USSR. This caused some consternation in Montenegro, given its historical links with Russia. Of all the Yugoslav republics, Montenegro had the highest per capita membership of the Communist Party, and it was highly represented in the army.

During the 1960s, the concentration of power in Belgrade became an increasingly testy issue as it became apparent that money from the more prosperous republics of Slovenia and Croatia was being distributed to the other republics, and not always fairly. Unrest reached a crescendo in 1971 when reformers called for greater economic autonomy and the loosening of ties within the Yugoslav federation, but nationalistic elements manifested themselves as well. Tito's 1974 constitution afforded the republics more autonomy, but the stage was set for the rise of nationalism and the wars of the 1990s.

Tito left a shaky Yugoslavia upon his death in May 1980. A presidency rotating among the six republics could not compensate for the loss of his steadying hand at the helm. The authority of the central government sank with the economy, and long-suppressed mistrust among Yugoslavia's ethnic groups resurfaced.

Union with Serbia, then Independence

As communism collapsed throughout Eastern Europe, Slobodan Milošević used the issue of Kosovo to ride to power in Serbia on a wave of nationalism. Montenegrins largely supported their Orthodox co-religionists.

In 1991 Slovenia and Croatia declared independence from the federation and the Yugoslav wars commenced. There was no fighting in Montenegro, but Montenegrin paramilitary groups, in conjunction with the Serb-dominated Yugoslav army, were responsible for the shelling of Dubrovnik and parts of the Dalmatian littoral. These acts appeared to serve no strategic purpose and were roundly criticised in the international press. In 1992, by which point BiH and Macedonia had also opted for independence, the Montenegrins voted overwhelmingly to remain in the Yugoslav state with Serbia. Admittedly there was some Montenegrin edginess about their place within 'Greater Serbia', and the autocephalous Montenegrin Church was revived in 1993.

As the bloody war in Bosnia wound down with the signing of the Dayton accords in 1995, Montenegrin Prime Minister Milo Đukanović began distancing himself from Milošević. Previously a Milošević ally, Đukano-

1979	**1980**	**1991**	**1997**
An earthquake registering 7.1 on the Richter scale causes large-scale devastation across the country; countless historic buildings collapse, rail lines are cut and 101 people die.	The death of President Tito prompts a genuine outpouring of grief. Tributes flow, but Yugoslavia is beset by inflation, unemployment and foreign debt, setting the scene for the difficulties to come.	Yugoslavia splits. As Slovenia, Croatia, BiH and Macedonia seek their independence, the question of Montenegrin independence is raised, but a year later Montenegrins vote to remain in Yugoslavia.	Milo Đukanović wins a further election victory. Montenegro adopts a pro-Western stance and distances itself from the Serbian position during the NATO raids in defence of Kosovo in 1999.

vić, who had been elected in 1991, realised that in the face of declining living standards and rising discontent, Montenegro would fare better if it adopted a more pro-Western course. In doing so he became the darling of Western leaders, who were trying to isolate and bring down Milošević. As the Serbian regime became an international pariah, the Montenegrins increasingly moved to re-establish their distinct identity. Political relations with Serbia rapidly cooled, with Đukanović winning further elections in Montenegro despite spirited interference from Belgrade. Nevertheless, Montenegro was bombed (though nowhere near as much as Serbia) during the NATO strikes of 1999, with Podgorica and its airport taking direct hits; eight civilians died.

In 2000 Milošević lost the election in Serbia, and in 2001 he was arrested; he died in prison in The Hague while on trial for war crimes. In 2003 the name Yugoslavia was consigned to the dustbin of history and Montenegro entered into a state union with Serbia. In theory, the union was based on equality between the two members but in practice, Serbia was such a dominant partner that the union proved infeasible from the outset. Again, this rankled, given the Montenegrins' historic self-opinion as the 'best of the Serbs'. In May 2006 a slim majority voted for independence and the modern state of Montenegro was formed.

In 1946 the Montenegrin capital was moved from Cetinje to Podgorica and renamed Titograd. In 1992 Titograd was changed back to Podgorica, which remains the capital.

The Đukanović decades

Đukanović and his Democratic Party of Socialists (DPS) maintained a tight grip on Montenegrin politics, with Đukanović himself switching between the role of prime minister and president several times. However, his tenure has been dogged by claims of corruption.

Montenegro's 2016 general election was a contentious affair, marked by protests. Đukanović alleged that Russia – with a little help from Serbia – was behind a coup plot to derail the elections due to his party's pro-NATO and EU stance. The Montenegrin prosecutor claimed the suspected would-be coup members planned to incite violence on election night, and to have Đukanović assassinated. Đukanović also accused his opposition of being funded by Russia, a charge they have denied. They in turn accused Đukanović's DPS of faking the attempted coup to improve their vote count. While opposition parties initially refused to accept the election results, the DPS was able to secure support in parliament from social democrats and parties of national minorities.

The DPS was finally unseated in the equally contentious 2020 parliamentary election, with a broad coalition comprising right-wing, left-wing and various nationalist and ethnicity-based parties taking control. Đukanović, however, remains as president – the next presidential elections are due to be held in 2025.

2003	2006	2007	2017
Yugoslavia expires and is replaced by the state union of Serbia and Montenegro. The union is intended to be an equal partnership but it rapidly proves unworkable.	In May Montenegrins vote in a referendum for independence from Serbia. With a slim majority (55%) voting in the affirmative, Montenegro declares independence in June.	Having the previous year become a member of the UN, Montenegro is admitted to the IMF and, continuing its pro-Western stance, signs a 'stabilisation and association' agreement with the EU.	Montenegro officially becomes the 29th member of NATO, despite domestic protests against joining the military alliance.

Montenegro's People

In this part of the world, questions of ethnicity are so thickly embroiled with history, politics and religion that discussions of identity can be a minefield. Yet to an outsider, the more you travel in the Balkans, the more you're struck by the similarities between its various peoples: the warm hospitality, the close family bonds, the social conservatism, the fiery tempers, and the passionate approach to life.

Ethnicity vs Nationality

Throughout the Balkans, people tend to identify more by ethnicity than citizenship. This is hardly surprising; a family that has never left its ancestral village may have had children born in Montenegro, parents born in Yugoslavia, grandparents born in the Kingdom of Serbs, Croats and Slovenes, and great-grandparents born in the Ottoman or Austro-Hungarian empires. Countries may come and go, but self-identity tends to stick around. It's understandable then that an Albanian, Bosniak (South Slav Muslim), Croat or Serb might not call themselves Montenegrin, even if their family has lived in the area that is now Montenegro for generations.

In the last census (2011), the country's main ethnic groups were Montenegrins (45%), Serbs (29%), Bosniaks (9%) and Albanians (5%). Tellingly, the next major group was 'Does not want to declare' at 5%. To give you an idea of the kind of ethnic knots people tie themselves in, smaller categories represented in the census include Montenegrin Serbs, Serb Montenegrins, Montenegrin Muslims, Muslim Montenegrins, Muslim Bosniaks, Bosniak Muslims, Bosnians and just plain Muslims.

In fact, these myriad ethnic identities have little to do with actual genetic heritage and despite the 29 ethnicities listed in the census, around 88% of the population could reasonably be labelled as some flavour of South Slav, with Albanians (5%) and Roma (1%) being the largest non-Slavic minorities. Scratch a little further and it's even more complicated, as numerous armies have raped and pillaged their way through these lands over the millennia.

Montenegrins are in the majority in most of the country, while Albanians dominate in the southeast (Ulcinj), Bosniaks in the far east (Rožaje and Plav), and Serbs in Herceg Novi (due to a large influx caused by the Yugoslav wars) and parts of the north and east (Plužine, Pljevlja, Bijelo Polje, Berane and Andrijevica).

Religion and ethnicity broadly go together in these parts. More than 72% of the population is Orthodox (mainly Montenegrins and Serbs), 19% Muslim (mainly Bosniaks and Albanians), 3% Roman Catholic (mainly Albanians and Croats) and only 1% atheist.

A popular self-belief is that Montenegro has a better tolerance of ethnic and religious minorities than many of its neighbours. This is possibly true, although you may still hear some mutterings from locals about the threat of a Greater Serbia/Albania/Croatia.

The fictional Nero Wolfe – of Rex Stout's famously hard-boiled detective stories – was a Montenegrin by birth. Stout chose Montenegro for Nero because he'd read that Montenegrin men were romantic, loyal, proud, brave and stubborn, traits that fit his intense character perfectly.

The Warrior Spirit

It's no surprise that the areas where people most strongly identify as Montenegrin are those that were part of Montenegro before the dawn of the 20th century, especially in the old heartland around Cetinje. This is where the archetype of the noble Montenegrin warrior, fierce in battle and devoted to freedom and the Orthodox Church, has its origins.

A staple feature of nearly every museum in Montenegro is a display of weapons. These aren't any old guns and swords. Inlaid with mother-of-pearl and set with precious jewels, these are finely crafted objects that have been handled with obvious love and care. The period architecture was solid and perfunctory and the paintings largely devotional, but when it came to making guns, the Montenegrins were happy to indulge themselves. Men weren't properly dressed without a pair of fancy pistols protruding from their waistbands; one can only imagine what kind of accidental injuries were sustained.

One of the most famous Montenegrin warrior stories (and there are many) is about Aleksandar Lekso Saičić, a volunteer in the Russian army in the Russo-Japanese War of 1904–1905. The oft-told tale – immortalised also in song – goes that the Russian commander asked for a volunteer to duel to the death with a legendary and hitherto invincible samurai. The cowardly Russian troops shuffled their feet, but the Montenegrin villager put his hand up and – in a whirl of savage sword clanging – decapitated the Japanese samurai, paid tribute to the body and gained instant *junak* (hero) status for life (and beyond).

The warrior spirit may traditionally have been at the heart of Montenegrin society, but today most people are keen to get on with their lives and put the turbulence of the last 25 years behind them. Gunshots can still be heard here but only in celebration. It's the traditional accompaniment to weddings and other festivities, as a flight from Ljubljana to Podgorica discovered when it took an accidental hit during celebrations for Orthodox Christmas Eve in 2008. There were no casualties.

Tied in with the warrior culture is the importance of *čojstvo i junašt-vo,* which roughly translates as 'humanity and bravery' – in other words, chivalry. In the past, it inspired soldiers to fight to the death rather than abandon their mates to the enemy or face the shame of being captured. While it might not have exactly the same practical application today, don't expect a Montenegrin to back down from a fight, especially if the honour of their loved ones is at stake. Luckily Montenegro doesn't (yet) attract stag-party groups – it doesn't take much to imagine the sort of reception that drunken louts would receive if they were stupid enough to be disrespectful to the local women.

Montenegrin Life

On a warm summer's evening, the main street of every town fills up, as they do throughout the Balkans, with a constant parade of tall, beautiful, well-dressed people of all ages, socialising with their friends, checking each other out and simply enjoying life. In summer, life is lived on the streets and in the cafes.

The enduring stereotype of Montenegrins is that they are lazy, an accusation that they themselves sometimes revel in. Certainly the cafes and bars are always full, but perhaps no more so than in the neighbouring countries. As a popular local joke goes, 'Man is born tired and lives to rest'. This accusation of indolence probably derived from the era when occupations other than fighting and raiding the neighbouring Turks were seen to be beneath a man's dignity. It's certainly not true of Montenegrin women, to whom all the actual heavy labour fell.

Montenegro's stirring national anthem – 'Oh, Bright Dawn of May' – celebrates its citizens' fierce independence and passion for the craggy country itself with lines like 'We love you, the rocky hills/And your awesome gorges/That never came to know/The chains of shameful slavery'.

MONTENEGRO'S PEOPLE THE WARRIOR SPIRIT

MONTENEGRIN VS SERB

The issue of identity is particularly thorny with regard to current Montenegrin–Serb relations. For centuries, Montenegrins considered themselves 'the best of the Serbs', keeping the flame of independent Serbian culture alive while their brethren elsewhere were under the Ottoman yoke. Pro-Serbian graffiti covers the country and while most Montenegrins feel a strong kinship to their closest siblings, this is usually coupled with a determination to maintain their distinct identity.

After negotiating a reasonably amicable divorce from the unhappy state union with Serbia in 2006, relations took a turn for the worse. In 2008 Serbia expelled Montenegro's ambassador after Montenegro officially recognised the former Serbian province of Kosovo as an independent country, joining around 50 other nations who had already done so. Serbia has vowed never to recognise Kosovo, which many Serbs view as their spiritual heartland.

The main unifying factor between Montenegrins and Serbs has traditionally been the Serbian Orthodox Church (SOC), but even that was shaken with the formation of the Montenegrin Orthodox Church (MOC) in 1993, claiming to revive the self-governing Church of Montenegro's *vladikas* (prince-bishops), which was dissolved in 1920. Furthermore, the MOC claims that all church property dating prior to 1920 should be returned to it. The SOC doesn't recognise the MOC and neither do the other major Orthodox denominations.

In December 2019 the Montenegrin government passed a law effectively transferring all SOC property built before 1918 to the state. Some international media have speculated that President Đukanović chose to ignite the ethnic divide in this way so as to divert attention from corruption allegations in advance of the 2020 elections. If that's the case, it backfired. The SOC promptly excommunicated President Đukanović and led major protests against the law, and Đukanović's party lost the election.

Montenegrin society has traditionally been rigidly patriarchal and women were expected to kiss a man's hand as a sign of respect. In 1855 Prince Danilo caused a scandal by publicly kissing the hand of his beloved fiancée; one of his officials berated him, saying: 'I would never kiss the hand of a woman or a Turk'. Despite major advances in education and equality for women during the communist years, distinct gender roles remain. If you're invited to a Montenegrin home for dinner, for example, it's likely that women will do all the cooking, serving of the meal and cleaning up, and it's quite possible that an older hostess may not sit down and eat with you but spend her whole time in the kitchen.

These days you'll see plenty of younger women out and about in cafes and bars. Literacy and employment levels are relatively equal, and basic rights are enshrined in law including (since 1945) the right to vote.

Montenegrin society has traditionally been tribal, with much emphasis placed on extended family-based clans. This can create the potential for nepotism; accusations that major employers and public officials favour family, friends or business associates are commonplace. Family ties are strong and people generally live with their parents until they are married. This makes life particularly difficult for gays and lesbians or anyone wanting a taste of independence. Many young people get a degree of this by travelling to study in a different town.

Although people have drifted away from the more remote villages, Montenegro isn't particularly urbanised, with about half of the populace living in communities of fewer than 10,000 people. Roughly a third of the population live in the two cities that have more than 20,000 people (Podgorica and Nikšić).

Football (soccer), basketball, water polo and handball are the national sporting obsessions. Given the national tendency towards tallness, it's little wonder you'll find Montenegrins playing in America's NBA. Current players include Orlando Magic's Nikola Vučević (2.13m), Nikola Mirotić (2.08m) of the Chicago Bulls and Minnesota Timberwolves' Nikola Peković (2.11m). Nikola is clearly a name of great stature.

Art & Architecture

Montenegro's historic preoccupation with religion and war focused its earliest artistic endeavours on sumptuously painted churches, beautifully crafted weapons and epic poetry. The modern stereotype of the bed-wetting poet whimpering on about romantic failures or fields of daffodils had no place in macho Montenegrin society; traditionally the role of the warrior and the poet went hand in hand. Peacetime in communist Yugoslavia saw a flourishing of divergent artistic expression, particularly in the fields of painting, sculpture, cinema and architecture.

Literature

Towering over Montenegrin literature is Petar II Petrović Njegoš (1813–51); towering so much, in fact, that his mausoleum overlooks the country from the top of the black mountain itself. This poet and prince-bishop produced the country's most enduring work of literature, *Gorski vijenac* (The Mountain Wreath; 1847), a verse play romanticising the struggle for freedom from the Ottomans. It's not without controversy, as the story glorifies the massacre of Muslims on Orthodox Christmas Eve in 1702, known as the Montenegrin Vespers. It's not certain whether it actually happened, but according to the story, Vladika Danilo, Njegoš's great-granduncle, ordered the leaders of the Montenegrin tribes to kill all of their kinspeople (men, women and children) who had converted to Islam. Some commentators have drawn a parallel between this story of ethnic cleansing and the atrocities that took place in Bosnia in the 1990s.

Following in the same epic tradition was Avdo Međedović (1875–1953), a peasant from Bijelo Polje who was hailed as the most important *guslar* (singer/composer of epic poetry accompanied by the *gusle*, a one-stringed folk instrument) of his time. If you think that 'Stairway to Heaven' is too long, it's lucky you didn't attend the marathon performance over several days where Međedović is said to have recited a 13,331-line epic.

He may have been born a Bosnian Croat, but Ivo Andrić (1892–1975), Yugoslavia's greatest writer, had a home in Herceg Novi. Andrić was awarded the Nobel Prize in 1961 for his brilliant *Bridge over the Drina* (1945). While you're rafting along the Tara River, it's worth remembering that the Tara becomes the Drina just over the Bosnian border.

Miodrag Bulatović (1930–91) was known for his black humour and graphic portrayals of dark subjects. His most famous books including *Hero on a Donkey* (1967), *The Red Rooster Flies Heavenward* (1959) and *The Four-Fingered People* (1975) are available in English.

Danilo Kiš (1935–89) was an acclaimed author of the Yugoslav period who had several novels translated into English, including *Hourglass* (1972) and *A Tomb for Boris Davidovich* (1976). He was born in what is now Serbia but moved to Cetinje with his Montenegrin mother after his Hungarian Jewish father was killed in the Holocaust.

Montenegrin-born Borislav Pekić (1930–92) was another significant name in Yugoslav literature. His huge oeuvre includes novels, dramas, science fiction, film scripts, essays and political memoirs. His work has been translated into many languages, but at present only the early novels

The Montenegrin language lends itself to poetry and it was once commonplace to frame formal language in verse. A British diplomat from the time of King Nikola reported that a government minister once delivered an entire budget in verse.

The Time of Miracles (1965), *The Houses of Belgrade* (1970) and *How to Quiet a Vampire* (1977) are available in English.

A popular modern author is Andrej Nikolaidis, whose novel *Sin* (The Son; 2011) won the European Union Prize for Literature and has been translated into English, alongside *Dolazak* (The Coming; 2009). Another one to watch is Ognjen Spahić, whose *Hansenova djeca* (Hansen's Children; 2004) – available in English – won a regional award.

Visual Arts

Northern Montenegro and other parts of the Western Balkans are a treasure trove of carved medieval tombstones known as *stećci*. Their origins and symbolism continue to puzzle archaeologists. A collection of *stećci* in Cetinje and the northern mountains were added to the Unesco World Heritage list in 2016.

Montenegro's fine-arts legacy can be divided into two broad strands: religious iconography and Yugoslav-era painting and sculpture.

The nation's churches are full of wonderful frescoes and painted iconostases (the screen that separates the congregation from the sanctuary in Orthodox churches). A huge number were produced by members of the Dimitrijević-Rafailović clan from Risan in the Bay of Kotor, who turned out 11 painters between the 17th and 19th centuries.

Earlier Serbian masters (predating Montenegro) include Longin, a monk from 16th-century Peć (in present-day Kosovo), whose unique approach to colour created otherworldly scenes of saints and Serbian royalty backed by blue mountains and golden skies. You'll find his work at Piva Monastery. Following him half a century later was Đorđe Mitrofanović from Hilandar (now in northern Greece), whose accomplished icons and frescoes feature in the Morača and Pljevlja monasteries. A talented contemporary of his was Kozma, who also worked at Morača.

Yugoslavia proved to be something of a golden age for the arts. Among the modern painters, an early great was Petar Lubarda (1907–74), whose stylised oil paintings included themes from Montenegrin history. Miodrag (Dado) Đurić (1933–2010) was known for his accomplished surrealist paintings and drawings, but he also produced engravings, sculpture and, in later years, digital work. In 2012 an offshoot of the Montenegrin Art Gallery devoted to 20th-century and contemporary art was opened in Cetinje and named in his honour.

Other names to look out for include Milo Milunović (1897–1967), Jovan Zonjić (1907–61), Vojo Stanić (born 1924), Filip Janković (born 1935), Dimitrije Popović (born 1951) and sculptor Risto Stijović (1894–1974). The best places to see the works of these and others are at Cetinje's Montenegrin Art Gallery and the museums and galleries of Podgorica.

MUSIC, SACRED & PROFANE

Archbishop Jovan of Duklja was producing religious chants in the 10th century, making him the earliest known composer in the region. Traditional instruments include the flute and the one-stringed *gusle*, which is used to accompany epic poetry.

The most famous Montenegrin musician of the moment is 30-year-old classical guitarist Miloš Karadaglić, who won the Breakthrough Artist prize at the 2012 Classical BRIT Awards and has been touring the world on the back of number-one recordings on the US, UK and Australian classical charts.

In the 1990s, the excruciatingly named Monteniggers carried the torch for homegrown hip-hop. Continuing on the unfortunate name theme, Rambo Amadeus is Montenegro's answer to Frank Zappa. He's been releasing albums since the late 1980s, flirting with styles as diverse as turbofolk, hip-hop and drum and bass – all with a large serving of laughs. In 2012 he created one of the more memorable Eurovision Song Contest moments, performing his song 'Euro Neuro' backed by a wooden 'Trojan donkey' and breakdancers.

If anyone doubts the relevance of Eurovision, they should travel through Montenegro. Montenegrins love their local pop, particularly if it's a gut-wrenching power ballad or a cheesy ditty played loud and accompanied by a thumping techno beat.

Of the contemporary crop, one to watch is Jelena Tomašević, whose paintings and video installations have been exhibited in New York, Berlin, Milan and Venice. Born in Belgrade to Montenegrin parents, performance artist Marina Abramović won the Golden Lion in the Venice Biennale in 1997. One of her most well-known pieces was *The Artist Is Present,* where she sat immobile in a chair in New York's Museum of Modern Art for 75 days while museum visitors took turns to sit opposite her.

Cinema

In the decade since independence, Montenegrin cinema has yet to set the world alight. Someone who's working hard to change that is Marija Perović, who is credited with being the country's first female film and TV director. She followed up her 2004 debut *Opet pakujemo majmune* (Packing the Monkeys, Again!) with *Gledaj me* (Look at Me) in 2008.

Montenegro-born Veljko Bulajić has been directing movies since the 1950s, with his most recent being *Libertas* in 2006. His *Vlak bez voznog reda* (Train Without a Timetable) was nominated for the Golden Palm at Cannes in 1959, while *Rat* (War) was nominated for the Golden Lion at the 1960 Venice Film Festival. In 1969 he wrote and directed *Bitka na Neretvi* (The Battle of Neretva), which was nominated for the Academy Award for Best Foreign Language Film.

Another noteworthy Yugoslav-era director was Živko Nikolić (1941–2001), who directed 24 features from the 1960s to 1990s.

Montenegro's biggest Hollywood success is cinematographer Bojan Bazelli, whose titles include *King of New York* (1990), *Kalifornia* (1993), *Mr & Mrs Smith* (2005), *Hairspray* (2007) and *Rock of Ages* (2012).

Ironically, the movie that springs to most people's minds when they think of Montenegro is the 2006 Bond flick *Casino Royale;* the Montenegrin scenes were actually shot in the Czech Republic. The Golden Palm–nominated *Montenegro* (1981), directed by Serb Dušan Makavejev, was set in Sweden.

Architecture

Traditional Montenegrin houses are sturdy stone structures with small shuttered windows and terracotta-tiled pitched roofs. In the mountainous regions a stone base is topped with a wooden storey and a steeply pitched cut-gable roof designed to let the snow slide off. The *kula* is a blocky tower-like house built for defence that's common in the country's far-eastern reaches. They are usually three to four storeys tall, with no windows on the lowest floor, and they sometimes have ornate overhanging balconies in wood or stone on the upper level.

The influence of Venice is keenly felt in the walled towns of the coast, which echo the spirit of Dubrovnik and other Dalmatian towns. Cetinje's streets include late-19th-century mansions and palaces remaining from its days as the royal capital.

It's easy to be dismissive of the utilitarian socialist architecture of the Yugoslav period, yet there are some wonderfully inventive structures dating from that time. James Bond would have been quite at home settling in with a martini beneath the sharp angles and bubbly light fixtures of some of the 1970s hotels. It would be a shame if those that haven't already been bowled over or modernised aren't restored to their period-piece glory.

As for the concrete apartment blocks of the cities, they may look grim but they're hardly the slums you'd expect of similar-looking housing projects in the West. While nobody seems to be charged with the upkeep of the exteriors, inside they're generally comfortable and well looked after.

ART & ARCHITECTURE CINEMA

The unusual *oro* is a circle dance accompanied by the singing of the participants as they tease each other and take turns to enter the circle and perform a stylised eagle dance. For a dramatic conclusion, the strapping lads form a two-storey circle, standing on each other's shoulders.

The Montenegrin Kitchen

Loosen your belt and pack pants one size up: you're in for a treat. Eating in Montenegro is generally an extremely pleasurable experience. By default, most of the food is local, fresh and organic, and hence very seasonal. Despite its small size, Montenegro has at least three distinct regional styles: the food of the old Montenegrin heartland, mountain food and coastal cuisine.

Montenegrin Heartland Specialities

The village of Njeguši on the edge of Lovćen (the black mountain) is famous for its *pršut* (smoke-dried ham) and *sir* (cheese). Anything with 'Njeguški' in its name is going to be a true Montenegrin dish and stuffed with these two goodies; this might be pork chops, veal, steak or spit-roasted meat *(Njeguški ražanj)*.

Old Montenegro extended to the Crnojević River and the upper reaches of Lake Skadar, where the cuisine is dominated by three main freshwater fish: eel *(jegulja)*, bleak *(ukljeva)* and carp *(krap)*.

Mountain Food

In the northern mountains, food was traditionally more stodgy, meaty and Serb-influenced, providing comfort and sustenance on those long winter nights. A traditional method of cooking is *ispod sača*, where meat and vegetables are roasted under a metal lid covered with hot coals, usually set in a hearth in the middle of the room for warmth. Lamb may also be slowly poached in milk with spices and potato *(brav u mljeku)* in a dish that's particularly popular in the Albanian areas. Beef is cooked with cabbage-like *raštan*, rice and red peppers to make a rich stew called *japraci*. You might eat it with *cicvara* (a cheesy, creamy polenta or buckwheat dish) or *kačamak* (similar but with potato). The best honey *(med)* is also produced in the mountains. The higher up you go, the better the *kajmak*, somewhat similar to a salty clotted cream. Slather it on bread, meat or potatoes, or just eat it straight.

Many people distil their own *rakija* (akin to schnapps or a very strong brandy). The most common variety in Montenegro is *loza*, made out of grapes, but it can be made from just about anything. It's offered as a sign of hospitality, so brace yourself – it typically ranges from 40% to 60% alcohol.

Coastal Cuisine

Sun-seeking holidaymakers, this is what you'll mainly encounter – and it's absolutely delicious. The food on the coast is indistinguishable from Dalmatian cuisine: lots of grilled seafood, garlic, olive oil and Italian-style dishes.

Hearty, flavoursome fish soup *(riblja čorba)* is a must-try, as is grilled squid *(lignje na žaru)* – the crispy tentacles coated in garlic and olive oil – and *punjene lignje*, served stuffed with *pršut* (smoke-dried ham) and *sir* (cheese). Nearly 400 years of Venetian rule have left a legacy of excellent risotto and pasta dishes. Black risotto *(crni rižot)* gets its rich colour and subtle flavour from squid ink and includes pieces of squid meat. Seafood risotto can also be white or red (made with a tomato-based sauce) and served hot or cold.

MONTENEGRIN WINE

Montenegro's domestic wine is eminently drinkable and usually the cheapest thing on the menu. *Vranac* is the indigenous red grape, producing excellent, full-bodied wines. It's traditionally aged in walnut rather than oak barrels and its history goes back an extremely long way. Illyrian Queen Teuta is said to have been particularly fond of the drop and encouraged its production in the 3rd century BC. Locally produced whites include chardonnay, sauvignon blanc and the native *krstač*.

While these dishes make filling mains, at a formal dinner they're just a precursor to the grilled fish. In most fish restaurants, whole fish *(ribe)* are presented to the table for you to choose from and sold by the kilogram according to a quality-based category. A standard portion is around 200g to 250g; ask for a rough price before you choose if you're unsure.

Local varieties tend to be small but tasty; the bigger ones are probably fresh but imported. Fish dishes are flavoured with wild herbs such as laurel and parsley as well as lemon and garlic. The traditional accompaniment is a delicious mixture of silver beet *(blitva)*, mushy boiled potato, olive oil and garlic, often referred to on English menus as a 'Dalmatian garnish'.

Regional Dishes

Various types of grilled meat are common throughout the former Yugoslavia, including *ćevapčići* (pieces of minced meat shaped into small skinless sausages), *pljeskavica* (spicy hamburger patties) and *ražnjići* (pork or veal kebabs). Grills are often served with fried potato chips and salad.

For dishes that have more than just meat (although not vegetarian), try *musaka* (layers of aubergine, potato and minced meat), *sarma* (minced meat and rice rolled in sour-cabbage leaves), *kapama* (stewed lamb, onions and spinach with yoghurt) and *punjene tikvice* or *paprike* (courgettes or capsicum stuffed with minced meat and rice). Other dishes include spicy Hungarian goulash *(gulaš)* and Turkish kebabs *(kebap)*.

The cheapest and most ubiquitous Balkan snack is *burek*, a greasy filo-pastry pie made with cheese, meat *(meso)*, potato *(krompir)* or occasionally mushrooms *(pečurke)*, most commonly consumed with yoghurt. Savoury or sweet pancakes *(palačinke)* are served from kiosks in busy areas. Toppings include chopped walnuts and almonds, jam and banana. For a major artery clog, go for a *slane* (salty) *palačinke* – a heart attack disguised as a crumbed, deep-fried, cheese-filled pancake.

The Main Meals

Breakfast *(doručak)* usually consists of fresh bread with slices of cheese and cured meat (salami or *pršut*) or perhaps a sweet pastry. Locals often skip breakfast and grab something like *burek* on their way to work. Omelette *(omlet)* is the most common cooked breakfast.

Lunch *(ručak)*, served midafternoon, has traditionally been the main family meal, but with Western working hours catching on, this is changing. A family lunch might consist of a soup followed by a salad and a cooked meat or fish dish of some description. Dinner *(večera)* would then be lighter, possibly just bread with cured meats, cheese and olives. However, if you're heading out for a proper sit-down evening meal, you'll probably start late (after 8pm) and eat a similar meal to the typical lunch.

Sweets are eaten at all times of the day, especially with coffee or after dinner. The most typical Montenegrin sweet dish is *priganice* (fritters) served with honey, cheese and jam *(džem)*. Incredibly sweet cakes and tortes are offered with coffee, including delicious baklava. The local ice cream *(sladoled)* is also excellent.

Though people round these parts tend to be a bit bewildered when faced with the prospect of people not eating meat (or – shock, horror – dairy products), there are ways around it. Thanks to the fairly common Orthodox tradition of not eating meat/animal products on certain holy days, many restaurants will have a *post* (Lent) menu on hand; ask your waiter for *posna hrana* (meatless food). Otherwise, pasta, pizza and salad are the best fall-back options; beware of ordering stuffed vegetables as they're likely to be stuffed with meat.

National Parks & Wildlife

'Wild Beauty', crows Montenegro's enduring tourism slogan, and indeed the marketing boffins are right to highlight the nation's extraordinary natural blessings. In the mountainous interior are pockets of virgin forest and large mammals, long since hunted out of existence on most of the continent, still hanging on – just.

Durmitor National Park

Montenegro's first three national parks were declared in 1952: Lovćen, Biogradska Gora and Durmitor. The most interesting and popular of the three is Durmitor, a magnificent place for nature lovers, blessed with springs of clear mountain water and glacial lakes that mirror the heavens. In 1980 it was recognised by Unesco as a World Heritage Site.

The 39,000-hectare park comprises the Durmitor mountain range and a narrow strip forming an elephant's trunk along the Tara Canyon. The Durmitor range has 48 peaks over 2000m including Bobotov Kuk (2523m), which is often referred to as the country's highest mountain. There's actually a higher peak in the Prokletije Mountains bordering Albania, but Bobotov Kuk is the highest mountain entirely within Montenegro. The Tara River is hidden in the deepest canyon in Europe (1300m at its apogee). It's not the sheer force of the water that has gouged such an impressive rift through the mountains, but rather the carbon dioxide in the water reacting with the hard limestone (calcium carbonate) to form soluble calcium bicarbonate.

Popular activities in the park include rafting (between April and October), skiing (from January to March), hiking, rock climbing and jeep safaris (best in summer). These can all be organised from Žabljak, the park's gateway town.

Lovćen National Park

Montenegro has 500 types of herbs with medicinal properties, many of which are harvested for essential oils and ingredients for natural remedies. Wormwood is an ingredient of absinthe and was once exported to Italy to make the bitter liqueur Amaro Montenegro.

Lovćen National Park's 6220-hectare offering is cultural as well as natural, encompassing the old Montenegrin heartland and the impressive mausoleum of the national hero, Njegoš. Like many of Montenegro's mountains, Lovćen is karstic in nature with craggy grey-white outcrops, sparse vegetation and, below, caves. Water disappears into the rock and bubbles up elsewhere to form springs.

Heading up Mt Lovćen (1749m), the lower slopes are covered in forests of black beech. Once these deciduous trees lose their leaves and their distinctive black trunks are bared, you'll understand why the Venetians named it the 'black mountain'. Higher up, the beech is joined by an endemic pine called munika. Healing and sweet-smelling herbs poke out from the rocky slopes, including sage, rosemary, balm, mint, chamomile and St John's wort.

Cetinje, Montenegro's historic capital, is a great place to base yourself while tackling the park's hiking and mountain-biking trails, although Kotor and Budva are also nearby.

Biogradska Gora National Park

The smallest of the national parks, Biogradska Gora covers a 5650-hectare chunk of the Bjelasica Mountains, which includes 1600 hectares of virgin forest – one of the most significant untouched stands remaining in Europe. Here you'll find groves of juniper, wild rose, pine, beech, maple, fir and elm trees, the tallest of which reach 60m.

There are no settlements within this park, but campsites and bungalows are available near the park office. Mojkovac is the nearest town, although Kolašin makes a better base. Hiking is great in summer but autumn is the best time to visit, when the leaves erupt in colour.

Lake Skadar National Park

In 1983 Lake Skadar became the country's fourth national park and the first non-mountainous one. Skadar is the largest lake in southern Europe, stretching between Montenegro and Albania, where it's called Shkodër. It's mainly fed by the Morača River in the northwest and drained into the Adriatic by the Bojana River at its opposite corner. The lake is what is known as a cryptodepression, meaning that the deepest parts are below sea level. The lake's marshy edges are carpeted with white and yellow water lilies, reeds, willows and edible water chestnuts. Rare endemic species of orchids may also be found.

Lake Skadar National Park protects 40,000 hectares on the Montenegrin side of the lake, but the whole lake is recognised by an international treaty, the Ramsar Convention, as a 'wetland of international importance'. It is home to a quarter of the world's population of pygmy cormorants and 262 other, mainly migratory, species including the great snipe and the great bustard (mind how you read that). Other fabulous flappers include the Dalmatian pelican, the largest of all pelicans, which is the poster bird of the park.

As well as birdwatching, activities include hiking, kayaking, swimming and boat trips to various island monasteries and fortresses. The weather is usually best in August. Virpazar is the main gateway, but other settlements include Murići, Vranjina and Rijeka Crnojevića.

Prokletije National Park

Montenegro's newest national park was declared in 2009, covering 16,000 hectares of the mountainous region on the border with Albania and Kosovo. It contains the country's highest peak, Kolac (2534m); on the Albanian side of the border, the Prokletije Mountains soar to 2694m. There has long been talk of declaring the entire range a cross-border Balkan Peace Park, but the politics have yet to be ironed out.

Ancient glaciers formed the Plav Valley on the edge of the mountains. Lake Visitor, in the mountain of the same name above Plav, has the unusual quirk of a floating island. Local legends say that it was once a raft used by the ancient shepherds to transport stock. Because it was well fertilised, it developed soil and foliage and now drifts around the lake.

Tourist infrastructure is limited in the gateway towns of Plav and Gusinje, but that is bound to improve. The park's potential for mountain biking, hiking and serious mountaineering has been realised with the establishment of the 192km Peaks of the Balkans transnational trail.

Wildlife

Many species of animals and birds have managed to find solace in Montenegro's hidden nooks. Precisely because those nooks are so hidden, you're unlikely to see any of the more dramatic mammals.

Birdwatchers are more likely to have their tendencies gratified with plenty of rare wetland birds congregating around Lake Skadar and near

The Bojana River occasionally performs the unusual trick of flowing upstream. This happens in winter when the swollen waters of its Albanian tributary, the Drim, cut across it and the volume of water forces part of the flow back into its source, Lake Skadar.

NATIONAL PARKS & WILDLIFE BIOGRADSKA GORA NATIONAL PARK

ENVIRONMENTAL ISSUES

Much of the credit for Montenegro's 'wild beauty' lies with the terrain itself. Its rugged contours haven't just hindered foreign invaders, they've limited population spread and the worst excesses of development. The Montenegrin government has realised the value of this by declaring the country the world's first 'ecological state', yet it remains to be seen what this means in a country where hunting is popular, recycling is virtually unknown and people litter as a matter of course. Despite trumpeting the existence of bears, lynx and wolves, no one knows what numbers remain. Hunting (illegal or otherwise) is of real concern.

On the coast, development continues unabated. With most of the Budva Riviera now given over to hulking resort complexes, attention has turned to the previously unspoiled Luštica Peninsula.

Ulcinj, and flashy birds of prey swooping over the mountains. King of them all is the golden eagle. It has a wingspan of up to 240cm and can sometimes supplement its rodent diet with lambs and small goats.

The big mammals (brown bear, grey wolves, Eurasian lynx) tend to keep their heads down so as not to have them blown off. Brown bears like to hang out in the forests at altitudes of 900m and higher. In 2000 there were estimated to be fewer than 130 remaining in Montenegro, concentrated in the northern and eastern mountains. Despite the male bears weighing up to 200kg, they pose little threat to humans unless they're protecting a cub or are startled.

Likewise, grey wolves don't pose much of a threat unless they're rabid or starving. They too fancy forest living, but may venture out into the meadows to make closer acquaintance with the odd bit of livestock. For this reason, there's still a price on their heads in some areas.

Look out for European otters going about their unspeakably cute business around Lake Skadar and the Tara River. Badgers hang out in Durmitor and Biogradska Gora national parks. Balkan chamois join roe deer in Durmitor, while the latter also wander the Lovćen and Bjelasica Mountains. Golden jackals are known to live around Bar and Ulcinj, with three packs spotted on Ada Bojana. Foxes, weasels, moles, groundhogs, hares, shrews, bats, wild boar, red squirrels and dormice complete the diverse mammalian picture.

More than half of Montenegro is more than 1000m above sea level and 15% is higher than 1500m.

If you're wandering the remote trails you'll often catch sight of something reptilian scurrying off the path. Montenegro has an impressive collection of lizards, newts, frogs, turtles and snakes. The isolated glacial lakes of the karstic mountain ranges harbour species such as the serdarski triton, a type of alpine newt that only exists in one small lake in Durmitor. The European pond turtle is listed as near-threatened but can still be spotted in both Lovćen and Lake Skadar national parks.

Of more interest or concern to most visitors are the snakes. Commonly spotted and often mistaken for a snake is the harmless slow-worm (sometimes called blindworm), a 50cm-long brown legless lizard. Rather less harmless is the horned viper. Reaching up to 95cm, this is the largest and most venomous snake in Europe. It likes rocky habitats (which doesn't rule out much in Montenegro) and has a zigzag stripe on its body and a distinctive scaly 'horn' on its nose. If you're close enough to spot the horn, you're probably a little too close. The good news is that this guy isn't at all aggressive and will only bite with extreme provocation, so mind where you tread.

Survival Guide

Directory A–Z

Accessible Travel

The mobility-impaired will find Montenegro's many cobbled lanes and numerous stairways – especially in 'old towns' – extremely challenging. There are very few specific facilities for either travellers or residents with disabilities. Some of the top-end hotels have wheelchair-accessible rooms.

Accommodation

Montenegro offers a great variety of accommodation. Booking ahead in the summer – especially on the coast – is essential.

Hotels Range from slick seaside offerings to off-the-beaten-track Yugoslav-style digs. Prices range accordingly.

Hostels Popping up in popular destinations but thin on the ground elsewhere.

Campgrounds Usually offer million-dollar views for penny-pinching prices. Facilities vary wildly.

PLAN YOUR STAY ONLINE

For more accommodation reviews by Lonely Planet authors, check out http://lonelyplanet.com/montenegro/hotels. You'll find independent reviews, as well as recommendations on the best places to stay.

Private accommodation Almost every town and village has private rooms (sobe) and/or apartments (apartmani) for rent.

Eco villages Wooden cabins in the countryside.

Camping & Caravan Parks

Facilities at camping grounds tend to be basic, often with squat toilets and limited water. Some national parks have cabin-style accommodation but most camping grounds don't. Charges are a combination of a nightly rate per vehicle, size of tent, number (and age) of guests and whether you require power or not. Camping grounds are most common along the coast (including the Bay of Kotor) and near Žabljak.

During summer, when shepherds in the mountainous areas take their flocks to the higher meadows, you can ask permission to pitch your tent next to one of their traditional katun dwellings. Some agencies, especially around Durmitor and Kolašin, can organise stays in a katun itself.

Though it's a Slovenian-based website, www.

avtokampi.si has a fairly thorough list of campsites in Montenegro.

Eco Villages

Traditional accommodation is offered in 'ethno' and 'eco' villages (etno i eko sela), particularly around Piva, and Durmitor and Prokletije National Parks. Quality can vary wildly, but generally accommodation is in rustic-style cabins, and meals come hot and hearty; rakija (fruit brandy) shots with the hosts are usually unavoidable. They're almost always run by families; if you're travelling with your brood, these are generally great for kids (think wide-open spaces, fresh air and plenty of livestock to pester).

Hostels

Hostels have made a relatively recent appearance on the scene, as they previously never fitted into tidy bureaucratic pigeonholes, being neither private accommodation nor a traditional hotel. Thankfully, that battle has been fought and won, and some great places have sprung up – particularly in Kotor, Budva, Ulcinj, Podgorica and Žabljak. Some are little different from private rentals split into dorms. The better custom-built places have well-thought-out communal spaces and offer a roster of activities. Most have

SLEEPING PRICE RANGES

Prices are very seasonal, and we've listed prices for the peak season (July and August). Expect to pay less in shoulder season (June and September) and considerably less in the off-season. In the ski resorts, the high season runs from January through to March, with the absolute peak around New Year. Discounts are often available for longer bookings.

All visitors are required to pay a small nightly tourist tax (usually less than €1 per person per night), which is sometimes included in the quoted rate but more often added to the bill at the end. This is almost always collected and paid by the accommodation provider; some private operators may leave it up to the guest to pay, but this is rare. The procedure varies from area to area and it can be nigh on impossible to find the right authority to pay it to. Theoretically you could be asked to provide white accommodation receipt cards (or copies of invoices from hotels) when you leave the country, but in practice this is almost never required.

The following price ranges refer to the cheapest option available for a couple.

€ less than €45

€€ €45 to €100

€€€ more than €100

some sort of kitchen; shared bathrooms are the norm.

Hotels

You'll find a large range of hotels of varying size and quality in the popular destinations. They usually have some form of restaurant attached and offer the option of half- or full board (breakfast plus one or two meals). In Montenegro, a hotel spa centre is called a 'wellness centre'.

Generally, the further you travel from Budva, the cheaper the average price. Tourist-focused Žabljak and Kolašin are the most (relatively) expensive of the northern centres, but you'll find bargains in the other towns.

Private Accommodation

The cheapest options in any given town are almost always private rooms and apartment rentals. These can be arranged through travel agencies or, in season, you may be approached at the bus stop or see signs hanging outside the houses (they often read 'Sobe/Zimmer/Rooms'). Some local tourist offices publish handy guides to private accommodation. Rooms in local homes shouldn't be

difficult to find, but some places will require minimum stays in high season (often a three-day minimum). Don't expect an en suite.

Apartments (apartmani) will always have their own bathroom and at least a kitchenette. Generally speaking, you'll get what you pay for. The cheaper options are usually a bit rougher and further from the attractions, but there shouldn't be a problem with cleanliness. For a range of luxurious apartments, some of which have swimming pools and cliff-top locations, try Explore Montenegro (www. montenegroholidays.com).

If you're armed with a bit of charm, an adventurous spirit, an unfussy attitude and a few words in the local lingo, it should be possible to turn up in remote villages and ask if anyone has any rooms to rent for the night. Some restaurants in out-of-the-way places also have rooms available that they don't otherwise advertise: just ask.

Children

Montenegrins absolutely adore babies and kids. For many parents this is half the battle won. Hotels, restaurants and cafes all warmly

welcome children, and we've even seen the occasional young teenager boogieing with their parents at beachside nightclubs.

With the relatively safe environment allowing them off the leash a little, older offspring should have a blast in Montenegro. You may find that they're kicking a ball around with the local scallywags in no time. The opposite is true for toddlers and small children, as a generally lower standard of safety regulations (missing railings, unfenced pools etc) means you'll have to keep a closer eye on them.

You'll struggle to get strollers along the cobbled lanes and stairways in the older towns and you'll often find yourself having to trundle them along dangerous roads due to parked cars blocking the footpaths. A baby carrier or sling takes up less luggage space and makes exploring easier. Still, bringing a pram is a good idea, if only so you can join the legions of other parents promenading with their sleeping babies on summer nights.

Any hurdles you may strike will be insignificant compared to the wonderfully family-friendly atmosphere, fresh air and gently lapping

Climate

Podgorica

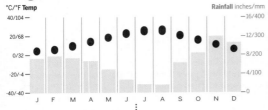

°C/°F **Temp**
40/104 —
20/68 —
0/32 —
-20/-4 —
-40/-40 —

Rainfall inches/mm
—16/400
—12/300
—8/200
—4/100
—0

J F M A M J J A S O N D

Mediterranean waters that Montenegro provides. Lonely Planet's *Travel with Children* offers further tips for hitting the road with the brood in tow.

Customs Regulations

➡ In a bid to stop tourists from neighbouring countries bringing all their holiday groceries with them, Montenegro restricts the quantity of food that can be brought into the country to a total of 5kg of fresh fruit and vegetables, and 1kg of other products.

➡ Restrictions apply to tobacco products (200 cigarettes or 50 cigars or 250g tobacco) and alcohol (1L spirits, 4L nonsparkling wine, 16L beer).

➡ Amounts greater than €10,000 of cash or travellers cheques must be declared when entering or leaving the country.

➡ Drug laws are similar to most other European countries. Possession or trafficking of drugs could

result in a lengthy jail sentence.

➡ When you enter the country you need to receive an entry stamp in your passport. If you don't, you may be detained or fined when you seek to leave for entering the country illegally.

➡ The Montenegro Customs Bureau has more information (some in English) at www. upravacarina.gov.me.

Discount Cards

➡ The **International Student Identity Card** (ISIC; www.isic.org), which is issued to full-time students aged 12 years and over, entitles the bearer to discounts on train trips and some admission charges, shops, eateries, accommodation and other services in Montenegro. It's available online, from student unions, hostelling organisations and some travel agencies.

➡ The same organisation issues the **International Youth Travel Card** (IYTC;

available to people who are between 12 and 26 years of age and not full-time students) and the **International Teacher Identity Card** (ITIC; available to teaching professionals), both of which give similar discounts to the ISIC.

Electricity

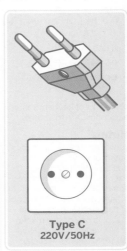

**Type C
220V/50Hz**

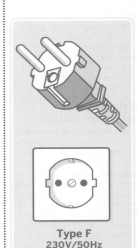

**Type F
230V/50Hz**

EATING PRICE RANGES

The following ranges refer to the average price of a main course.

€ up to €5

€€ €5 to €15

€€€ over €15

Embassies & Consulates

For a full list of foreign missions in Montenegro, see www.gov.me. The following are all in Podgorica, unless otherwise stated:

Albanian Embassy (Map p104; ☎020-667 380; www.mfa.gov. al; Capital Plaza, Bul Džordža Vašingtona 98)

Bosnia & Hercegovina Embassy (Map p104; ☎020-618 105; www.mvp.gov.ba; Atinska 58)

Croatian Embassy & Consulate Podgorica (☎020-269 760; www.mvep.hr; Vladimira Ćetkovića 2); **Kotor** (Map p48; ☎032-323 127; Trg od Oružja bb, Kotor)

French Embassy (Map p104; ☎020-655 348; www.amba-france-me.org; Atinska 35)

German Embassy (Map p104; ☎020-441 000; www.auswaertiges-amt.de; Hercegovačka 10)

Serbian Embassy & Consulate Podgorica (Map p104; ☎020-667 305; www.podgorica.mfa. gov.rs; Ivana Crnojevića 10); **Herceg Novi** (Map p39; ☎031-350 320; www.herceg novi.mfa.gov.rs; Trg Hercega Stjepana 15, Herceg Novi; ◷9.30am-1.30pm)

UK Embassy (Map p104; ☎020-618 010; www.gov.uk/government/world/montenegro; Ulcinjska 8)

US Embassy (Map p104; ☎020-410 500; www.podgorica. usembassy.gov; Ljubljanska bb)

The following countries are represented from offices in nearby countries:

➡ Australian Embassy
➡ Canadian Embassy
➡ Dutch Embassy
➡ Irish Embassy

Etiquette

Greetings Some Montenegrins (especially those of Serbian heritage) engage in a three-kiss hello.

Visiting Take off your shoes when entering a home. Montenegrins are typical Slavs and are obsessed with draughts and cold extremities; they'll have slippers for you. Bring a small gift, like wine or bag of coffee.

Conversation Politics, religion, history and ethnicity can be minefields; tread cautiously.

Religion Walk backwards out of a shrine.

Personal space Don't expect much; Montenegrins love to touch and huddle.

Dress Be modest when visiting religious buildings. Topless sunbathing is usually reserved for nudist beaches.

Eating If you're dining with locals, arrive hungry. This is a nation of feeders.

Drinking Engaging in a toast without eye contact may result in calamity, as will pouring your own *rakija* (fruit brandy).

Health

Good, affordable health care is readily available in Montenegro and for minor illnesses, pharmacists can give valuable advice and sell over-the-counter medication. They can also advise when more specialised help is required and point you in the right direction. The standard of dental care is usually good, but it is sensible to have a dental check-up before a long trip.

Recommended Vaccinations

There are no specific vaccinations required for visiting Montenegro. However, if you are over 18 and do not have evidence of being fully vaccinated for Covid-19 you will have to present evidence of:

➡ a negative PCR test taken within the previous 72 hours,

➡ or a negative rapid antigen test taken within the previous 48 hours,

➡ or a positive PCR or rapid antigen test which is older than 10 days and not older than 180 days since the date of issuing the test's result.

The World Health Organization (WHO) also recommends that all travellers be covered for diphtheria, hepatitis B, measles, mumps, pertussis (whooping cough), polio, rubella, tuberculosis, tetanus and varicella (chickenpox), regardless of their destination. You should also consider being vaccinated for hepatitis A. Since most vaccines don't produce immunity until at least two weeks after they're given, visit a physician at least six weeks before departure.

Tick-borne encephalitis is spread by tick bites and is thought to exist in forested areas of Montenegro. It is a serious infection of the brain and vaccination is advised for those in risk areas who are unable to avoid tick bites (such as campers and hikers).

The US Center for Disease Control recommends a rabies vaccination for long-term travellers, those involved in outdoor activities in remote areas, and people working around animals.

Sea Urchins

Watch out for sea urchins around rocky beaches; if you get some of their needles embedded in your skin, olive oil will help to loosen them. If they are not removed, they could become infected. As a precaution, wear rubber shoes while walking on the rocks and take care while bathing.

Snake Bites

To avoid getting bitten by snakes, do not walk barefoot or stick your hands into holes or cracks. Half of those bitten by venomous snakes are not actually injected with poison (envenomed). If bitten by a snake, do not panic. Immobilise the bitten limb with a splint (eg a stick) and apply a

EMERGENCY & IMPORTANT NUMBERS

International access code ☑00

Country code ☑382

Police ☑122

Ambulance ☑124

Roadside assistance ☑9807

bandage over the site firmly, similar to a bandage over a sprain. Do not apply a tourniquet, or cut or suck the bite. Get medical help as soon as possible so that antivenene can be administered if necessary.

Tap Water

As a general rule, tap water is drinkable in Montenegro but there can be problems. For instance, it's advisable not to drink the water in Herceg Novi in May as they close off and clean the pipes from the main reservoir (in Croatia) and revert to a local reservoir. Bottled water is cheap and readily available.

Insurance

A watertight travel insurance policy covering theft, loss and medical problems is recommended. While theft isn't a huge problem, rental cars are sometimes targeted by opportunists and Montenegro's roads aren't the world's safest. There are plenty of policies to choose from – compare the fine print and shop around.

If you're an EU citizen, you will be covered for most emergency medical care except for emergency repatriation home. Citizens from other countries should find out if there is a reciprocal arrangement for free medical care between their country and Montenegro. Strongly consider a policy that covers you for the worst possible scenario, such as an accident requiring an emergency flight home. Find out in advance if

your insurance plan will make payments directly to providers or if it will reimburse you later for any overseas health expenditures. The former option is generally preferable, especially if your finances are limited.

Some policies specifically exclude designated 'dangerous activities' such as scuba-diving, parasailing, paragliding, canyoning, white-water rafting, skiing and even hiking. If you plan on doing any of these things (a distinct possibility in Montenegro), make sure the policy you choose covers you fully and includes ambulances and emergency medical evacuation.

If you need to make a claim, ensure you obtain and keep all relevant documentation. This may involve a police report in case of theft and invoices for medical expenses incurred. Some policies ask you to call back (reverse charges) to a centre in your home country where an immediate assessment of your problem is made.

Internet Access

Most accommodation providers (including the majority of private accommodation, unless you're really in the back of beyond) offer free wireless connections, although they may not always penetrate to every part of the building and can be limited to the reception area. Many bars and cafes also offer wireless. You'll find free wireless access at tourist hotspots in bigger cities.

Some libraries and hotels offer terminals for guests to use, but this practice appears to be on the way out with the proliferation of personal devices.

We've used the internet symbol for accommodation that has a computer linked to the internet for guests to use. Places that have a wireless connection are marked with the wireless symbol. Note that the symbols don't imply that the service is free, but in most cases it will be.

Legal Matters

It may seem obvious, but while you are in Montenegro you're covered by Montenegrin laws, which may differ from those in your home country.

➡ If you're arrested, you have the right to contact your country's embassy or consulate and arresting officers have a responsibility to help you to do so. They're also required to immediately notify you of the charges you're facing in a language you understand and to inform you that you're not required to give any statement. You have the right to a defence counsel of your own choosing during any interrogation.

➡ A lower court can choose to detain you for three months pending trial, while a higher court can extend this for a further three months. Minors may not be held for more than 60 days.

➡ The Montenegrin constitution enshrines the right to a fair and public trial with a defence, legal aid if required and a presumption of innocence.

➡ Montenegro has outlawed the death penalty. If you're caught with drugs you may face a lengthy stint in a local jail.

➡ You are required to register with local police within 24 hours of arriving in

Montenegro and whenever you change address. Accommodation providers usually do this on your behalf (which is the reason you're asked to hand over your passport when you arrive at a hotel).

➡ There have been incidences of traffic police asking for money upfront for alleged violations. If this happens to you, ask for a full explanation of the situation from the officer and, if it's not forthcoming, ask to speak to your embassy.

LGBTIQ+ Travellers

Where's the party? The answer's nowhere. Although homosexuality was decriminalised in 1977 and discrimination outlawed in 2010, you won't find a single gay or lesbian venue in Montenegro. Don't be fooled by all the men walking arm in arm, or hand in hand in the Albanian areas. Attitudes to homosexuality remain hostile and life for gay people is extremely difficult, exacerbated by the fact that most people are expected to live at home until they're married.

In recent years there have been high-profile incidents of violence against gay activists. The country's first Pride parade was held in Budva in 2013; an Orthodox priest consecrated the town afterwards to 'stop the disease spreading'. Since then, Podgorica has held annual parades, the most recent of which have passed without serious incident.

Many gay men connect via apps or take their chances at a handful of cruisy beaches. These include Jaz Beach near Budva (eastern end), Ada Bojana and below the ruins of Ratac near Bar. Lesbians will find it harder to access the local community.

Check out Queer Montenegro (www.queermontenegro.org) for details on Pride,

arts and cultural events, and news updates.

Money

➡ Though they're not in the EU, Montenegro uses the euro (€) and we quote all prices in that currency, unless otherwise stated.

➡ You'll find banks with ATMs (bankomat) in all the main towns, most of which accept Visa, MasterCard, Maestro and Cirrus. ATMs tend to dish out big notes, which can be hard to break.

➡ Don't rely on restaurants, shops or smaller hotels accepting credit cards.

Opening Hours

Montenegrins have a flexible approach to opening times. Even if hours are posted on the door of an establishment, don't be surprised if they're not heeded. Many tourist-orientated businesses close between November and March.

Banks 8am to 5pm Monday to Friday, 8am to noon Saturday.

Post offices 7am to 8pm Monday to Friday, sometimes Saturday. In smaller towns they may close midafternoon, or close at noon and reopen at 5pm.

Restaurants, cafes & bars 8am to midnight. If the joint is jumping, cafe-bars may stay open until 2am or 3am.

Shops 9am to 8pm. Sometimes they'll close for a few hours in the late afternoon.

Post

Every town has a post office that locals use for paying their bills, so be prepared for horrendous queues. Parcels should be taken unsealed for inspection. You can receive mail, addressed poste restante, in all towns for a small charge. International postal services are slow.

Public Holidays

New Year's Day 1 and 2 January

Orthodox Christmas 6, 7 and 8 January

Orthodox Good Friday & Easter Monday Date varies, usually April/May

Labour Day 1 and 2 May

Independence Day 21 and 22 May

Statehood Day 13 and 14 July

Safe Travel

➡ Montenegro is generally safe and street violence is uncommon.

➡ The roads are usually in good condition but many are narrow and have sheer drops on one side. Local motorists have no qualms about overtaking on blind corners while talking on their mobile

---

PRACTICALITIES

Print Media Vijesti (The News), Dan (The Day), Dnevne Novine (Daily Newspaper) and Pobjeda (Victory) are all daily newspapers. Monitor, a weekly news magazine, joins local-language versions of international titles on the news-stands.

Radio & Television RTCG (Radio TV Montenegro) is the state broadcaster, with two radio stations and three TV channels. In total there are 11 more-or-less national TV channels and six regional channels. There are dozens of independent radio stations broadcasting around the country.

Weights & Measures The metric system is used.

phones. It's best to keep your cool and stick to the speed limit: the traffic police (some of whom are wont to ask for bribes) are everywhere.

➡ Montenegro has two types of venomous vipers but they'll try their best to keep out of your way. If bitten, head immediately to a medical centre for the antivenene.

Smoking

Smoking on public transport and in bars, clubs and restaurants is apparently banned in Montenegro, but someone forgot to tell the Montenegrins. While you won't find passengers lighting up on a bus, the same doesn't necessarily hold true for the driver. As for the rest: good luck. Cigarettes and coffee/booze go together like fish and soup in Montenegro, and if you get between a local and their after-dinner cigarette, you'd better have insurance.

A few eating establishments are starting to offer nonsmoking sections, and many hotels don't permit smoking in the rooms.

Telephone

➡ The international access prefix is 00, or + from a mobile phone.

➡ The country code is 382.

➡ Press the *i* button on public phones for dialling commands in English.

➡ Mobile numbers start with 06.

➡ The prefix 80 indicates a toll-free number.

➡ You can make phone calls at most larger post offices. Phone boxes are otherwise few and far between.

Mobile Phones

Local SIM cards are a good idea if you're planning a longer stay and can be used in most unlocked handsets. The main providers (T-Mobile, M:tel and Telenor) have shopfronts in most towns.

Time

➡ Montenegro is in the Central Europe time zone (an hour ahead of GMT).

➡ Clocks go forward by an hour for daylight saving at the end of March and return to normal at the end of October.

➡ Outside the daylight-saving period, when it's midday in Montenegro it will be 3am in Los Angeles, 6am in New York, 11am in London, 9pm in Sydney and 11pm in Auckland.

➡ Montenegrins use the 24-hour clock, so hours are usually listed as '9–17' rather than '9am–5pm'.

Visas

Visas are not required for citizens of European countries, Turkey, Israel, Singapore, South Korea, Japan, Australia, New Zealand, Canada and the USA. In most cases this allows a stay of up to 90 days. If your country is not covered by a visa waiver, you will need a valid passport, verified letter of invitation, return ticket, proof of sufficient funds and proof of medical cover in order to obtain a visa. Go to www.mvpei.gov.me and follow the links to 'Overview of visa regimes for foreign citizens'; find your country on the drop-down map for visa regulations.

Volunteering

Montenegro isn't high up on international volunteering agencies' agendas, but there are ways you can get involved in local projects.

➡ **Responsible Travel** (www.responsibletravel.com) runs voluntourism projects in Montenegro.

➡ **Green Home** (www.greenhome.co.me) is a Podgorica-based NGO dedicated to sustainable development, environmental protection and biodiversity conservation; contact it for volunteering opportunities in any of the national parks.

➡ Drop the good people at **Undiscovered Montenegro** (☎069-402 364; www.undiscoveredmontenegro.com; Boljevići bb; week incl accommodation €645-745; ☺Apr-Oct) an email about volunteer work in the Lake Skadar region.

➡ While Montenegro doesn't have a national WWOOF (World Wide Opportunities on Organic Farms) organisation, there are still opportunities to volunteer in the country. See www.

TOURIST INFORMATION

Official tourist offices (usually labelled *turistička organizacija*) are hit and miss. Some have wonderfully helpful English-speaking staff, regular opening hours and a good supply of free material, while others have none of the above.

The **National Tourism Organisation** (Map p104; ☎080-001 300; www.montenegro.travel) operates a free call centre and an excellent website, which includes a listing of the country's regional tourist offices.

wwoofindependents.org for regularly updated lists of hosts and vacancies.

Women Travellers

Other than a cursory interest shown by men towards solo women travellers, travelling in Montenegro is hassle-free and easy. In Muslim areas, some women wear a head-scarf but most don't.

Work

Montenegro doesn't issue working visas, and working here is a complicated business that involves a forest's worth of paperwork and bucketloads of patience.

A work permit, permission for permanent or temporary residence and a work contract are all required. The Employment Bureau of Montenegro (www.zzzcg.me, in Montenegrin) ostensibly can assist with the process. The www.gov.uk/guidance/living-in-montenegro website has more information.

Transport

GETTING THERE & AWAY

Whether you choose to fly, train, ferry, bus or drive, it's not difficult to get to Montenegro these days. New routes – including those served by low-cost carriers – are continually being added to the busy timetable at the country's two airports. It's also possible to make your way from neighbouring countries, especially Croatia. Dubrovnik's airport is very close to the border and the beautiful city makes an impressive starting point to a Montenegro holiday. Flights, cars and tours can be booked online at lonelyplanet.com/bookings.

Entering the Country

Entering Montenegro doesn't pose any particular bureaucratic challenges. In fact, the country's dead keen to shuffle tourists in. Unfortunately, Croatia seems less happy to let them go, if the long waits at their side of the Adriatic highway checkpoint are any indication; if you need to be somewhere at a certain time, it pays to allow an hour. The main crossing from Serbia at Dobrakovo can also be slow at peak times.

See Recommended Vaccinations (p167) for entry requirements pertaining to Covid-19.

Passport

Make sure that your passport has at least six months left on it. You'll need a visa if you're not from one of the many countries with a visa-waiver arrangement. There are no particular nationalities or stamps in your passport that will deny you entry. Make sure that your passport is stamped when you enter the country or else there may be difficulties when you leave.

Air

Airports & Airlines

➡ Montenegro's largest and most modern airport is immediately south of the capital, **Podgorica** (TGD; ☏020-444 244; www.montenegroairports.com). If you're wondering about the airport code, it's a hangover from Podgorica's previous name, Titograd. Locals sometimes call it Golubovci airport, as it's close to a village with that name.

➡ The second international airport, at **Tivat** (TIV; ☏032-670 930; www.montenegroairports.com; Jadranski Put bb), is well positioned for holidaymakers heading to the Bay of Kotor or Budva and now welcomes over 1.1 million passengers annually.

➡ Montenegro's de facto third airport is actually in neighbouring Croatia. **Dubrovnik Airport** (DBV, Zračna luka Dubrovnik;

CLIMATE CHANGE & TRAVEL

Every form of transport that relies on carbon-based fuel generates CO_2, the main cause of human-induced climate change. Modern travel is dependent on aeroplanes, which might use less fuel per kilometre per person than most cars but travel much greater distances. The altitude at which aircraft emit gases (including CO_2) and particles also contributes to their climate change impact. Many websites offer 'carbon calculators' that allow people to estimate the carbon emissions generated by their journey and, for those who wish to do so, to offset the impact of the greenhouse gases emitted with contributions to portfolios of climate-friendly initiatives throughout the world. Lonely Planet offsets the carbon footprint of all staff and author travel.

☎020-773 100; www.airport-dubrovnik.hr; Čilipi) is a modern facility only 17km from the border and the closest airport to Herceg Novi. Commonly referred to locally as Čilipi airport, it's used by more than 2.3 million travellers annually.

➡ The word for airport in Montenegrin is *aerodrom* (аеродром). This was also used in Croatia until independence, but in a fit of French-style linguistic nationalism the official Croatian term has been changed to a direct translation of the words for 'air' and 'port', *zračna luka* – a potential trap for English speakers.

➡ Montenegro Airlines is the national carrier, running a small fleet of 116-seater planes. Apart from a skid at Podgorica Airport while landing in snowy conditions in 2005, its safety record has been unsullied during its 14-plus years of operation. It has code-share agreements with Adria, Air France, Air Serbia, Alitalia, Austrian, Etihad and Russia's S7 Airlines.

Land

Montenegro may be a wee slip of a thing but it borders five other states: Croatia, Bosnia and Hercegovina (BiH), Serbia, Kosovo and Albania. You can easily enter Montenegro by land from any of its neighbours.

Bicycle

There are no problems bringing a bicycle into the country, though there are not many cyclists here so road-users are not cycle savvy – and remember that there's a *monte* (mountain) in the country's name for a reason.

If you want to bring your own bike, most airlines allow you to put a bicycle in the hold for a fee. You can either take it apart and pack all the pieces in a bike bag or box, or simply wheel it to the check-in desk, where it should be treated as a piece of check-in luggage. You may have to remove the pedals and turn the handlebars sideways so that it takes up less space in the aircraft's hold; check all this with the airline before you pay for your ticket. If your bicycle and other luggage exceed your weight allowance, ask about alternatives or you may find yourself being charged a small ransom for excess baggage.

Bus

There's a well-developed bus network linking Montenegro with the major cities of the former Yugoslavia and onward to Western Europe and Turkey. At the border, guards will often enter the bus and collect passports, checking the photos as they go. Once they're happy with them they return them to the bus conductor who will return them as the driver speeds off. Make sure you get yours back and that it's been stamped.

Useful websites include www.busticket4.me, www.eurolines.com, www.getbybus.com and www.vollo.net.

Albania Direct services from Tirana to Podgorica, Ulcinj, Budva and Kotor.

Austria Buses between Vienna and Kotor.

Bosnia & Hercegovina Buses head from Mostar to Kotor via Trebinje, Podgorica, Cetinje, Budva and Tivat. There are also services from Sarajevo to Herceg Novi, Kotor, Budva, Ulcinj and Podgorica.

Croatia Direct buses from Zagreb to Podgorica via Split, Makarska, Dubrovnik, Herceg Novi, Kotor and Budva.

Kosovo Buses from Pristina to Ulcinj via Peja and Podgorica.

North Macedonia Buses head all the way from Skopje to Herceg Novi via Podgorica, Budva, Kotor and Tivat.

Serbia Coaches from Belgrade to Žabljak, Podgorica, Cetinje, Ulcinj, Budva, Tivat, Kotor and Herceg Novi.

DEPARTURE TAX

Departure tax is included in the price of tickets.

Car & Motorcycle

Crossing into Montenegro with a private or hire car won't pose any problems as long as you have all of your papers in order. You must have vehicle registration/ownership documents and a locally valid insurance policy such as European Green Card vehicle insurance. Be sure to check your hire car insurance cover as some Western European companies will not cover you for travel in Montenegro.

From the major border crossings with Croatia, Serbia, Kosovo and Albania, you won't have to drive more than 25km to find a petrol station or assistance with mechanical repairs. From the Bosnian crossings, don't expect to find anything before Herceg Novi, Nikšić or Pljevlja. You'll see the words *'auto šlep'* and an adjoining phone number spray-painted along all the roadways in the country; this is low-cost advertising for local towing services.

There have been incidences of attacks on cars with Montenegrin plates in Croatia (particularly around Dubrovnik) and on cars with Croatian plates in Montenegro (particularly around Herceg Novi). These are usually limited to minor vandalism, such as cars being keyed while parked on the road.

Hitching

Although we don't recommend it, it's entirely possible to hitch in or out of Montenegro. As with any border crossing, be sure you have your passport and any relevant visas. Some drivers may ask for money, but it's not a common practice.

TRANSPORT LAND

Train

Montenegro's main train line starts at Bar and heads north through Podgorica and into Serbia. At least two trains head between Bar and Belgrade daily (€21, 11¾ hours). You'll find timetables on the website of **Montenegro Railways** (www.zcg-prevoz.me). From Belgrade it's possible to connect to destinations throughout Europe; see the website of **Serbian Railways** (www.serbianrailways.com) for timetables.

Montenegro is one of the countries included on the **Eurail** (www.eurail.com, for non-European residents) and **InterRail** (www.interrail.eu, for European residents) **Global Passes**. It's also included on the **Balkan Flexipass**, sold by Montenegro Railways, which covers rail travel in Montenegro, BiH, Serbia, North Macedonia, Bulgaria, Greece, Romania and Turkey.

Border Crossings

Albania There are two main crossings: Sukobin (between Shkodra and Ulcinj) and Hani i Hotit (between Shkodra and Podgorica). If you're paddling about on Lake Skadar, remember that the border runs through the lake and be careful not to cross it. Because of problems with trafficking (of cigarettes, drugs and women), the Montenegro police patrol the lake. The same caution should be applied while hiking in the Prokletije Mountains; you'll need a cross-border permit.

Bosnia & Hercegovina There are four main crossings: Zupci-Sitnica (between Trebinje and Herceg Novi), Klobuk–Ilino Brdo (between Trebinje and Nikšić), Hum–Šćepan Polje (between Foča and Nikšić) and Metaljka (between Sarajevo and Pljevlja). Other more remote crossings are marked on some maps but these may only be open to local traffic (if they are open at all) and we've heard of travellers being turned back at some crossings.

Croatia Expect delays at the busy Debeli Brijeg checkpoint on the Adriatic highway (between Herceg Novi and Dubrovnik). You can avoid them by taking a detour down the Prevlaka Peninsula to the Konfin-Kobila border post, although this has become more popular and sometimes also has queues. To reach it from the Croatian side, turn right off the highway a few kilometres before the main border crossing and pass through Pločice and Vitaljina. The road rejoins the highway on the Montenegro side just before Igalo.

Kosovo There's only one crossing, Kulina, on the road between Rožaje and Peć.

Serbia The busiest crossing is Dobrakovo (north of Bijelo Polje), followed by Dračenovac (northeast of Rožaje) and Ranče (east of Pljevlja). The train crosses at Dobrakovo.

Sea

Montenegro Lines (www.montenegrolines.com) has boats from Bar to Bari (Italy), at least weekly from May to November (deck ticket €44 to €48, cabin €63 to €210, 11 hours); and from Bar to Ancona (Italy), at least weekly from July to August (deck €60, cabin €80 to €230, 16 hours). Cars cost €56 to €90.

FLIGHT-FREE TRAVEL

If you fancy a guilt-free, low-carbon journey from London to Montenegro, log on to www.seat61.com and click on 'Montenegro' on the side navigation. You'll find detailed instructions on how to get from London to Belgrade by train and then connect through to Montenegro, including departure times, fares and travel-pass information.

GETTING AROUND

Air

Though there are two airports in Montenegro, there are no domestic flights available within the country.

Bicycle

Cyclists are a rare species even in the cities and there are no special bike lanes on the roads. Don't expect drivers to be considerate; wherever possible, try to get off the main roads. The wearing of helmets is not compulsory.

However, the outlook for cyclists isn't as grim as it sounds. The **National Tourism Organisation** (Map p104; ☑080-001 300; www.montenegro.travel) has developed a series of wilderness mountain-biking trails, making a two-wheeled tour of Montenegro an excellent proposition. As most of the country is mountainous, you'll have to be exceedingly fit to attempt it.

The key to a successful bike trip is to travel light, and don't overdo it on the first few days. Even for the shortest and most basic trip, it's worth carrying the tools necessary for repairing a puncture. You might want to consider packing spare brake and gear cables, spanners, Allen keys, spare spokes and strong adhesive tape. At the risk of stating the obvious, these won't be much use unless you know what to do with them. Maintenance is also important: check over your bike thoroughly each morning and again at night when the day's touring is over. Take a good lock and always use it when you leave your bike unattended.

A seasoned cyclist can average about 80km a day, but this depends on the terrain and how much weight is being carried. Again, don't overdo it – there's no point burning yourself out during the initial stages.

The cycling enthusiasts at **Montenegro Bed and Bike** (www.bedandbike.me) can help with trails, bike rental and accommodation ideas.

Boat

There are no regular ferry services within Montenegro, but taxi boats are a common sight during summer. They can be hailed from the shore for a short trip along the coast or to one of the islands. They're harder to find outside the high season; look for them at the marinas. Some boats advertise set cruises, but normally they operate on an ad hoc basis.

Bus

The local bus network is extensive and reliable. Buses are usually comfortable and air-conditioned; they're rarely full.

Up-to-date timetable information and online booking can be found on www.busticket4.me. It's usually not difficult to find information on services and prices from the bus station. Most have timetables prominently displayed. As with many service-industry types in Montenegro, some station staff are more helpful than others. Where English isn't spoken, they'll usually write down the price and time of the bus for you.

It's a bit cheaper to buy your ticket on the bus rather than at the station, but a station-bought ticket theoretically guarantees you a seat. Reservations are only worthwhile for international buses, at holiday times, or where long-distance journeys are infrequent. Luggage carried below is charged at €1 per piece.

Smoking is forbidden on buses and this rule is generally enforced. The standard of driving is no better or worse than that of anyone else on the roads.

Car & Motorcycle

Independent travel by car or motorcycle is an ideal way to gad about and discover the country; some of the drives are breathtakingly beautiful. Traffic police are everywhere, so stick to speed limits and carry an International Driving Permit.

Allow more time than you'd expect for the distances involved as the terrain will slow you down. You'll rarely get up to 60km/h on the Bay of Kotor road, for instance. The standard of roads is generally fair with conditions worsening in rural areas, especially in winter and after bad weather. A particularly notorious road is the Podgorica–Belgrade highway as it passes through the Morača Canyon, which is often made dangerous by bad conditions and high traffic. It's a good idea to drive defensively and treat everyone else on the road as a lunatic – when they get behind the wheel, many of them are. That said, no matter how much they toot at you or overtake on blind corners, you should avoid confrontation.

The only toll in Montenegro is the Sozina tunnel between Lake Skadar and the sea (€3.50 per car).

Automobile Associations

The **Automobile Association of Montenegro** (Auto Moto Savez Crne Gore; ☑020-9807) offers roadside assistance, towing and repairs. The **UK Automobile Association** (www.theaa.com) has excellent information on its website, with specific driving advice for Montenegro.

Bring Your Own Vehicle

As long as you have registration/ownership papers with you and valid insurance cover, there should be no problem driving your car into Montenegro. If your vehicle has obvious signs of damage, the border guards should provide you with a certificate that must be produced upon leaving to prove that the damage didn't occur inside the country.

Driving Licences

It's recommended that you arrange an International Driving Permit from your home country before the trip. Although many rental companies will hire out a car based on your foreign driver's licence, there's no assurance that the traffic police will accept it and it doesn't pay to give them any excuse to fine you.

Fuel & Spare Parts

Filling up is no problem in any medium-sized town, but don't leave it until the last drop. There are few late-night petrol stations. Diesel, unleaded 95 and 98 octane are easy to find. Spare parts for major makes will be no problem in the cities, and mechanics are available everywhere for simple repairs.

Hire

It's not difficult to hire a car in the bigger towns. Budva, in particular, is overflowing with options. The major European car-hire companies have a presence in various centres including the airports, but the local alternatives are often cheaper. If you're flying into Dubrovnik, it will certainly be more convenient to arrange to collect your car at the airport, but this will need to be balanced against the (albeit minor) risk of vandalism against cars with Croatian plates in Montenegro.

Alamo (www.alamo.com) Pick up from Podgorica, Tivat or Dubrovnik airports.

Avis (www.avisworld.com) Pick up from Budva or Bar, or Podgorica, Tivat or Dubrovnik airports.

Europcar (www.europcar.com) Pick up from Podgorica, Tivat or Dubrovnik airports.

Hertz (www.hertz.me) Pick up from Podgorica or Budva, or Podgorica, Tivat or Dubrovnik airports.

Meridian Rentacar (www.meridian-rentacar.com) A reliable local option with offices in Budva, Podgorica and Bar, and Tivat and Podgorica airports; one-day hire starts from €30.

National (www.nationalcar.com) Pick up from Podgorica, or Tivat, Podgorica or Dubrovnik airports.

Sixt (www.sixt.com) Pick up from Herceg Novi, Tivat, Budva, Podgorica or Bar, or Podgorica, Tivat or Dubrovnik airports.

Insurance

Third-party insurance is compulsory and you'll need to be able to prove you have it in order to bring a car into Montenegro. You should get your insurer to issue a Green Card (which may cost extra), an internationally recognised proof of insurance, and check that it lists all the countries you intend to visit. You'll need this in the event of an accident outside the country where the vehicle is insured. The European Accident Statement (known as the 'Constat Amiable' in France) is available from your insurance company and is copied so that each party at an accident can record information for insurance purposes. The Association of British Insurers (www.abi.org.uk) has more details. Never sign accident statements you cannot understand or read – insist on a translation and sign that only if it's acceptable.

Some insurance packages (particularly those covering rental cars) do not include all European countries and Montenegro is often one of those excluded – make sure you check this before you rent your car. When you're renting a car, ensure you check all aspects of the insurance offered, including the excess (you may wish to pay extra to reduce it) and rules regarding where you may or may not drive it (on dirt roads, for example).

Parking

Local parking habits are quite carefree, so it's possible you can be blocked in by someone double-parking next to you. Sometimes parking that looks illegal (eg on footpaths) is actually permitted.

Road Rules

→ As in the rest of continental Europe, people drive on the right-hand side of the road and overtake on the left. Keep right except when overtaking, and use your indicators for any change of lane and when pulling away from the kerb.

→ School buses can't be overtaken when they stop for passengers to board or alight.

→ Vehicles entering a roundabout have right of way.

→ Standard international road signs are used.

→ You are required by law to wear a seatbelt (including in the back seat if they're fitted), drive with dipped headlights on (even during the day) and wear a helmet on a motorbike.

→ Children's car seats aren't compulsory but kids under 12 and intoxicated passengers are not allowed in the front seat.

→ Using a mobile phone while driving is prohibited, although plenty of people do it anyway.

→ Driving barefoot is a no-no.

→ Penalties for drink-driving are severe and could result in jail time. The legal limit is 0.03% of alcohol in your bloodstream. Police can issue an on-the-spot fine but cannot collect payment.

→ Standard speed limits are 50km/h in built-up areas, 80km/h outside built-up areas and 100km/h on certain roads. Often the limit will change several times on a single stretch of the road because of the mountainous conditions. Excessive speeding (30km over the limit) could lead to your driver's licence being temporarily confiscated.

→ Cars must carry a set of replacement bulbs, a first-aid kit, a warning triangle and a reflective jacket.

→ If you're involved in an accident resulting in major injury or material damage to your or another vehicle, you're legally obliged to report it to the police.

Hitching

Hitching is never entirely safe but it is a common practice in Montenegro. Wherever you are, there's always a risk when you catch a ride with strangers. It's safer to travel in pairs and to let someone know where you're planning to go. Once you've flagged down a vehicle, it's safer if you sit next to a door you can open. Ask the driver where they are going before you say where you are going. Trust your instincts if you feel uncomfortable about getting in, and get out at the first sign of trouble.

Local Transport

Most Montenegrin towns, even Podgorica, are small enough to be travelled by foot. Podgorica is the only city to have a useful local bus network, costing 80c per trip. Taxis are easily found in most towns. If they're not metered, be sure to agree on a fare in advance. Some Budva taxis have their meters set at extortionate rates, so ask to be let out if you suspect something's amiss.

Train

Montenegro Railways (Željeznički prevoz Crne Gore; www.zpcg.me) has limited services heading north from Bar and crossing the country before disappearing into Serbia; useful stops include Virpazar, Podgorica, Kolašin, Mojkovac and Bijelo Polje. A second line heads northwest from Podgorica to Danilovgrad and Nikšić.

The trains are old and can be hot in summer, but they're priced accordingly and the route through the mountains is spectacular. Apart from a derailment in 2006 and a crash in 2012, the trains are generally a safe option.

Language

Montenegrin belongs to the western group of the South Slavic language family. It is very similar to other languages in this group (Serbian, Croatian and Bosnian), and there are only slight variations in pronunciation and vocabulary between them.

Both Latin and Cyrillic alphabets are used in Montenegro. It's worth familiarising yourself with the latter in case you come across it on menus, timetables or street signs – see the box on the following page.

If you read our coloured pronunciation guides as if they were English, you'll be understood. The stressed syllables are indicated with italics – in most cases the stress falls on the first syllable in a word.

Some Montenegrin words have masculine and feminine forms, indicated after the relevant phrases in this chapter by 'm' and 'f'. Polite ('pol') and informal ('inf') alternatives are also included where necessary.

BASICS

Hello.	Zdravo.	zdra·vo
Goodbye.	Do viđenja.	do vi·je·nya
Yes.	Da.	da
No.	Ne.	ne
Please.	Molim.	mo·leem
Thank you.	Hvala.	hva·la

WANT MORE?

For in-depth language information and handy phrases, check out Lonely Planet's phrasebooks series. You'll find it at **shop.lonelyplanet.com**.

You're welcome.	Nema na čemu.	ne·ma na che·moo
Excuse me.	Oprostite.	o·pro·stee·te
Sorry.	Žao mi je.	zha·o mee ye

How are you?
Kako ste/si? (pol/inf) ka·ko ste/see

Fine. And you?
Dobro. do·bro
A vi/ti? (pol/inf) a vee/tee

My name is ...
Zovem se ... zo·vem se ...

What's your name?
Kako se zovete/ ka·ko se zo·ve·te/
zoveš? (pol/inf) zo·vesh

Do you speak (English)?
Govorite/ go·vo·ree·te/
Govoriš go·vo·reesh
li (engleski)? (pol/inf) lee (en·gle·skee)

I (don't) understand.
(Ne) Razumijem. (ne) ra·zoo·mee·yem

ACCOMMODATION

Do you have a room available?
Imate li slobodnih ee·ma·te lee slo·bod·neeh
soba? so·ba

Is breakfast included?
Da li je doručak da lee ye do·roo·chak
uključen? ook·lyoo·chen

How much is it (per night/per person)?
Koliko košta ko·lee·ko kosh·ta
(za noć/po osobi)? (za noch/po o·so·bee)

Do you have a ... room?	Imate li ... sobu?	ee·ma·te lee ... so·boo
single	jednokrevetnu	yed·no· kre·vet·noo
double	dvokrevetnu	dvo· kre·vet·noo

air-con	klima-uredaj	klee·ma·oo·re·jai
bathroom	kupatilo	koo·pa·tee·lo
bed	krevet	kre·vet
campsite	kamp	kamp
cot	dječji krevet	dyech·yee kre·vet
guesthouse	privatni smještaj	pree·vat·nee smyesh·tai
hotel	hotel	ho·tel
wi-fi	bežični internet	be·zheech·nee een·ter·net
window	prozor	pro·zor
youth hostel	omladinsko prenoćište	om·la·deen·sko pre·no·cheesh·te

DIRECTIONS

Where is ...?
Gdje je ...? — gdye ye ...

What's the address?
Koja je adresa? — ko·ya ye a·dre·sa

Can you show me (on the map)?
Možete li da mi pokažete (na mapi)? — mo·zhe·te lee da mee po·ka·zhe·te (na ma·pee)

at the corner	na uglu	na oo·gloo
at the traffic lights	na semaforu	na se·ma·fo·roo
behind	iza	ee·za
in front of	ispred	ees·pred
far (from)	daleko (od)	da·le·ko (od)
left	lijevo	lee·ye·vo
near	blizu	blee·zoo
next to	pored	po·red
opposite	nasuprot	na·soo·prot
right	desno	de·sno
straight ahead	pravo naprijed	pra·vo na·pree·yed

EATING & DRINKING

What would you recommend?
Šta biste preporučili? — shta bee·ste pre·po·roo·chee·lee

I'm a vegetarian.
Ja sam vegetarijanac/ vegetarijanka. (m/f) — ya sam ve·ge·ta·ree·ya·nats/ ve·ge·ta·ree·yan·ka

That was delicious!
To je bilo izvrsno! — to ye bee·lo eez·vr·sno

Please bring the menu/bill.
Molim vas donesite jelovnik/račun. — mo·leem vas do·ne·see·te ye·lov·neek/ra·choon

CYRILLIC ALPHABET

In 2009 two new letters – indicated in the following list with an asterisk (*) – were introduced to the Montenegrin alphabet.

А а	a	short as the 'u' in 'cut'; long as in 'father'
Б б	b	as in 'but'
В в	v	as in 'van'
Г г	g	as in 'go'
Д д	d	as in 'dog'
Ђ ђ	j	as in 'joke'
Е е	e	short as in 'bet'; long as in 'there'
Ж ж	zh	as the 's' in 'measure'
З з	z	as in 'zoo'
* З́ з́		soft zh
И и	i	short as in 'bit'; long as in 'marine'
Ј ј	y	as in 'young'
К к	k	as in 'kind'
Л л	l	as in 'lamp'
Љ љ	ly	as the 'lli' in 'million'
М м	m	as in 'mat'
Н н	n	as in 'not'
Њ њ	ny	as in 'canyon'
О о	o	short as in 'hot'; long as in 'for'
П п	p	as in 'pick'
Р р	r	as in 'rub' (but rolled)
С с	s	as in 'sing'
* С́ с́		soft sh
Т т	t	as in 'ten'
Ћ ћ	ch	as in 'check'
У у	u	short as in 'put'; long as in 'rule'
Ф ф	f	as in 'fan'
Х х	h	as in 'hot'
Ц ц	ts	as in 'cats'
Ч ч	ch	as in 'change'
Џ џ	j	as in 'judge'
Ш ш	sh	as in 'shop'

I'd like a table for ...	Htio/Htjela bih sto za ... (m/f)	htee·o/htye·la beeh sto za ...
(eight) o'clock	(osam) sati	(o·sam) sa·tee
(two) people	(dvoje) ljudi	(dvo·ye) lyoo·dee

I don't eat ...	Ne jedem ...	ne ye·dem ...
fish	ribu	ree·boo
meat	meso	me·so
nuts	orahe	o·ra·he

Signs

Izlaz	Exit
Muški	Men
Otvoreno	Open
Ulaz	Entrance
Zabranjeno	Prohibited
Toaleti/WC	Toilets
Zatvoreno	Closed
Ženski	Women

Key Words

bar	*bar*	bar
bottle	*boca*	bo·tsa
breakfast	*doručak*	do·roo·chak
cafe	*kafić*	ka·feech
cold	*hladno*	hlad·no
dinner	*večera*	ve·che·ra
fork	*viljuška*	vee·lyoosh·ka
glass	*čaša*	cha·sha
knife	*nož*	nozh
lunch	*ručak*	roo·chak
plate	*tanjir*	ta·nyeer
restaurant	*restoran*	re·sto·ran
spoon	*kašika*	ka·shee·ka
warm	*toplo*	top·lo

Meat & Fish

beef	*govedina*	go·ve·di·na
carp	*šaran*	sha·ran
chicken	*piletina*	pi·le·ti·na
cod	*bakalar*	ba·ka·lar
crabs	*račići*	ra·chi·chi
hake	*oslić*	o·slich
ham	*šunka*	shun·ka
lamb	*jagnjetina*	yag·nye·ti·na
lobster	*jastog*	ya·stog
mussels	*dagnje*	dag·nye
oysters	*školjke*	shkoly·ke
pork	*svinjetina*	svi·nye·ti·na
prawns	*škampi*	shkam·pi
salmon	*losos*	lo·sos
sausage	*kobasica*	ko·ba·si·tsa
squid	*lignje*	lig·nye
trout	*pastrmka*	pas·trm·ka
turkey	*ćuretina*	chu·re·ti·na
veal	*teletina*	te·le·ti·na

Fruit & Vegetables

apple	*jabuka*	ya·bu·ka
apricot	*kajsija*	kai·si·ya
banana	*banana*	ba·na·na
beans	*pasulj*	pa·suly
beetroot	*cvekla*	tsve·kla
cabbage	*kupus*	ku·pus
capsicum	*paprika*	pa·pri·ka
carrot	*šargarepa*	shar·ga·re·pa
cauliflower	*karfiol*	kar·fi·ol
cherry	*višnja*	vish·nya
cucumber	*krastavac*	kra·sta·vats
fig	*smokva*	smok·va
grapes	*grožđe*	grozh·je
lemon	*limun*	li·mun
lettuce	*zelena salata*	ze·le·na sa·la·ta
melon	*dinja*	di·nya
mushrooms	*pečurke*	pe·chur·ke
olives	*masline*	mas·li·ne
onion	*crni luk*	tsr·ni luk
orange	*pomorandža*	po·mo·ran·ja
peach	*breskva*	bres·kva
pear	*kruška*	kru·shka
peas	*grašak*	gra·shak
plum	*šljiva*	shlyi·va
potato	*krompir*	krom·pir
spinach	*spanać*	spa·nach
strawberry	*jagoda*	ya·go·da
tomato	*paradajz*	pa·ra·daiz
watermelon	*lubenica*	lu·be·ni·tsa

Other

bread	*hljeb*	hlyeb
cheese	*sir*	seer
egg	*jaje*	ya·ye
honey	*med*	med
pepper	*biber*	bee·ber
rice	*pirinač*	pee·ree·nach
salt	*so*	so
sugar	*šećer*	she·cher

Drinks

beer	*pivo*	pee·vo
coffee	*kafa*	ka·fa
(fruit) juice	*(voćni) sok*	(voch·nee) sok
milk	*mljeko*	mlye·ko

tea	*čaj*	chai
(mineral) water	*(mineralna) voda*	*(mee*·ne·ral·na) *vo*·da
(red/white) wine	*(crno/bijelo) vino*	*(tsr*·no/*bye*·lo) *vee*·no

bank	*banka*	*ban*·ka
market	*pijaca*	*pee*·ya·tsa
post office	*pošta*	*posh*·ta
tourist office	*turistički biro*	too·*ree*·steech·kee *bee*·ro

EMERGENCIES

Help!
Upomoć! — oo·po·moch

Leave me alone!
Ostavite me na miru! — o·sta·vee·te me na *mee*·roo

I'm lost.
Izgubio/ Izgubila sam se. (m/f) — eez·*goo*·bee·o/ eez·*goo*·bee·la sam se

Call a doctor!
Zovite ljekara! — zo·vee·te lye·*ka*·ra

Call the police!
Zovite policiju! — zo·vee·te po·*lee*·tsee·yoo

I'm ill.
Ja sam bolestan/ bolesna. (m/f) — ya sam bo·le·stan/ bo·le·sna

I'm allergic to ...
Ja sam alergičan/ alergična na ... (m/f) — ya sam a·*ler*·gee·chan/ a·*ler*·geech·na na ...

Where are the toilets?
Gdje su toaleti? — gdye soo to·a·*le*·tee

SHOPPING & SERVICES

I'd like to buy ...
Želim da kupim ... — zhe·leem da koo·peem ...

I'm just looking.
Samo razgledam. — sa·mo raz·gle·dam

May I look at it?
Mogu li da pogledam? — mo·goo lee da po·gle·dam

How much is it?
Koliko košta? — ko·lee·ko kosh·ta

That's too expensive.
To je preskupo. — to ye pre·skoo·po

Do you have something cheaper?
Imate li nešto jeftinije? — ee·ma·te lee nesh·to yef·tee·nee·ye

There's a mistake in the bill.
Neka je greška na računu. — ne·ka ye gresh·ka na ra·choo·noo

Question Words
How?	*Kako?*	ka·ko
What?	*Šta?*	shta
When?	*Kada?*	ka·da
Where?	*Gdje?*	gdye
Who?	*Ko?*	ko
Why?	*Zašto?*	za·shto

TIME & DATES

What time is it?
Koliko je sati? — ko·lee·ko ye sa·tee

It's (10) o'clock.
(Deset) je sati. — (de·set) ye sa·tee

Half past (10).
(Deset) i po. — (de·set) ee po

morning	*jutro*	yoo·tro
afternoon	*poslijepodne*	po·slee·ye·*pod*·ne
evening	*veče*	ve·che
yesterday	*juče*	yoo·che
today	*danas*	da·nas
tomorrow	*sjutra*	syoo·tra
Monday	*ponedjeljak*	po·*ne*·dye·lyak
Tuesday	*utorak*	oo·to·rak
Wednesday	*srijeda*	sree·ye·da
Thursday	*četvrtak*	chet·*vr*·tak
Friday	*petak*	pe·tak
Saturday	*subota*	soo·bo·ta
Sunday	*nedjelja*	ne·dye·lya
January	*januar*	ya·noo·ar
February	*februar*	feb·roo·ar
March	*mart*	mart
April	*april*	ap·reel
May	*maj*	mai
June	*jun*	yoon
July	*jul*	yool
August	*avgust*	av·goost
September	*septembar*	sep·tem·bar
October	*oktobar*	ok·to·bar
November	*novembar*	no·vem·bar
December	*decembar*	de·tsem·bar

TRANSPORT

Public Transport
boat	*brod*	brod
bus	*autobus*	a·oo·*to*·boos
plane	*avion*	a·*vee*·on
train	*voz*	voz

Numbers

1	jedan	ye·dan
2	dva	dva
3	tri	tree
4	četiri	che·tee·ree
5	pet	pet
6	šest	shest
7	sedam	se·dam
8	osam	o·sam
9	devet	de·vet
10	deset	de·set
20	dvadeset	dva·de·set
30	trideset	tree·de·set
40	četrdeset	che·tr·de·set
50	pedeset	pe·de·set
60	šezdeset	shez·de·set
70	sedamdeset	se·dam·de·set
80	osamdeset	o·sam·de·set
90	devedeset	de·ve·de·set
100	sto	sto
1000	hiljadu	hee·lya·doo

I want to go to (Dubrovnik).
Htio/Htjela bih
da idem u
(Dubrovnik). (m/f)
htee·o/htye·la beeh
da ee·dem oo
(doo·brov·neek)

Does it stop at (Budva)?
Staje li u (Budvi)? sta·ye lee oo (bood·vee)

What time does it leave?
U koliko sati kreće? oo ko·lee·ko sa·tee kre·che

What time does it get to (Podgorica)?
U koliko sati stiže
u (Podgoricu)?
oo ko·lee·ko sa·tee stee·zhe
oo (pod·go·ree·tsoo)

Could you tell me when we get to (Cetinje)?
Možete li mi reći
kada stignemo do
(Cetinja)?
mo·zhe·te lee mee re·chee
ka·da steeg·ne·mo do
(tse·tee·nya)

I'd like to get off at (Kotor).
Želim da izađem
u (Kotoru).
zhe·leem da ee·za·jem
oo (ko·to·roo)

A ... ticket.	Jednu ... kartu.	yed·noo ... kar·too
1st-class	prvo- razrednu	pr·vo· raz·red·noo
2nd-class	drugo- razrednu	droo·go· raz·red·noo
one-way	jedno smjernu-	yed·no· smyer·noo
return	povratnu	po·vrat·noo
first	prvi	pr·vee
last	poslednji	pos·led·nyee

aisle seat	sjedište do prolaza	sye·deesh·te do pro·la·za
platform	peron	pe·ron
ticket office	blagajna	bla·gai·na
timetable	red vožnje	red vozh·nye
station	stanica	sta·nee·tsa
window seat	sjedište do prozora	sye·deesh·te do pro·zo·ra

Driving & Cycling

I'd like to hire a ...	Htio/Htjela bih da iznajmim ... (m/f)	htee·o/htye·la beeh da eez·nai·meem ...
4WD	džip	jeep
bicycle	bicikl	bee·tsee·kl
car	auto	a·oo·to
motorcycle	motocikl	mo·to·tsee·kl

bicycle pump	pumpa za bicikl	poom·pa za bee·tsee·kl
child seat	sjedište za dijete	sye·deesh·te za dee·ye·te
diesel	dizel gorivo	dee·zel go·ree·vo
helmet	kaciga	ka·tsee·ga
mechanic	auto- mehaničar	a·oo·to· me·ha·nee·char
petrol	benzin	ben·zeen
service station	benziska stanica	ben·zeen·ska sta·nee·tsa

Is this the road to (Herceg Novi)?
Je li ovo put za
(Herceg Novi)?
ye lee o·vo poot za
(her·tseg no·vee)

(How long) Can I park here?
(Koliko dugo)
Mogu ovdje da
parkiram?
(ko·lee·ko doo·go)
mo·goo ov·dye da
par·kee·ram

The car/motorbike has broken down (at Bar).
Automobil/
Motocikl se
pokvario (u Baru).
a·oo·to·mo·beel/
mo·to·tsee·kl se
pok·va·ree·o (oo ba·roo)

I need a mechanic.
Treba mi
automehaničar.
tre·ba mee
a·oo·to·me·ha·nee·char

I have a flat tyre.
Imam probušenu
gumu.
ee·mam pro·boo·she·noo
goo·moo

I've run out of petrol.
Nestalo mi je
benzina.
ne·sta·lo mee ye
ben·zee·na

I've lost the keys.
Izgubio/
Izgubila
sam ključeve. (m/f)
eez·goo·bee·o/
eez·goo·bee·la
sam klyoo·che·ve

GLOSSARY

aerodrom – airport
autocamp – camping ground for tents and caravans
Avars – Eastern European people who waged war against Byzantium from the 6th to 9th centuries

bb – in an address the letters 'bb' following a street name (eg Jadranski Put bb) stand for *bez broja* (without number), indicating that the building has no street number
Bokelj – inhabitant of Boka Kotorska (Bay of Kotor)
Bosniak – Slavic Muslim, not necessarily from Bosnia
burek – heavy pastry stuffed with meat or cheese

čaršija – old market area
Cattaro – Venetian name for Kotor
ćevapčići – small spicy beef or pork sausages
čojstvo i junaštvo – literally 'humanity and bravery' (ie the concept of chivalry present in Montenegrin culture)
crkva – church
Crna Gora – Montenegrin name for Montenegro (literally 'black mountain')

Dom kulture – cultural centre
Dom zdravlja – medical centre
donji (m), donja (f) – lower
Duklja – early Serbian state considered a precursor of Montenegro
džamija –mosque

galerija – gallery
garderoba – left-luggage office
Glagolitic – ancient Slavic alphabet (precursor of the Cyrillic alphabet) created by Greek missionaries Cyril and Methodius
gora – mountain
gornji (m), gornja (f) – upper
gorske oči – literally 'mountain eyes'; name for glacial lakes in mountainous regions
grad – city
guslar – singer/composer of epic poetry accompanied by the *gusle*
gusle – one-stringed folk instrument

hammam – Turkish bathhouse
Hitna pomoć – emergency clinic

Illyrians – ancient inhabitants of the Adriatic coast, defeated by the Romans in the 2nd century BC
ispod sača – (meat) roasted under a metal lid covered with hot coals

jezero – lake

karst – highly porous limestone and dolomitic rock
katun – traditional shepherds' mountain hut
klapa – a traditional form of unaccompanied singing from Dalmatia
klima – air conditioning
kolo – lively Slavic round dance in which men and women alternate in the circle
konoba – the traditional term for a small, intimate dining spot, often located in a cellar; now applies to a wide variety of restaurants; usually a simple, family-run establishment
kula – a blocky tower-like house built for defence

mali (m), mala (f) – little
manastir – monastery
most – bridge
muzej – museum

novi (m), nova (f) – new

obala – waterfront
oro – traditional Montenegrin circle dance
ostrvo – island

palačinke – pancakes
Partisans – communist-led WWII resistance fighters
pivo – beer
plaža – beach
polje – field
pršut – smoke-dried ham
put – path; road; trail

rakija – fruit brandy
ražnjići – small chunks of pork grilled on a skewer
restoran – restaurant
rijeka – river
rruga – Albanian word for 'street' (used in Ulcinj street names)

šetalište – walkway
sladoled – ice cream
sobe (pl) – rooms (available for hire)
stara maslina – literally 'old olive', a famous 2000-year-old tree in Bar
stari (m), stara (f) – old
Stari Grad – Old Town
stećci – mysterious carved stone monuments from the Middle Ages found throughout northern Montenegro
sveti (m), sveta (f) – saint

trg – square
turbofolk – version of Serbian music, a mix of folk and pop

ulica – street

veliki (m), velika (f) – large
vladika – bishop-prince
vrh – peak; summit

Zakonik – legal code (historic term)
Zdravstvena stanica – medical centre or emergency clinic
Zeta – early Serbian state considered a precursor of Montenegro
zimmer – German word for 'rooms' (available for hire)

Behind the Scenes

SEND US YOUR FEEDBACK

We love to hear from travellers – your comments keep us on our toes and help make our books better. Our well-travelled team reads every word on what you loved or loathed about this book. Although we cannot reply individually to your submissions, we always guarantee that your feedback goes straight to the appropriate authors, in time for the next edition. Each person who sends us information is thanked in the next edition – the most useful submissions are rewarded with a selection of digital PDF chapters.

Visit **lonelyplanet.com/contact** to submit your updates and suggestions or to ask for help. Our award-winning website also features inspirational travel stories, news and discussions.

Note: We may edit, reproduce and incorporate your comments in Lonely Planet products such as guidebooks, websites and digital products, so let us know if you don't want your comments reproduced or your name acknowledged. For a copy of our privacy policy visit lonelyplanet.com/privacy.

OUR READERS

Many thanks to the travellers who used the last edition and wrote to us with helpful hints, useful advice and interesting anecdotes:

Anne Daetz, Barbara Fischer, Charlotte Burton, Grace Gardner, Kerstin Köstler, Luis Lanz Tienda, Rob Van Elburg, Vildana Cicic

WRITER THANKS
Tamara Sheward
Mnogo hvala na (many thanks to) Drago, Andja, Miša, Rajan, Lola, Dutch and the rest of the Lučići, the Lješević crew, Srdjan, Gordana and Aleksa, Zoran and uncountable more. On the Lonely Planet front, heartfelt high-fives to Brana Vladisavljević, Peter Dragicevich and the beleaguered geniuses on the help team. Greatest thanks and love always to Dušan

and Masha: you are the *kajmak* to my bread, the squid to my risotto, the *urnebes* to my *pljeskavica*.

Peter Dragicevich
Researching in Montenegro and Croatia is always a joy but even more so with company – so many thanks to Robert Carpenter and Catherine Cole for joining me on the road. Once again I'm indebted to Vojko and Marija Dragičević for their wonderful hospitality.

ACKNOWLEDGEMENTS

Climate map data adapted from Peel MC, Finlayson BL & McMahon TA (2007) 'Updated World Map of the Köppen-Geiger Climate Classification', Hydrology and Earth System Sciences, 11, 163344.

Cover photograph: Perast, Bay of Kotor; Jan Wlodarczyk/Alamy ©

THIS BOOK

This 4th edition of Lonely Planet's *Montenegro* guidebook was curated by Tamara Sheward, and researched and written by Tamara and Peter Dragicevich. This guidebook was produced by the following:

Senior Product Editor Kate Chapman

Product Editor Kate Mathews

Senior Cartographer Mark Griffiths

Book Designer Virginia Moreno

Assisting Editors Janet Austin, Imogen Bannister, Monique Choy, Kate James, Charlotte Orr, Branislava Vladisavljevic

Cover Researcher Naomi Parker

Thanks to Parveen Qureshi

Index

NOTES

Map Legend

Sights

- Beach
- Bird Sanctuary
- Buddhist
- Castle/Palace
- Christian
- Confucian
- Hindu
- Islamic
- Jain
- Jewish
- Monument
- Museum/Gallery/Historic Building
- Ruin
- Shinto
- Sikh
- Taoist
- Winery/Vineyard
- Zoo/Wildlife Sanctuary
- Other Sight

Activities, Courses & Tours

- Bodysurfing
- Diving
- Canoeing/Kayaking
- Course/Tour
- Sento Hot Baths/Onsen
- Skiing
- Snorkelling
- Surfing
- Swimming/Pool
- Walking
- Windsurfing
- Other Activity

Sleeping

- Sleeping
- Camping

Eating

- Eating

Drinking & Nightlife

- Drinking & Nightlife
- Cafe

Entertainment

- Entertainment

Shopping

- Shopping

Information

- Bank
- Embassy/Consulate
- Hospital/Medical
- Internet
- Police
- Post Office
- Telephone
- Toilet
- Tourist Information
- Other Information

Geographic

- Beach
- Gate
- Hut/Shelter
- Lighthouse
- Lookout
- Mountain/Volcano
- Oasis
- Park
- Pass
- Picnic Area
- Waterfall

Population

- Capital (National)
- Capital (State/Province)
- City/Large Town
- Town/Village

Transport

- Airport
- Border crossing
- Bus
- Cable car/Funicular
- Cycling
- Ferry
- Metro station
- Monorail
- Parking
- Petrol station
- Subway station
- Taxi
- Train station/Railway
- Tram
- Underground station
- Other Transport

Note: Not all symbols displayed above appear on the maps in this book

Routes

- Tollway
- Freeway
- Primary
- Secondary
- Tertiary
- Lane
- Unsealed road
- Road under construction
- Plaza/Mall
- Steps
- Tunnel
- Pedestrian overpass
- Walking Tour
- Walking Tour detour
- Path/Walking Trail

Boundaries

- International
- State/Province
- Disputed
- Regional/Suburb
- Marine Park
- Cliff
- Wall

Hydrography

- River, Creek
- Intermittent River
- Canal
- Water
- Dry/Salt/Intermittent Lake
- Reef

Areas

- Airport/Runway
- Beach/Desert
- Cemetery (Christian)
- Cemetery (Other)
- Glacier
- Mudflat
- Park/Forest
- Sight (Building)
- Sportsground
- Swamp/Mangrove

OUR STORY

A beat-up old car, a few dollars in the pocket and a sense of adventure. In 1972 that's all Tony and Maureen Wheeler needed for the trip of a lifetime – across Europe and Asia overland to Australia. It took several months, and at the end – broke but inspired – they sat at their kitchen table writing and stapling together their first travel guide, *Across Asia on the Cheap*. Within a week they'd sold 1500 copies. Lonely Planet was born.

Today, Lonely Planet has offices in the US, Ireland and China, with a network of over 2000 contributors in every corner of the globe. We share Tony's belief that 'a great guidebook should do three things: inform, educate and amuse'.

OUR WRITERS

Tamara Sheward

Bay of Kotor, Adriatic Coast, Central Montenegro, Northern Mountains After years of freelance travel writing, rock'n'roll journalism and insalubrious author-dom, Tamara leapt at the chance to join the Lonely Planet ranks in 2009. Since then, she's worked on guides to an incongruous jumble of countries including Montenegro, Australia, Serbia, Russia, the Samoas, Bulgaria and Fiji. She's written a miscellany of travel articles for the BBC, *The Independent*, *Sydney Morning Herald* et al; she's also fronted the camera as a documentary presenter for Lonely Planet TV, Nat Geo and Al-Jazeera. Tamara's based in far northern Australia, but you're more likely to find her roaming elsewhere, tattered notebook in one hand, the world's best-travelled toddler in the other. Tamara wrote the Plan Your Trip, Understand and Survival Guide sections of this book.

Peter Dragicevich

Dubrovnik (Croatia) After a successful career in niche newspaper and magazine publishing, both in his native New Zealand and in Australia, Peter finally gave into Kiwi wanderlust, giving up staff jobs to chase his diverse roots around much of Europe. Over the last 15 years he's written over 100 books for Lonely Planet on an oddly disparate collection of countries, all of which he's come to love. He once again calls Auckland, New Zealand his home – although his current nomadic existence means he's often elsewhere. Peter wrote the Welcome To Montenegro and Montenegro's Top Experiences chapters for this guide.

Published by Lonely Planet Global Limited
CRN 554153
4th edition – May 2022
ISBN 978 1 78701 721 4
© Lonely Planet 2022 Photographs © as indicated 2022
10 9 8 7 6 5 4 3 2 1
Printed in China